A Poetics of Jonah

A Poetics of Jonah

Art in the Service of Ideology

by Kenneth M. Craig, Jr.

University of South Carolina Press

Published in Columbia, South Carolina, by the
University of South Carolina Press

Manufactured in the United States of America

Library of Congress Cataloging-in-Publication Data

Craig, Kenneth M., 1960–
    A poetics of Jonah : art in the service of ideology / by Kenneth
M. Craig, Jr.
        p.   cm.
    Includes bibliographical references and index.
    ISBN 0-87249-890-5 (alk. paper)
    1. Bible. O.T. Jonah—Criticism, interpretation, etc. 2. Bible.
O.T. Jonah—Criticism, Narrative. 3. Bible. O.T. Jonah—
Language, style. I. Title.
BS1605.2.C73 1993
224′.92066—dc20   93–7999

To Niki

Contents

Tables

Preface

With warm tears in his eyes, Patroclus, obviously distressed and troubled, turns to his friend Achilles and says something like, "Who can do anything with you?"[1] An expression similar to this one from the *Iliad* might occur to anyone who writes about Jonah. With such a large number of books and articles available, what more can or needs to be said about the prophetic book?

My first attempt to answer this question appeared in 1989 as my doctoral dissertation. My original objectives and design have been modified in each chapter of this present study. Several factors have contributed to these changes: my discovery of some of the writings of Mikhail Bakhtin and his followers; the appearance of the New Revised Standard Version of the Bible; and the publication of Jack Sasson's commentary on Jonah. Sasson's book, perhaps the largest to date on Jonah, confirmed several of my initial thoughts, but more often his work caused me to rethink and recast my earlier positions. His work stands out among the commentaries for the simple reasons that he understands what's going on in Jonah and he explains himself well. Other exceptional studies on Jonah—the writings of George Landes, Phyllis Trible, and Hans Walter Wolff come quickly to mind—helped me to develop many of my ideas.

My work is largely the result of generous funds that Chowan College provided both to cover manuscript costs and travel expenses to professional conferences. Participants at the 1990 regional Society of Biblical Literature meeting in Charlotte, North Carolina, and at the 1990 annual Society of Biblical Literature meeting in New Orleans, Louisiana, listened to my papers on Jonah and offered good critical evaluation. A slightly different form of chapter 4 appeared in *Journal for the Study of the Old Testament* (47 [1990], pp. 103–14), published by the Sheffield Academic Press, Sheffield, England, and I wish to thank the editor for permission to reprint a version of it here. I wish also to thank Princeton University Press for permission to reprint material from *Ancient Near Eastern Texts Relating to the Old Testament*, edited by James B. Pritchard, copyright © 1950 (renewed) by Princeton University Press. Scripture quotations are from the New Revised Standard Version of the Bible, copyright 1989 by the Division of Christian Education of the National Council of the Churches of Christ in the U.S.A.

It is with pleasure that I express my gratitude for the advice, encouragement, and criticism that I received from scholars who showed interest in my work from the earliest stages. The lectures Meir Sternberg gave in the "Poetics of Biblical Narrative" seminar at the Porter Institute for Poetics and Semiotics at Tel Aviv University proved to be an asset. I am grateful for the generosity of the tutorial sessions, his extensive comments on the papers I wrote while studying in Israel, and for his help in correcting my translation of articles from Hebrew. I would also like to thank Itamar Even-Zohar and Brian McHale at the Porter Institute for their valuable assistance. John D. W. Watts and Marvin Tate called my attention to mistakes and omissions in my dissertation. Their friendship, comments, and suggestions have helped me more than they know. I am grateful to George Landes and Terence Fretheim for offering numerous suggestions after reading a later version of my manuscript with the kind of care and critical sensitivity that is evident in their own published work on Jonah. I wish to thank John Joseph Owens who helped me iron out a technical point in chapter 2. I have also been helped by Katherine Wood and Betty Harrelle who provided me with assistance and full support in the library at Chowan College, and by Steve Siebert and the support staff at Nota Bene who make writing enjoyable. Finally, I am particularly grateful to my partner in life. The dedication of these pages to her is a poor return on a large and selfless investment of love, friendship, and unfailing encouragement.

Abbreviations

Books, Periodicals, and Serials

ATANT	Abhandlungen zur Theologie des Alten un Neuen Testaments
BASOR	*Bulletin of the American Schools of Oriental Research*
BDB	F. Brown, S. R. Driver, and C. A. Briggs, *Hebrew and English Lexicon of the Old Testament*
BHK	*Biblia Hebraica*, ed. Kittel
BHS	*Biblia Hebraica Stuttgartensia*
Bib	*Biblica*
BKAT	Biblischer Kommentar Altes Testament
BMik	*Bet Mikra*
BTB	*Biblical Theology Bulletin*
BZ	*Biblische Zeitschrift*
CBQ	*Catholic Biblical Quarterly*
CI	*Critical Inquiry*
CompLit	*Comparative Literature*
CTJ	*Calvin Theological Journal*
EJ	*Encyclopedia Judaica*
ExpT	*Expository Times*
GKC	*Gesenius' Hebrew Grammar*, ed. E. Kautzsch, trans. A. E. Cowley
HTR	*Harvard Theological Review*
HUCA	*Hebrew Union College Annual*
IB	*The Interpreter's Bible*
ICC	The International Critical Commentary
IDB	*Interpreter's Dictionary of the Bible*
Int	*Interpretation*
JBL	*Journal of Biblical Literature*
JNES	*Journal of Near Eastern Studies*
JPOS	*Journal of the Palestine Oriental Society*
JQR	*Jewish Quarterly Review*
JSOT	*Journal for the Study of the Old Testament*
NICOT	New International Commentary on the Old Testament
NLH	*New Literary History*

PMLA	*Publications of the Modern Language Association*
PTL	*A Journal for Descriptive Poetics and Theory of Literature*
RB	*Revue biblique*
RHPR	*Revue d'histoire et de philosophie religieuses*
TLS	*Times Literary Supplement*
TynBul	*Tyndale Bulletin*
TZ	*Theologische Zeitschrift*
VT	*Vetus Testamentum*
VTSup	Vetus Testamentum, Supplements
YR	*Yale Review*
ZAW	*Zeitschrift für die alttestamentliche Wissenschaft*
ZNW	*Zeitschrift für die neutestamentliche Wissenschaft*

Modern Translations

AB	Anchor Bible
ASV	American Standard Version
GNB	Good News Bible
JB	Jerusalem Bible
KJV	King James Version
NAB	New American Bible
NEB	New English Bible
NIV	New International Version
NRSV	New Revised Standard Version
RSV	Revised Standard Version
RV	Revised Version

Other Abbreviations

Ev(v)	English verse(s)
hi.	hiph'il
hit.	hitpa'el
impf.	imperfect
impv.	imperative
inf.	infinitive
LXX	Septuagint
MT	Masoretic Text
n(n).	note(s)
ni.	niph'al

pf.	perfect
pi.	piel
pol.	polel
ptc.	participle
SBL	Society of Biblical Literature
vs(s).	verse(s)

A Poetics of Jonah

Introduction

Only in recent years have writers working in the area of biblical studies focused on literary art's role in Hebrew narrative. The changes in the field that have come from looking at (instead of behind) the Bible are producing an important new discourse. Thus Robert Alter concludes his popular book on biblical narrative with this sober observation: "Subsequent religious tradition has by and large encouraged us to take the Bible seriously rather than to enjoy it, but the paradoxical truth of the matter may well be that by learning to enjoy the biblical stories more fully as stories, we shall also come to see more clearly what they mean to tell us about God, man [and woman], and the perilously momentous realm of history."[1]

Yet the days of undervaluing the Bible's art have not passed. Since criticism continues to be leveled against literary interpretations of biblical prose and verse, a few words of general orientation may be in order.[2] The aim of this study is to shed light on the four chapters of Jonah *without* denying the book its historical or normative context. To anticipate my argument in small measure, it seems reasonably safe to assume (based on the Bible's art of arrangement) that the first hearers or readers would have attempted to fill one of the book's most important and extended gaps—What motivates the prophet to flee from the Lord?—with the same alacrity as their modern counterparts. They, like us, would have been surprised on learning at the end that Jonah, much more than the Ninevites, is the one who needs to mend his ways. Since reading is a time-art—unlike the painting on the wall, the story proceeds and is perceived *only in time*—readers are invited to formulate hypotheses whenever information relevant to the unfolding plot is suppressed. Reading presupposes writing, and writers ancient or modern appeal to certain linguistic means to communicate to an audience. Since a network of givens governs both sides of the communication coin, no one can escape the notion that the Bible *is* literature. Readers are interpreters who make decisions based on their linguistic knowledge, and they, like Jonah, sometimes take wrong turns. Herein lies the fun.

While many have written about Jonah, such fundamental questions about how we make sense of the story have too often been overlooked. This study on one of the Bible's most famous tales seeks to elucidate the conditions of meaning by highlighting the close inter-dependence between descriptive poetics and interpretation. A few questions reveal the scope: How are the two fundamental principles (the artistic and the ideological) combined in this story, and how do they set it apart from other biblical stories? What are the various rhetorical resources at the command of the narrator? What distin-guishes literary from everyday experience? In sum, *how* is this biblical story about a recalcitrant prophet told?

On the surface, the story of Jonah appears to be a simple one (if we compare it to a work by Dickens, Balzac, Proust, or Woolf), but I seek to show that the seemingly elementary art of the book of Jonah is enormously varied, rich, and complex. Even the choice of what might appear to be "small" words is calculated. A close rela-tionship between words in dialogue and narration exists, and at times, the narrator confirms the words of the characters in an interplay of repetition, a hallmark of biblical narrative. The narrator, who emerg-es as a master of the art of indirection, describes action, introduces speakers, and often tells us what characters think and feel, but refrains from providing explicit praise or condemnation for a single character. By the end of the tale, readers have, however, had ample opportunity to find fault with one character in particular—and perhaps even with themselves.

This book is written for anyone whose interests lie in narrative, and it may appeal to readers who study narrative outside the Bible if only because the Bible has a great deal to teach about the basics of narrative through its deceptively simple art. My research builds upon the work of a number of scholars who have, convincingly to my mind, shown that the Bible does have its own distinctive poetics. I have attempted to present an intelligible argument for the general reader as well as for specialists in the field. Occasionally it has been necessary to consider examples outside Jonah and outside the Bible itself to make a particular point, and it has also been necessary to employ Hebrew words from time to time, especially when I refer to wordplays and syntax. However, no special expertise in Hebrew, or knowledge of the Bible, is assumed. When it has been necessary to quote in Hebrew, an English translation has been supplied.

I have chosen to transliterate two Hebrew words, *kikayon* and *ḥesed*, because they are notoriously difficult to transplant from one language system to another. The first word, appearing nowhere in the Hebrew Bible but the final chapter of Jonah, identifies the plant that grows to a considerable height in less than a day and then withers. Ancient and modern translators have classified this plant by using a host of different names. Among these, "gourd" and "castor bean plant" appear to be the most popular, but others are also frequently found. Based on the failed attempts to recover the precise identification of this shade plant, it seems prudent to render this Hebrew word only by transliteration. By contrast, the word *ḥesed* is a favorite among the writers of the Hebrew Bible. It is rich in meaning and is often translated as "goodness," "kindness," or "steadfast love." The challenge for the translator is finding one- or two-word equivalents that do not sound hollow. In essence, the word refers to an attitude: the desire to pursue goodness without respect to cost, or to intervene on behalf of a sufferer, or to provide the kind of protection and goodness that is often evident only in parent-child relationships. Again, it seems prudent to approximate the sound of the Hebrew word instead of attempting to translate it. The special name for God, uttered to Moses in Exod. 3:14, is given throughout as Lord.

Chapter 1

What Is Poetics?

The various usages to which the word *poetics* has been put is a considerable study in itself. The term has appeared in titles of doctoral dissertations, books and articles in the area of biblical studies, as well as in books from other fields of study. Several academic journals are also committed to the discipline in a systematic fashion.[1] While acknowledging the reader's involvement with texts, *poetics* eludes easy definition. The word is associated with Aristotle and medieval theories of rhetoric. Beginning in 1968, Benjamin Hrushovski set the stage for modern discussions of poetics and its compass by inaugurating three journals: *Hasifrut* (first published in 1968 with articles in Hebrew and today the foremost journal of literary theory published in Israel), *PTL: A Journal for Descriptive Poetics and Theory of Literature* (published from 1976 to 1979), which was superseded by the widely circulated *Poetics Today* (1979–present). *Poetics*, in Hrushovski's view, is a systematic and scientific study of literature,[2] committed to the comprehensive investigation of texts, ancient and modern. In an attempt to define its boundaries, Hrushovski describes *poetics* as a unified theory of texts in the light of two approaches to literature: the subjective experiences that take place when one reads for pleasure, knowledge about society or culture, insight into the mind, or any such activity properly belonging to the sphere of aesthetic experience, as distinct from the study of the objects which give rise to it.[3]

The word *science* carries strong connotations of the natural sciences, and Hrushovski points out that one may (indeed, should) question the extent to which the study of social sciences, including literature, may be discussed in the same instance as the natural sciences.[4] The word *science* as it relates to poetics, and for the design of this study, is best conveyed by the modern Hebrew word מדע or the German *Wissenschaft*.[5] Thus understood, poetics involves the rigorous application of various analytical tools to the study of literature and may be contrasted with *literary criticism*, essentially an intuitive enterprise that lacks methods and objective rules. Since the boundaries and tasks of all fields of study, especially in the humanities and natural sciences, are hardly agreed upon and are shaped in large measure by the continuing work of researchers in each discipline, the general description of poetics offered here will not (and cannot) serve to define the full compass of this "science." It only provides a preliminary orientation.

In addition to the problems attending the phrase "science of literature," one also has to overcome the specious notion that studies of this kind establish incontrovertible principles or facts. Hrushovski's conclusion in his introductory remarks on "the fields and responsibilities of the study of literature" serves to correct the popular misconception: "Of course, there is no reason to assume that the word 'science' should imply any kind of absolute truth, devoid of the difficulties and problems obsessing the methodologies of other social sciences. It is a *horizon* rather than a strait jacket. . . . The expression 'science of literature' . . . is a short-cut for a whole series of terms such as: 'a systematic and integrated study of literature,' 'a body of knowledge,' plus 'theory,' plus 'methodology,' plus 'research,' etc."[6] The moment one begins to assume that a single theory is definitive, able to solve all questions or problems, and thus never in need of modification, then he or she operates under false pretense, one certainly alien to the spirit of poetics as defined and practiced by the scholars mentioned above.

But why a "science" of literature, and why the story of Jonah? What will form the core of this poetics? Instead of discovering or assigning meaning, poetics strives to elucidate the *conditions* of meaning. While calling attention to the activity of reading, the goal is to see how the Jonah text *made* and *makes* sense based on various interpretive operations. Just as a child assembles a complex grammar which enables him or her to "read" a series of sounds made by other children and adults, so too the reader of Jonah forges all types of questions and answers, consciously or unconsciously, in an attempt to concretize the projected world: How does the narrator's communicativeness in terms of reader-elevated experiences (in Jonah 1:7a, for example) or character-elevated experiences (in Jonah 4:2, for example) influence interpretation? What is the significance of the narrator's reticence at key moments of the narrative? How important is the concretization of narratorial omniscience as opposed to the human norm throughout? How does repetition on both small and large scales shape the reader? What is achieved in the modulations to and from prose and poetry? And what are the implications of the reader's shifting expectations in terms of surprise all along the text continuum? We, like the author(s) and first hearers of the book of Jonah, live in a world of words. Thus, the reading of the story requires us to form multiple linkages, and to simultaneously discriminate between contrasting and similar words, thoughts, and actions.

The poetics I am arguing for does not exclude historical questions. In fact, before the conditions for meaning of any biblical text can be established, one must know something about the conditions of the text itself (see "The Text and Translation" discussion below). However, this poetics will resist speaking of the Jonah story by means of nontextual historical assumptions projected onto the text. Historical criticism has by and large failed to provide definitive answers to external questions such as the book's historical setting and date of composition,[7] while internal issues—the book's art— have often been ignored.[8] Yet what does Aristotle and twenty-five hundred years of literary history have to do with the son of Amittai?

Aristotle's Influence

Aristotle's *Poetics*, twenty-five hundred years old, is the first work devoted entirely to a systematic study of literature. Many consider it among the most important critical works of antiquity, and its influence on subsequent generations is inestimable.[9] While Aristotle did not found literary criticism, he did more for it than any other ancient we know. Ronald S. Crane calls attention to "the beginnings of systematic criticism" as reflected in the *Poetics*, and his under- standing of the nature of the "science" is similar to Hrushovski's views: "The *Poetics* is a statement, or at least an outline sketch, of a science, and as such it deals with principles. . . . Poetics, therefore, can never be thought of as something fixed and determined. It must aim, rather, to be a progressive science, always lagging somewhat behind . . . but never, if it is to keep alive, remaining indifferent to what new [writers] are trying to do."[10]

Aristotle discussed a range of issues in the *Poetics*, and some have little or no bearing on Jonah (history of drama, comparisons of epic and tragedy, the tragic chorus, etc.). More relevant discussions in terms of the prophetic book relate to plot, character, surprise, and temporal ordering. A question may arise concerning the relationship between Aristotle's work as reflected in the *Poetics* (and subsequent studies) and the Hebrew story of Jonah.[11] On the surface, the answer is simple: with different goals in mind, both the Hebrew author of

Jonah and the Greek philosopher knew that *certain conditions distinguish literary from everyday experience.*

Meir Sternberg's monumental volume, *The Poetics of Biblical Narrative,* is the single most significant work on poetics and biblical narrative. His pioneering work began more than twenty years ago when he first published articles on the subject in *Hasifrut,* and his subsequent publications have helped generate a powerful discourse on the Bible's art.[12] Sternberg describes biblical narrative as a complex discourse regulated by three principles: the ideological (evident, for example, in the law passages from Exodus, the prophetic speeches, and the various promise-fulfillment themes), the historiographical (emphasized by recurring dates, genealogies, and aetiological tales), and the aesthetic (the art of indirection, gapping, repetition, deformation of chronological ordering, variations in quotation, and access to privileged information in the form of interior monologue). These three basic principles serve to define the essence and uniqueness of biblical narrative distinguishing it from other ancient and modern literature. But how are they related? What relation does the overall aesthetic function bear on the historiographic and the ideological? How do they *co*operate? These are the questions which his book answers. In the abstract, the three principles

> form natural rivals, with different goals in view and different forms of communication to match. Ideology would above all establish a world view and, if militant, a consensus. It accordingly presses for transparent representation that will (and in didactic writing, does) bring the world into the appropriate doctrinal pattern, schematized in equal disregard for the intractability of historical fact and the ordering niceties of art. Historiography has no eye but for the past: at its quintessential, as in chronicle, it would like nothing better than to tack fact onto fact in an endless procession, marching across all artistic and ideological design. For aesthetics, the play's the thing, ideally (as in abstract painting or the fantastic) with no strings attached to what is, was, or should be. Given free rein, therefore, each would pull in a different direction and either win the tug of war or tear the work apart.[13]

As the quotation suggests, the ideological principle is not to be confused with didactic discourse.[14] Most often, biblical characters are realistic, and only occasionally ideal. Whereas, as Sternberg points out, a didactic work subordinates language, plot, and character to the requisites of indoctrination, the Hebrew Bible often goes out of its way to generate ambivalence. Characterization of Jacob, Aaron, Gideon, Saul, David, Solomon, and certainly of Jonah, serves to illustrate the point with the Bible foregrounding the discordance of divine election and moral stature rather than aligning them.

According to Sternberg, once the Bible's ideological *and* antididactic moves are recognized as a policy, we see how the aesthetic rules and codes function. Moreover, the combination of these three principles (ideological, historiographical, and aesthetic) is what makes the Bible "such exciting if difficult reading and . . . forms its main claim to poetic originality and theoretical notice: the transformation of ideological discourse into art of the highest order, without compromising either but enriching both."[15] The result, from the reader's side, is what he calls "the drama of reading."

While Sternberg's triad has much to offer in terms of an extended discussion on Hebrew biblical narrative, a different model applies for the book of Jonah. Two functional principles are operative: (*a*) the ideological (as emphasized by the natural order's consistent response to the Lord's acts, the narrator's direct statements such as "and God saw their deeds, how they turned from their evil ways, and God was sorry concerning the evil which he had said he would do to them, and he did not do it" [3:10], as well as the characters' own speech such as "for I knew that you are a gracious God, and compassionate, slow in coming to anger and great in *ḥesed* and repenting of evil" [4:2b] and "may I not be concerned about Nineveh, the great city, where there are more than 120,000 people who do not know their right hand from their left and many cattle?" [4:11]), and (*b*) the artistic (the antichronological moves in 4:2, 5; the maneuvering through repetition of the sailors' increasing "fear" [1:5, 10, 16] and Jonah's pleas for death [4:3, 9], and the play between direct speech and the narrator's statements). The twin principles will serve as a foundation in showing *how* art serves ideology, both in descriptive and functional terms.

Since ideology (like its cognate, ideologue) often carries a pejorative connotation, it is necessary to set a proper context for this study. In the tradition of Boris Uspensky, Mikhail Bakhtin, and more recently, Robert Polzin, I employ the word to mean a deeply held and interlocking set of religious, social, and political beliefs or attitudes about the world and how the world works.[16] In addition,

I accept the premise that objective knowledge free of ideological taint exists only as a fiction in the mind. The ancient Israelites, like people of all cultures, had their own ideas about the world, truth, and value, and such views are reflected in their literature. The unifying factor for the book of Jonah that keeps contrasting images, themes, characters—in short, art—together is its ideological or evaluative point of view. Such artistic and ideological functions will often diverge, yet neither will ultimately oppose the other. Both are full partners. A central concern is therefore what unity of effects does the author pursue? We seek to explore the worldview of one of the Bible's most famous stories and to demonstrate how the artful ideologist brings it home.

Jonah and Other Literary Traditions

As soon as attention shifts from history behind the text to the issue of *how* meaning gets produced, a range of issues comes into focus. In an attempt to draw some loose threads together and to set the sails for the journey, excerpts from other literary traditions will provide a preliminary orientation.

With respect to the artistic side of the coin, one notices distinct parallels (between the book of Jonah and other texts from approximately the same time period right up to the English novel) as characters deprived of essential information quite naturally ask a series of questions. After the sailors determine through the casting of lots that Jonah is responsible for their misfortune (1:7b), they bombard him with five questions (vs. 8), and the cumulative weight reflects their frenzied state of mind:

> And they said to him, "Tell us, we pray, on whose account has this evil happened to us? What is your occupation? And from where do you come? What is your country? And from what people are you?"

Consider a few scenes from the *Odyssey*. Of the Greek heroes who survived the Trojan War, only Odysseus had not returned home, for he had been detained by Calypso, the powerful goddess who kept him in a cave on the lonely island of Ogygia. With Poseidon away visiting the Ethiopians and with the help of Zeus and Hermes, Odysseus is able to escape from Calypso, and to begin his return home to Ithaca. In the palace of Alcinous and Arete, Odysseus speaks with the king and queen after the guests return to their homes. Arete recognizes some of the clothes that Odysseus is wearing and asks him a series of questions which provide Odysseus an opportunity to relate the story about his escape from Calypso. Arete asks,

"Who are you? Where do you hail from? And who gave you those clothes?"[17]

In book 10, Odysseus and his crew continue to travel hoping to return to Ithaca. They arrive on the island of Aeaea, the home of the beautiful and formidable goddess Circe. At Odysseus' request, some men go to Circe's house and while there become the drugged victims of the goddess's magic. When Odysseus learns what has happened to his men, he enters Circe's house. She mixes poison in with the pottage and then offers it to Odysseus. After noticing that her drug has no effect, she asks Odysseus:

"Who on earth are you? . . . What parents begat, what city bred such a man?"[18]

When Odysseus finally arrives in Ithaca, he meets his most faithful steward, Eumaeus, the swineherd. Eumaeus, unaware of Odysseus' true identity, offers his former master meat and wine and proceeds to tell him about the exploits of the suitors and that Telemachus, Odysseus' son, is now in danger. Eumaeus' extended speech provides Odysseus with important information about some of the events that have transpired since he has been held by Calypso. Odysseus attempts to persuade Eumaeus that the former king of Ithaca will in fact return, but is unable to convince the swineherd. Finally, Eumaeus asks Odysseus a series of questions:

"Who are you and where do you come from? What is your city? Who are your family? And since you certainly can't have come on foot, what kind of vessel brought you here? How did its crew come to land you in Ithaca; and who did they claim to be?"[19]

In chapter 19, just before the famous scene where Eurycleia recognizes her former master's scar as she washes the disguised beggar's feet and legs, Odysseus describes his plan of attack to Telemachus. Odysseus succeeds in temporarily deceiving his wife, Penelope (who is completely unaware of his identity), with a fantastic tale after she asks a few questions about his past:

"Who are you and where do you hail from? What is your city and to what family do you belong?"[20]

Parallels to the sailors' questions in chapter 1 of Jonah are not limited to contemporary examples. In act 3 of *Julius Caesar*, for example, Antony is able to convince the crowd that those who have killed Caesar are conspirators. Just after scene ii, Antony reads Caesar's will, and the crowd becomes so anxious for revenge they murder Cinna the poet, an innocent man who happens to have the same name as one of the conspirators. The plebians knew the poet was innocent, but they kill him anyway after determining his innocence through a series of questions:

"What is your name?"
"Whither are you going?"
"Where do you dwell?"
"Are you a married man or a bachelor?"[21]

In yet a third example, shortly after young Oliver meets the Artful Dodger in *Oliver Twist*, he finds himself in the midst of a gang of young thieves. On his first mission, Oliver is caught and taken to the police station. There he is rescued by Mr. Brownlow, the man whose pocket the young boy had been accused of picking and the man who becomes Oliver's benefactor. Oliver receives a new suit, a cap, and a pair of shoes from Mr. Brownlow and is later invited into the study. After a short conversation on books, Brownlow attempts to learn more about Oliver by asking him a few questions:

"Let me hear your story; where you come from; who brought you up; and how you got into the company in which I found you."[22]

These examples, drawn from different eras, are not intended to suggest any direct borrowing or influence,[23] but they do reveal that at the level of plot, characters deprived of essential information ask questions routinely and that the cumulative weight of such questions enhances psychological portrayal. Rhetorical strategies, suggested in these examples, are what we seek to explore in this study.

The Text and Translation

While readers have recently emerged as distinguished participants in the hermeneutical circle (as the multiplying qualifiers—

"competent," "actual," "ideal," "implied"—reveal), concern with and respect for "the" text remains an important consideration in biblical studies. The well-preserved Masoretic text (MT) of Jonah contains few variants. Even the Targum, which is significantly expansionistic in other books of the Minor Prophets, contains a relatively small number of explanatory glosses.[24]

Phyllis Trible's thorough study of the text included Hebrew, Greek, Latin, Aramaic, and Syriac witnesses. She indicated that the manuscripts catalogued by Kennicott, de Rossi, and others agree for the most part with each other and with the text of BHK. While literally hundreds of variants are listed, most of these relate to the absence and presence of *matres lectionis* which do not affect the text. With respect to the Hebrew manuscripts, she concludes, "None of these variants, however, is sufficient either in kind or in number to merit closer study. Their unimportance demonstrates clearly the uniformity existing among *Jonah* mss."[25] The variations between the LXX and MT of Jonah (such as the *hapax* קיקיון, "*kikayon*," which is rendered differently in the LXX most likely because the translators did not know the precise meaning of the term) are also minor.[26]

Acknowledging that there are textual variations lying alongside or behind MT, the present study proceeds from an unemended text. While it is certainly true that MT should not be maintained at every verse of the Hebrew Bible,[27] the purpose here is not to reconstruct but to defend; or, in Robert Polzin's words, we assume "an artful narrative rather than a clumsy redaction."[28] Several good textual studies are available for Jonah.[29] While MT is followed (and defended) throughout this study, a few comments about the translation are necessary and are given in the notes below. The translation of the book of Jonah is my own. Other passages from the Bible follow the text of the New Revised Standard Version, except as noted.

Chapter 1. (1) And the word of the Lord was to Jonah, son of Amittai, saying, (2) "Arise, go to Nineveh, the great city, and call to her, for her wickedness has come up before me." (3) But Jonah arose to flee towards Tarshish away from the presence of the Lord, and he went down to Joppa and he found a ship going to Tarshish and he gave the fare and he went down in it to go with them towards Tarshish away from the presence of the Lord.

(4) But the Lord hurled a great wind upon the sea and a great

tempest was on the sea, and the ship thought about breaking up. (5) And the sailors were afraid and they cried out each to his god(s) and they hurled the cargo which was on the ship into the sea to be lightened from them, and Jonah ªhad gone downª into the inner recesses of the ship, and ªhad lain down,ª and had fallen into a trance. (6) And the captain of the sailors came to him and he said to him, "How can you fall into a trance?!ᵇ Arise, call upon your god(s). Perhaps the god(s) will give a thought to us so that we will not perish." (7) And they said each to the other, "Come and let us cast lots so that we may know on whose account this evil has happened to us." And they cast lots and the lot fell unto Jonah. (8) And they said to him, "Tell us, we pray, on whose account has this evil happened to us? What is your occupation? And from where do you come? What is your country? And from what people are you?" (9) And he said unto them, "I am a Hebrew, and the Lord, the God of the heavens, I fear, who made the sea and the dry land." (10) And the men were afraid, greatly afraid, and they said unto him, "What is this which you have done?" for the men knew that he was fleeing from the presence of the Lord ᶜfor he had told

------

a–a. The options for rendering these verbs illustrate the axiom that translation involves interpretation. Biblical Hebrew has no grammatical indicators for a pluperfect construction to signal events anterior to what is narrated. Jack Sasson, citing S. R. Driver (*A Treatise on the Use of the Tenses in Hebrew* [Oxford: The Clarendon Press, 1892], 22, 84–89 [§16, 76]; cited in Sasson, *Jonah*, 99), argues that pluperfects can be defended, and in fact a great many translations offer such (JB, NAB, NAS, NIV, NRSV, RSV). Coming just after the scenario in vs. 5a ("and the sailors were afraid and they cried out each to his god(s) and they hurled the cargo which was on the ship into the sea to be lightened from them"), the translation of vs. 5b as either past tense ("and [then] Jonah went down into the inner recesses of the ship and lay down") or in a pluperfect sense ("[but Jonah had previously] gone down into the inner recesses of the ship, and had lain down") certainly affects interpretation. Does Jonah seek to forget his troubles by descending to the inner recesses just after boarding the ship? Or does he seek to withdraw at the moment the others on board are doing all they can to save the ship and their lives? For the sake of clarity, I have translated the verbs as pluperfects, but as part of my thesis that ambiguity operates on both large and small scales in the book, I acknowledge that *both* translations are desirable.

b. נרדם ("fall into a trance") is a ni. ptc. and not a vocative as the English translations (such as RSV, but not NRSV) frequently render. Cf. GKC §120b, Snaith, *Notes*, 15, and Sasson's translation and comments, *Jonah*, 89, 103.

c–c. כי הגיד להם ("for he had told them") is an example of indirect quotation and should *not* be omitted as Wellhausen, Nowack, and others (cf. Snaith, *Notes*, 19) have suggested. I disagree with Wolff's observation that this clause is "stylistically unpleasing" (*Obadiah and Jonah*, 107). Sasson, who does not regard the phrase as a gloss, offers a succinct reconstruction of events in vss. 9–11 (*Jonah*, 121–22).

them.[c] (11) And they said unto him, "What shall we do to you so that the sea may quiet down for us, for the sea is storming tempestuously?" (12) And he said to them, "Lift me up and hurl me into the sea and the sea will quiet down for you, for I know that it is because of me that this great tempest is upon you." (13) And the men rowed hard (trying) to return to the dry land but they could not, for the sea was storming tempestuously against them. (14) And they called unto the Lord and they said, "We pray,[d] O Lord, do not let us perish on account of this man's life, and may you not put innocent blood upon us, for you, Lord, as you have pleased you have done." (15) And they lifted Jonah up and they hurled him into the sea and the sea ceased from its raging. (16) And the men were afraid, [e]greatly fearing the Lord,[e] and they slaughtered a slaughter-meal to the Lord and they vowed vows.

Chapter 2. (1) And the Lord appointed a great fish to swallow Jonah, and Jonah was in the body[f] of the fish three days and three nights. (2) And Jonah prayed to the Lord, his God, from the body[f] of the fish. (3) And he said,

> "[g]I called from my distress;
>   Unto the Lord and he answered me.
> From the belly of Sheol I cried out;
>   You heard my voice.
> (4) And you cast me to deep, into the heart of the seas,
>   And a river encircled me.
> All your breakers and your waves
>   Passed over me.
> (5) And I said,
>   'I was cast away from your sight.

---

d. אנה, rendered here as "pray," is a combination of two particles of entreaty אה and נה (sometimes נא). It represents a strong supplication to God. (cf. BDB, 58 and Snaith, *Notes*, 21). The word is translated "pray" throughout the study to emphasize the stress on praying in each of the four chapters of Jonah (see chapter 5). It might also be translated with a stronger or more emphatic word such as "beseech," etc. The variety of translations in the versions is summarized by Sasson (*Jonah*, 132).

e–e. Cf. the comments in "Inside Views in Jonah: Degree, Reliability, Duration" of Chapter 7 (n. 15 esp.).

f. מעה may be translated with different English words ("internal organs," "inward parts," "intestines," "bowels," "belly," cf. BDB, 588). It is translated "body" here to distinguish it from בטן ("belly") in vs. 3.

g–g. Temporal ordering is especially complex in 2:3–10. Cf. the discussion at "The Prayers of Chapter 2" in chapter 5.

^hYetⁱ I will again look^h
 Upon your holy temple.'
(6) Waters encompassed (my) neck;^j
 (The) deep swirled around me.
Reeds were wrapped around my head
 (7) To/At^k the roots of the mountains,
I descended to the underworld;^l
 Bars were upon me forever.
Yet you brought my life up from the Pit,
 O Lord, my God.
(8) My soul fainted within me;
 I remembered the Lord.
And my prayer came unto you,
 Unto your holy temple.

---

h–h. אַךְ אוֹסִיף לְהַבִּיט, "yet I will again look," is an idiomatic expression (Trible, "Studies," 36). יסף (hi.) followed by an inf. (with or without לְ, "to") is best translated as "do again" (cf. BDB, 415 - Hiph. 2.a.).

i. MT has אַךְ, "yet," "nevertheless." An imposing list of scholars (Wellhausen, Bewer, Sellin, Wade, Weiser, Robinson, Aalders and Wolff) follow Theodotion's reading of אֵיךְ, "how" (cited in part by Allen, *Books*, 216, n. 17). אֵיךְ continues the mood of despair which is well in place before vs. 5 and certainly continues through vs. 8a, but it is certainly possible that the prophet's shift in mood reflected by MT (despair—> hope) could begin at vs. 5. In vs. 7 the prophet's mood shifts once again: "I descended / Yet (וּ) you brought my life up" (cf. also vss. 8–10). Sasson summarizes the history of these two translations nicely (*Jonah*, 179–80). His conclusion is persuasive: "Emending the Hebrew of Jonah because of a variant reading located in an ancient translation is not a useful approach, especially because we have repeatedly observed how translators adapt whenever it suits their (or their audience's) theology" (p. 180).

j. For the translation of נפש as "neck," see W. F. Albright, "Are the Ephod and the Teraphim Mentioned in Ugaritic Literaure?" *BASOR* 83 (1941): 41, n. 15; Lor. Dürr, "Hebr. נֶפֶשׁ=akk. napištu=Gurgel, Kehle.," *ZAW* 43 (1925): 262 and 264; and Sasson, *Jonah*, 184.

k. לקצבי "to/at the roots." See the "Grammar and Interlinear Relationships" in chapter 6 for an explanation of these two English words for the simple Hebrew preposition. Sasson (*Jonah*, 186–87) admits that it is possible for the Hebrew prepositions to accommodate both applications in this verse, but he argues for "to" instead of "at."

l. The translation of ארץ as "underworld" is now well-attested with examples from Akkadian, Ugaritic, Aramaic, and biblical literature. See, N. J. Tromp's examples in *Primitive Conceptions of Death and the Nether World in the Old Testament* (Rome: Pontifical Biblical Institute, 1969), 23–46; Frank M. Cross and David Noel Freedman, "The Song of Miriam," *JNES* 14 (1955): 247–48, n. 39; Sasson, *Jonah*, 188; Mitchell Dahood, *Psalms I:1–50*, AB, vol. 16 (Garden City: Doubleday, 1966), 106.

(9) Those who regard vain idols,
   Abandon their *ḥesed*.[m]
(10) But I, in a voice of thanksgiving,
   I will sacrifice to you.
What I have vowed, I will pay.
   Salvation is of the Lord![g]"

(11) And the Lord spoke to the fish and it vomited up Jonah to the dry land.

Chapter 3. (1) And the word of the Lord was to Jonah a second time, saying, (2) "Arise, go to Nineveh, the great city, and call to her the message which I am speaking to you." (3) And Jonah arose and he went to Nineveh according to the Lord's word, and Nineveh was [n]an exceedingly great city,[n] a journey of three days. (4) And Jonah began to go into the city, a journey of one day, and he cried out and he said, "Yet in forty days and Nineveh will be overthrown!" (5) And the people of Nineveh believed in God, and they called a fast and dressed themselves in sackcloth from the greatest to the least. (6) And the word reached the king of Nineveh and he arose from his throne and he removed his mantle from himself, and he covered himself with sackcloth and he sat upon the ashes. (7) And he cried out and he said throughout Nineveh by the decree of the king and his great-ones, saying, "Neither people nor cattle, herd nor flock, shall taste anything; nor shall they pasture, and water they shall not drink. (8) But they shall cover themselves with sackcloth, [o]people and animals,[o] and they shall call to God with

---

m. חסדם, "their *ḥesed*"; Marti, Nowack, and others suggest that MT's חסדם ("their *ḥesed*") is unusual here and emend it to מחסהם ("their refuge") or מחמדם ("their desire") without any textual support (cf. Snaith, *Notes*, 30). Sasson surveys the literature and concludes that he can offer no definite solution. At the end of his discussion he reasons that "v 9b is consequential to 9a; that the verb in 9b is chosen to contrast with 9a; and that *ḥesed* is a gratification that is not available to individuals attached to ["vain idols"], whether it be for them to receive or dispense it" (*Jonah*, 199). I suggest in chapter 5 that this and other emendations throughout the prayer are unnecessary.

n–n. For this translation of עיר גדולה לאלהים, literally "a great city to God," see the comments at "Chapter 3" in the seventh chapter. Cf. also Sasson, *Jonah*, 228–29, 310.

o–o. Wolff (*Obadiah and Jonah*, 144–45) is certainly correct in suggesting that this phrase should not be removed either partially (Bewer, Rudolph) or entirely (Wellhausen), *especially* since no ancient text supports such an omission.

might, and they shall turn each from their evil ways and from the wrongdoing which is in their hands. (9) Who knows? God may turn and be sorry, and turn from the flaming of his anger so that we will not perish." (10) And God saw their deeds, how they turned from their evil ways, and God was sorry concerning the evil which he had said he would do to them, and he did not do it.

Chapter 4. (1) [p]And it displeased Jonah, a great evil, and he became hot with anger.[p] (2) And he prayed unto the Lord and he said, "I pray,[d] Lord, was this not my word when I was in my country? This is why I made haste to flee towards Tarshish, for I knew that you are a gracious God, and compassionate, slow in coming to anger and great in *ḥesed* and repenting of evil. (3) And now Lord, take, I pray, my life from me, for I prefer death to life." (4) And the Lord said, "Is it right for you to become inflamed?" (5) [q]And Jonah went out from the city and he sat down east of the city, and he made for himself there a booth and he sat under it in the shade until he could see what would happen in the city.[q] (6) And the Lord God appointed a *kikayon,* and it came up over Jonah to be a shade over his head to shade him from his evil, and Jonah was happy about the *kikayon,* extremely happy. (7) And God appointed a worm when the next dawn came up, and it struck the *kikayon* and it withered. (8) And it was as the sun rose and God appointed a cutting east wind and the sun struck upon the head of Jonah and he became faint, and he asked that his soul might die, and he said, "I prefer death to life." (9) And God said to Jonah, "Is it right for you to become inflamed about the *kikayon*?" And he said, "It is right for me to become inflamed, even to the point of death." (10) And the Lord said, "You were concerned about the *kikayon* for which you did not labor nor cause to grow, which as a child of night came to be and as a child of night perished. (11) And may[r] I not be concerned about Nineveh, the great city, where there are

p–p. The translation of 4:1 is difficult primarily because the subject of וירע, rendered here as "and it displeased," is elusive. Cf. the discussion in "Chapter 4" of the seventh chapter.

q–q. The disagreement concerning the (dis)placement of this verse is discussed in chapter 3.

r. The translation of this modal auxiliary is explained in the "Major Characters: Jonah and the Lord" section of chapter 3.

more than 120,000 people who do not know their right hand from their left and many cattle?"[s]

---

s. Trible points out ("Studies," 57) that all the versions correctly understand vs. 11 as an interrogative sentence, although the Hebrew lacks an interrogative ה which corresponds to the English interrogative "do." As in English, a question need not be introduced by an interrogative word (or letter). The arrangement or emphasis on words may indicate a question (cf. GKC §150a).

Chapter 2

The RSV, NRSV, and Jonah

The scope of this chapter is influenced by conclusions reached in the preceding one. While a single English translation of Jonah based on an unemended (and remarkably well preserved) Hebrew text is followed in this study, the matter of differences in English translations and the whole issue of why hundreds of them exist are worth considering because these issues have a bearing on this study. The discussion will focus on matters that will be examined in subsequent chapters though some observations may have implications for Bible translation in general. We set the stage for this study wherein we ask how language functions to carry ideology.

Since excellent textual studies are available for the book of Jonah and since the New Revised Standard Version (NRSV) has recently become available, it may be instructive to consider what type of changes have recently been made to the English text of Jonah. The Revised Standard Version (RSV), first published in 1946 (New Testament alone) and 1952 (containing both Jewish and Christian Scriptures),[1] has for many years been widely used by Jews, Roman Catholics, Protestants, Anglicans, and Eastern Orthodox. The large number of changes made to it recently—forty-seven of the forty-eight verses in Jonah have been altered in the NRSV—suggests that translation itself is an on-going process that is necessary as our understanding of language and culture, both ancient and modern, increases.

A small sampling of the two translations suggests the flavor of change. Genesis 1:1 incorporates a footnote from the RSV and now reads, "In the beginning when God created the heavens and the earth" (NRSV). Adam and Eve no longer make "aprons" (RSV) in Genesis 3:7, but, apparel more fitting for the time, "loincloths" (NRSV). In 1 Samuel 25:3 Abigail was "of good understanding" (RSV), but is now "clever" (NRSV). Nabal was "churlish and ill-behaved" (vs. 3; RSV); now he's "surly and mean" (NRSV). And, in the interest of clarity, Psalm 50:9 has been changed from "I will accept no bull from your house" (RSV) to "I will not accept a bull from your house" (NRSV). Numerous changes have also been made to the New Testament. After Jesus appoints his disciples, the crowd is no longer just concerned that he is "beside himself" (RSV) in

Mark 3:21, but that he has "gone out of his mind" (NRSV). In the ancient hymn of Philippians 2, Christ is described as "not regard[ing] equality with God as something to be exploited" (vs. 6; NRSV), instead of "not count[ing] equality with God a thing to be grasped" (RSV). What is behind all of these changes? What motivates a group of scholars to meet over an extended period of time for the sake of overhauling a translation that is relatively young? Why so many changes? As mentioned above, a comparison of the RSV and NRSV reveals that only one verse in Jonah (2:1) has escaped the NRSV translators' surgical knife! Answers to questions such as these could take us far beyond the general scope of the present study. The four chapters of Jonah provide a small area from which to make observations about language, translation, and interpretation that are relevant for this study. A few general remarks provide some background for comparing these two English translations of Jonah.

On 30 September 1990, after fifteen years of work by the Standard Bible Committee of the National Council of Churches, the NRSV was published.[2] The adjective "new" is misleading. This Bible is only a newcomer to a venerable line of English Bible translations that began with the "authorized" successor to William Tyndale's 1534 translation of Scripture into English, the King James Version (KJV) of 1611. In spite of all the changes that have recently been introduced, the NRSV is the latest revision. In this sense, it is not a new translation of the Bible. It stands in a tradition of three committee-produced Bibles: a) the KJV (1604–1611); b) the Revised Version (1881–95) and what is generally speaking its American edition, the American Standard Version (published in 1901 and based on the work of the American RV members), and c) the RSV (1946–1957).[3] The dates in this succession do not account for the plethora of other translations. From 1952, the year both testaments of the RSV were first published, and 1990, the year the NRSV appeared, twenty-six translations of the Bible appeared in English, as did twenty-five other English translations of the New Testament alone.

Thus, the NRSV is most accurately described as an up-to-date version, rather than a new translation. And it is only one of many. It is not like other versions of the Bible that claim to be new translations based exclusively on the ancient manuscripts. Unlike the Bibles that Jerome, Luther, and Tyndale produced, the NRSV is the result of work that was carried out by a committee. The work was involved, spread out over a long period, and the revision process itself often took many turns.

The procedure for dealing with the separate books of the Bible was very simple. At least one member in each group was assigned a particular book for study, and for as much research as necessary. When the member's study was finished, he or she then drew up a detailed list of all the changes he or she felt were either necessary or desirable. These agendas were then discussed *seriatim*, each item being either accepted immediately (as many were, of course, being in accordance with previous decisions) or discussed until a consensus was reached. In rare instances, discussion of a single item could go on for an hour or two. If, finally, no consensus seemed possible, the issue was decided by simple majority vote. At the end of the week all the changes voted by all of the subcommittees, after further discussion when it seemed necessary, were ratified at a general meeting. Since the committee's work went on for some fifteen years, with many changes in personnel, a large number of the Old Testament books were reviewed a second time by another subcommittee, following an agenda prepared by yet another scholar, since in the course of time the committee's understanding of its task had changed and matured; new general rules were formulated and the whole process of revision had become more thorough-going (some might say more radical) than had originally been envisaged.[4]

It is interesting to compare the time frame between these translations. Two hundred and seventy years elapsed from the time of the KJV to the RV (1611–1881); seventy-one years from the time of the RV to the RSV (1881–1952); and thirty-eight years from the RSV to the NRSV (1952–90).[5] The consistent decline in these intervals and the comparatively short period of time that stands between the RSV and NRSV can be explained by two factors: (1) significant discoveries of ancient biblical manuscripts at Qumran and elsewhere have transformed our understanding of the Bible, and (2) the technological revolution has enhanced the way scholars go about their work. Today, researchers work in a different academic setting where scholars with earned, advanced degrees number in the thousands, where a burgeoning number of publishers are interested in their monographs, and where sophisticated text storage and retrieval systems allow for more work in less time. When future translation-by-committee projects are undertaken, the members will no doubt be working from CD-ROM and the Bible on computer disk where changes and searches are completed with a few keystrokes. Nonelectric concordance checks are time-consuming and are now unnecessary since computers gather information much more quickly and efficiently. With such technology available, we should not expect another two hundred and seventy years to elapse before we reach the next stage! One is left only to wonder how much time will pass before a major translation will be available that overcomes the God-as-male problem (mentioned below).

One of the reasons that such a large number of single-language translations are available is that the rendering of words and phrases from one language to another involves more than finding the right modern word for each ancient Hebrew (or Aramaic, Greek, Syriac, Latin, etc.) word. To put it simply: translating from one language to another requires that *interpretive* decisions be made. For example, Hebrew, unlike English, does not have a pluperfect tense. Does this mean the translator should consistently refrain from using the tense to stay "true" to the Hebrew? Or should the translator follow contextual clues (as in Jonah 1:5) and use the pluperfect tense from time to time? Second, at virtually every stage, translators must choose from several words when translating an individual word. For example, קום (and derivational forms) is a Hebrew word found frequently in Jonah. The NRSV, unlike the RSV, translates with several different English equivalents ("go," "get up," "set out"). The NRSV provides some variety by rendering different nuances of the single Hebrew word. In choosing the same English word, "arise," (or derivational forms, such as "rise") for the Hebrew word קום, the RSV translators re-create for the modern reader an experience similar to what the first hearers or readers might have had. Third, Hebrew words taken together, עיר גדולה לאלהים in Jonah 3:3, for example, often mean something other than what they suggest when simply added together ("a"+"great"+"city"+"to"+"God"). Fourth, the problems that translators of ancient texts face are astounding. Often, a single passage is preserved in multiple forms, and since the dates of manuscripts can often only be determined in a general sense, ascertaining the meaning of words is difficult. Texts are sometimes damaged. Punctuation—even spaces between words—does not exist in the oldest manuscripts, and our understanding of ancient languages is also developing. Like interpretation, translation is a developing science.

In general, committees since the KJV have attempted to remove some of (and at times only a little of) the ancient words and awkward expressions of the English language, while preserving some of the majesty and beauty of the older versions. At the first three stages of translation (KJV, RV, RSV), words like "wherefore," "lest," "whence," "beguile," and a host of others are frequently found. Such out-of-date words have been largely eliminated in the NRSV.

The appearance of new translations may also be explained by another factor. Social changes that took place from the late 1950s to the early 1970s contributed to the need for further revisions to the RSV. Today, on the whole, the dress and manner of people are more relaxed than a generation or two ago. Social relationships are more informal, and such factors as these have contributed to a more informal style of expression. These changes in the public sphere have had an impact on places of worship. Formal language for God ("thou," "thy") is much less common today in worship settings than it once was. The RSV had already made progress in the direction of bringing the Bible into contemporary English, but with one exception. Archaic forms ("thou," "dost," "art," "hast") were maintained even in the RSV, especially in the poetry. A comparison of Psalm 23 in the KJV and RSV reveals that the RSV essentially duplicates the KJV while adding footnotes that suggest alternative translations. Robert Dentan, commenting on the tremendous influence of the KJV, points out that with respect to Psalm 23, members of the RSV committee regarded the footnotes as preferable to their own translations on at least three occasions. Yet the KJV language was maintained with the better readings being relegated to the margins.[6] Other passages from Psalms, Job, and Jeremiah were also retained from the KJV without significant change.

Two major areas of change are reflected in the NRSV. Much exclusive language has been eliminated. That is, words intended to refer to all human beings are now translated with English words that refer to both sexes. As such, the NRSV is the first major translation to eliminate linguistic sexism, at least when reference is made to people. Traditional masculine pronouns for God are maintained: "so God created humankind in his image, in the image of God he created them" (Gen. 1:27). The Hebrew Bible does, if only on occasion, employ feminine metaphors for God (Isa. 42:14 [the pregnant woman]; Isa. 66:13 [the mother]; Ps. 22:9 [the midwife]; Job 38:29 [the woman who gives birth]; Deut. 32:11, 18 [the mother eagle]; Num. 11:12 [God who conceives]).[7] A few passages illustrate the switch to inclusive language when reference is made to people. The familiar lines of Ps. 8:4, "what is man that thou art mindful of him, and the son of man that thou dost care for him?" (RSV), now read, "what are human beings that you are mindful of them, mortals that you care for them?" (NRSV). Mark 4:9 is no longer "he who has ears to hear, let him hear" (RSV), but "let anyone with ears to hear listen" (NRSV). Revelation 21:3 has been changed from "the dwelling of God is with men" (RSV) to "the home of God is among mortals" (NRSV). And, significantly, Phoebe is now "a deacon of the church" (NRSV), instead of "a deaconess" (RSV) in Rom. 16:1. The translators might have used more discretion in their attempt to avoid exclusive language. For example, when Sisera, completely un-aware that a woman will deliver Israel for the first time (as we know from Judges 4:9), tells Jael to deny any אִישׁ entrance into the tent in vs. 20, the Hebrew writer may in fact imply that Sisera is ironically unconcerned about any women who might pose a threat. The RSV rendering of אִישׁ as "man" highlights this discrepancy in awareness between Sisera and the informed readers and is arguably a better translation than the more inclusive "anybody" found in the NRSV. But any loss like this pales when compared to the removal of exclusive, androcentric language.

Quite apart from the inclusive language change, a number of adjustments to the RSV have been generated by recent discoveries of ancient biblical manuscripts. Following the publication of the RSV, the discovery of Hebrew and Aramaic texts found alongside the Dead Sea advanced the interpretation of the Hebrew Bible, and several early New Testament manuscripts of the Gospel of Luke and John and other portions have also become available since the publication of the RSV. Such discoveries have shed light on Hebrew and Greek passages that were previously difficult or impossible to understand. Discoveries advance our understanding of original lan-guages and require us to look again at existing English translations. Other studies (paleographical, sociological, and archaeological in nature) also shed light on these ancient words. Such combined forces work together to give us a new picture of Hebrew, Aramaic, and Greek vocabulary and syntax.

Many readers of the Bible are aware of these two major areas of improvement. A comparison of the Jonah stories (!) found in the RSV and NRSV reveals that much more is at work (and at stake) here. *Any* change in language works at different levels, and to understand these, thirteen categories are isolated below. Several of these distinctions overlap and some points that are raised here will be discussed further in the remaining chapters. Comparisons are made based on two critical editions of the Oxford Annotated Bibles.[8] Whenever a character's speech is quoted, the speaker is indicated after the RSV excerpt, and when no indication is given, the voice is that of the narrator.

1. Changes in the Narrator's Voice

a. (1:5) "Then the mariners were afraid." (RSV)
"Then the mariners were afraid." (NRSV)

b. (1:10) "Then the men were exceedingly afraid." (RSV)
"Then the men were even more afraid." (NRSV)

c. (1:16) "Then the men feared the Lord exceedingly." (RSV)
"Then the men feared the Lord even more." (NRSV)

d. (1:3) "so he paid the fare" (RSV)
"so he paid his fare" (NRSV)

e. (3:4) "and he cried, [proclamation]" (RSV)
"and he cried out, [proclamation]" (NRSV)

f. (1:4) "And there was a mighty tempest on the sea, so that the ship threatened to break up." (RSV)
"And such a mighty storm came upon the sea that the ship threatened to break up." (NRSV)

g. (3:7) "And [the king] made proclamation and published through Nineveh." (RSV)
"Then [the king] had a proclamation made in Nineveh." (NSRV)

h.   (4:1)   "But it displeased Jonah exceedingly, and he was
              angry." (RSV)
              "But this was very displeasing to Jonah, and he
              became angry." (NRSV)

The story of Jonah is told by a narrator and talking characters.
Always free to tell it all, this dialogue maker often allows characters
to speak for themselves. The implications of the narrator's voice as
compared to the dialogists themselves will be considered in chapter
3. Our present purpose is to isolate the NRSV's changes to the
narrator's voice. We learn of the fear (a.–c.) the sailors experience
in the first chapter from the narrator who describes their mounting
anxiety: (a.) וייראו → (b.) וייראו . . . ייראה גדולה → (c.) וייראו
ייראה גדולה את יהוה. . . . By comparing the two translations we
see that the NRSV highlights the accelerating fear with the words
"even more" in the second and third instance: "were afraid"→ "were
even more afraid"→ "feared the Lord even more." The RSV, on
the other hand, does show in c. that the sailors fear *the* Lord, but
its translation of b. and c. does not underscore the fact that their
fear accelerated as events transpired on board. The action Jonah
takes just before boarding the ship (d.) ויתן שכרה is notoriously
difficult to translate. A feminine pronominal suffix is attached to
"fare," that is "her fare," though it may be understood in a neuter
sense.[9] Some commentators use the suffix to argue that Jonah hired
the entire ship and crew, but such an image is not necessarily suggested by these Hebrew words.[10] Both the RSV and NRSV suggest
that Jonah simply paid his fare, and both alter the MT's pronominal
suffix attached to "fare." It might be argued that the NRSV improves
the RSV's translation at e. by more accurately introducing Jonah's
proclamation in Nineveh. Jonah "cries out" here just as he had been
charged to do in 1:2 (and as the NRSV had translated it). This type
of expression, perhaps more vivid than the image suggested by
"cried," is also evident in f. where we now learn that it is not simply
that "there was a mighty tempest on the sea" (RSV) but that "such
a mighty storm came upon the sea." The NRSV translation, "mighty
storm came upon" (in place of "there was a mighty tempest") highlights the Lord's role as a causal agent. The NRSV translation of
g. ויזעק ויאמר ("had a proclamation made") accords with BDB.[11]
This change alters the RSV in two respects: The action is no longer
reported in the active voice (the king no longer makes the procla-

mation but has someone else do it), and, by combining the two verbal forms of the RSV, the king is no longer portrayed as one who "publishes" the proclamation through Nineveh.

In Jonah the first verse of each chapter launches a new scene. The opening at chapter 4 is especially important because an entirely new crisis and set of issues are at work, quite unlike the action in the first three chapters. Several changes have been made to the narrator's words (h.) that introduce the fourth chapter. The change from "it displeased Jonah" to "this displeased Jonah" leaves little doubt in the mind of the reader that the turn of events in Nineveh (3:5–10) is what causes Jonah to boil. Second, the intensifier, "exceedingly," which follows "Jonah" in the RSV, has been incorporated in a more lucid phrase, "very displeasing to Jonah." Third, Jonah "was angry" before; the NRSV indicates that "he became angry." Both verbal forms are valid translations of the *vav consecutive* attached to the qal imperfect verb in 4:1. The NRSV, however, in each of these three portions of the verse ("this . . . very displeasing to Jonah . . . he became angry") draws more attention to the prophet who becomes angry because of what took place in Nineveh. The causal connection between the outcome in Nineveh and Jonah's subsequent response as reflected in the NRSV is important, we will later discover, because of its impact on characterization.

2. Changes in Quoted Speech

a. (1:6)   "'What do you mean, you sleeper?'" (RSV) [captain of the sailors]
"'What are you doing sound asleep?'" (NRSV)

b. (4:2)   "'That is why I made haste to flee to Tarshish.'" (RSV) [Jonah]
"'That is why I fled to Tarshish at the beginning.'" (NRSV)

c. (4:4)   "'Do you do well to be angry?'" (RSV) [Lord]
"'Is is right for you to be angry?'" (NRSV)

d. (4:9)   "'Do you do well to be angry for the plant?' And he said, 'I do well to be angry, angry enough to die.'" (RSV) [Lord/narrator/Jonah]

"'Is it right for you to be angry about the bush?'
And he said, 'Yes, angry enough to die.'" (NRSV)

The Hebrew word נרדם ("sleeper," "sound asleep") in a. is notoriously difficult to translate.[12] It may be a participle serving as an
accusative of state (GKC 385 [§ 120.b]) and thereby suggesting
something like, "What's with you sleeping?" It may also be translated
as a vocative (as RSV). By not translating as a vocative, the NRSV
has given a less condescending tone to the captain's pointed question.
We will have occasion to notice the importance of Jonah's delayed
verbal explanation for why he flees from the Lord in 4:2, but the
translations at b. allow for some preliminary observations. קדמתי
לברח does not necessarily mean "made haste to flee" as the RSV
has it.[13] Here the verb קדמתי may very well function as an auxiliary
to the infinitive construct (לברח), and the NRSV correctly understands the construction as a temporal qualifier. Such a translation as
found in the NRSV also highlights for the reader the antichronological nature of Jonah's important speech. This rendering of "at
the beginning" represents an improvement over other English translations that do not include it (JB, KJV, NASB, NEB, NIV). In c.
and d. the different translations are explained by the various shades
of meaning suggested by היטב, which carries the force of "to do
well," "to act ethically to/toward someone," but also "to do [an act]
thoroughly, skillfully."[14] The new translation, which calls into question Jonah's *right* to protest, had in fact recently been suggested by
Leslie Allen.[15] In addition to the type of changes discussed in the
introduction to this chapter, the incorporation of insight suggested
by post-RSV commentators is also an important feature of this new
translation. Both the RSV and NRSV make it clear that Jonah should
not be angry. The NRSV translation, however, presents Jonah in
an even less favorable light.

3. Inclusive Language

a. (3:7) "'let neither man nor beast'" (RSV) [king of
Nineveh]
"'no human being or animal'" (NRSV)

b. (3:8) "'but let man and beast'" (RSV) [king of Nineveh]
"'human beings and animals'" (NRSV)

c. (3:8) "'his evil way'" (RSV) [king of Nineveh]
"'their evil ways'" (NRSV)

d. (3:8) "'in his hands'" (RSV) [king of Nineveh]
"'in their hands'" (NRSV)

As mentioned above, one the most far-reaching changes is the NRSV's consistent use of language that refers to people with non-gender specific words. Members of the NRSV committee also considered eliminating exclusive, male terms applied to the deity ("King," "Lord," "Father"), but eventually decided against such a move. Thus, masculine references to God are maintained in Jonah as they are throughout the Bible: "when God saw what they did, how they turned from their evil ways, God changed *his* mind about the calamity that *he* had said *he* would bring upon them; and *he* did not do it" (3:10; NRSV). The decision to purge exclusive language that refers to people was one that committee members adopted, but they did not begin the process with such a mandate. Walter Harrelson, a member of the committee, describes the process behind the decision to eliminate some exclusive language:

> The decision was taken along the way, and in stages, as the work of the committee proceeded. The first formal statement on the subject was a page produced by the late George MacRae, S.J., containing guidelines for avoiding masculine language in cases in which it was clear that both men and women were intended. It was a modest statement indeed and was soon outgrown, but it served us well for several sessions. We did not engage in extended discussion about avoiding masculine references to the Deity, although we reviewed the matter as the draft of the Inclusive Language Lectionary was being produced, at which time the translation committee reaffirmed its decision not to attempt to eliminate masculine references to God.[16]

The translators of the RSV did, if only on occasion, use inclusive terms for Hebrew words they otherwise translated as masculine. For example, in Jonah 4:11, אדם was rendered as "person" in the RSV, a translation that did not have to be altered in the revision. With respect to the change to inclusive language in the Jonah story, alterations were required at four places, and on each occasion, it is the king's direct speech that was modified (a.–d.) In addition to the

inclusive language issue, a. and b. reflect a change from the word
"beast" to "animal(s)." The word "beast" in the RSV survives from
the KJV. The word "animal" never appears in the KJV (and is found
only infrequently in the RSV), but in the NRSV, the word is often
used.[17] Sometimes the translators changed the number of adjectives
and nouns (from singular to plural) to facilitate the change to inclusive language. The RSV's, "his evil way" c., a literal translation
of the Hebrew, is now "*their* evil ways." Working from the dictum
included in the preface to the NRSV, "as free as possible, as literal
as necessary," this alteration of the Hebrew text—which I have
followed—moves from a literal rendering to a freer one. One also
notices a change in number in d. where "his hands" is now "their
hands." In this case, the inclusive "their hands" more accurately
reflects the Hebrew (כפיהם).

4. Up-to-Date Language

a. (1:5)   "they threw the wares" (RSV)
             "they threw the cargo" (NRSV)

b. (1:8)   "'And whence do you come?'" (RSV) [sailors]
             "'Where do you come from?'" (NRSV)

c. (1:9)   "'I fear the Lord.'" (RSV) [Jonah]
             "'I worship the Lord.'" (NRSV)

d. (1:12   "'tempest' . . . tempestuous" (RSV) [Jonah/
    –13)   narrator]
             "'storm' . . . stormy" (NRSV)

e. (2:7)   "'when my soul fainted within me'" (RSV) [Jonah]
             "'As my life was ebbing away'" (NRSV)

f. (3:8)   "'yea'" (RSV) [king of Nineveh]
             — (NRSV)

g. (3:9)   "'so that we perish not?'" (RSV) [king of Nineveh]
             "'so that we do not perish'" (NRSV)

h. (4:11)   "'and also much cattle'" (RSV) [Lord]
             "'and also many animals'" (NRSV)

An examination of these brief passages reveals that archaic or seldom used words such as "wares," "whence," "tempest(uous)," and "yea" have either been replaced (with "cargo," "where," "storm[y]") or eliminated altogether (a., b., d., f.). Such a number of changes in a relatively small narrative space might suggest that many words have virtually dropped out of the English vocabulary since the RSV first appeared in the 1940s. In fact, this number considered in isolation would be misleading because the RSV often preserves words that appeared in the KJV. The change in c. is different from what we have observed in other examples. "Fear" and "worship" are both defensible translations of the Hebrew word ירא, a word that conveys several shades of meaning. It does mean "to be afraid of," and had in fact been used by the narrator in this sense as recently as vs. 5 (and will be used again in this sense in vs. 10). But it may also convey the idea of "standing in awe of," "respecting," and hence "worshipping." Here in vs. 9, the audience encounters the word a second time, unlike the sailors aboard ship (vs. 9), and are in position to appreciate the author's skill. From the reader's side, this single word functions to contrast the moods aboard ship. The pagan sailors take drastic measures because they literally fear for their lives; Jonah, on the other hand, in a comparatively calmer mood, responds to their series of questions by admitting that his fear is in God alone. Such a contrast revolving around a single word allows us to formulate questions on our own about this laconic prophet who says that he יראs the Lord, but whose flight demonstrates that he apparently lacks respect for God. This is an important word in the first chapter of Jonah, and the RSV consistently translates it as "fears," whereas the NRSV renders it with two different words to reflect these shades of meaning. Yet, even though the worshipping aspect is suggested again at 1:16 ("the men feared the Lord even more, and they offered a sacrifice to the Lord and made vows"), the word "worship" is not used here in the NRSV. The changes in language have also made certain images clearer. The RSV translates e. in a literal fashion. The obscure image of a "fainting soul" in chapter 2 is now a life described as "ebbing away." The NRSV's omission of the word "yea" from the king of Nineveh's edict in f. appears to be another attempt to avoid antiquated expressions. In fact, the RSV's "yea" is retained from the KJV, and the Hebrew simple conjunction ו does not have to be translated as an interjection. Other awkward sounding phrases (g. and h.) have also been updated.

5. Adversive vs. non-Adversive Conjunctions

(1:17) "and the Lord appointed" (RSV)
"but the Lord provided" (NRSV)

Biblical Hebrew knows at least three ways of expressing the conjunction "but." It may be introduced by כי אם, כי alone, or even with a prefixed ו (GKC §163a). While the examples above have suggested that translation *is* interpretation, the principle may be even more obvious when considering how the Hebrew conjunction ו is rendered. This conjunction, typically translated as "and," may also be translated as an adversive, "but" or "however," and in making the choice the translator is provided with only one clue: context. In the new translation, the ו is understood as an *adversive vav* on ten occasions;[18] whereas in the RSV it is understood in this manner on eleven occasions.[19] Sometimes, the translators of both the RSV and NRSV agree on their understanding of adversive conjunctions (1:3, 4, 13; 2:9; 4:1, 7, 9). The translation, "but the Lord provided," subtly draws attention to the contrasting actions of the mortal sailors who pick Jonah up and hurl him into the sea with the actions of God who is able to summon a large fish. The sailors do one thing; God does another.

6. And→ Then, etc.

a. (2:10) "And the Lord spoke to the fish." (RSV)
"Then the Lord spoke to the fish." (NRSV)

b. (3:7) "And he made proclamation." (RSV)
"Then he had a proclamation made." (NRSV)

c. (4:10) "and the Lord said" (RSV)
"then the Lord said" (NRSV)

d. (1:14) "Therefore they cried to the Lord." (RSV)
"Then they cried to the Lord." (NRSV)

e. (3:1) "Then the word of the Lord came to Jonah a second time." (RSV)
"The word of the Lord came to Jonah a second time." (NRSV)

f.   (3:6)   "then tidings reached the king" (RSV)
             "when the news reached the king" (NRSV)

g.   (4:3)   "'Therefore now, O Lord, take my life from me.'"
             (RSV) [Jonah]
             "'And now, O Lord, please take my life from me.'"
             (NRSV)

Biblical Hebrew does have its own word for "then" (אז), but the force of the temporal sequence may also be suggested by a *vav consecutive* attached to an imperfect (GKC §49, §100i, §112oo). In examples a.–f. above, a *vav consecutive* is attached to an imperfect verb. Quite often the RSV and NRSV translate such constructions as "then" (1:5, 8, 10, 11, 12, 16; 2:1, 4; 4:5). On four separate occasions (a.–d.), the NRSV translates the conjunction in a more temporal sense. On the fourth occasion (d.), the RSV implies a causal connection between the failed effort of the sailors to row the ship back to land and their supplication to the Lord ("*therefore* they cried to the Lord"). In the NRSV such a causal connection is only tacitly implied. On one occasion (e.), the trend is reversed. The NRSV ignores the conjunction altogether and simply translates the beginning of the new scene as "the word of the Lord came to Jonah." The RSV had taken the conjunction into account: "then the word of the Lord came." In f. the force of the *vav consecutive* onto an imperfect verbal form is rendered differently. The two adverbs, "then" (RSV) and "when" (NRSV), bridge the actions of the people of Nineveh (vs. 5) and the parallel actions of the king (vs. 6). The sequence of these activities has been explained in various ways and are summarized nicely by Sasson.[20] The best explanation may be that the actions of the citizens precede those of the king. The king's subsequent edict may then be understood as an official response to their actions. In both English translations under consideration, it is obvious that the news reaches the king. The issue at hand is: when does he receive the disturbing notification? Is the interval between the actions of the people and king minutes, hours, days? The NRSV's translation of "when the news reached the king" is more open-ended. The RSV's rendering, "then the news," while also indefinite, suggests that the time lapse is, most likely, short. The contrast reflected in g. is different from the other examples above. Here a conjunction is attached to עתה ("now"), a Hebrew word that typically signals a change in time, point of view, or the like. It marks the event as a significant one. The RSV offers a translation of greater force, "therefore now," unlike the slightly more subdued NRSV rendering of "and now."

7. Key Thematic Words Rendered Differently

a. (3:9) "'God may yet repent and turn from his fierce anger.'" (RSV) [king]
"'God may relent and change his mind; he may turn from his fierce anger.'" (NRSV)

b. (3:10) "God repented of the evil." (RSV)
"God changed his mind about the calamity." (NRSV)

c. (4:2) "'Thou art a gracious God . . . [who] repentest of evil.'" (RSV) [Jonah]
"'You are a gracious God . . . ready to relent from punishing.'" (NRSV)

d. (4:10) "'You pity the plant.'" (RSV) [Lord]
"'You are concerned about the bush.'" (NRSV)

e. (4:11) "'And should I not pity Nineveh?'" (RSV) [Lord]
"'And should I not be concerned about Nineveh?'" (NRSV)

On a few occasions one notices different translations of thematic words, as, for example, with the word יָרֵא ("fear" or "worship") discussed above. Two other key words have been rendered differently in the NRSV translation of Jonah. On three different occasions the Hebrew word נחם is applied to God (a.–c.).[21] The RSV consistently uses a form of the verb "repent." The Hebrew word does carry this shade of meaning, but when applied to God a question arises: Since the English word implies repentance *from wrongdoing*, why does God repent? The NRSV translators, apparently aware of the problem, never translate the Hebrew word as "repents" when God is the subject of the verb. In all three instances above, reference is made to actions that God considers but never carries out, and, as scholars have recently observed, in these instances the word is best translated as "changing one's mind" or "relenting."[22] In a., two synonymous Hebrew words שוב and נחם are used in the initial clause. The RSV captures the construction with "yet repent." The NRSV renders the words in a more literal and dramatic fashion, "relent and change his mind." In b., God is described as "chang[ing] his mind" (NRSV), instead of "repent[ing] of the evil" (RSV). With c., we observe that the NRSV translators render the verb נחם as "relent" on a second occasion. The NRSV's image of God who either relents or has a change of mind improves upon the picture of God who repents of evil in the RSV.

Commentators have frequently called attention to the important word חוס at the end of the book. Both of the words which the translators use to bring the Hebrew word into English (d.–e.), "pity" (RSV) and "concerned" (NRSV), are possible according to the standard lexicons, but the NRSV's choice is to be preferred on contextual clues. The word "concerned" better conveys the import of the Hebrew word because Jonah in fact does not "pity the plant" (RSV). That is, he does not feel sorry *for the withered plant*. Instead, he is *concerned* about it because it no longer provides him with what he wants: shade. Thus understood, the contrast is between Jonah's concern (חוס) over a plant and God's concern (חוס) over Nineveh.

8. New Paragraphs

The oldest Hebrew manuscripts do not have paragraph markings. In fact, the first readers did not even have the good fortune of spaces between words! The division of Jonah into four chapters can only be dated from the Middle Ages. The NRSV division of chapter 4 into three scenes (4:1–5; 4:6–8; 4:9–11) and the RSV division into two (4:1–5; 4:6–11) is, as far as I can tell, not based on early manuscript evidence,[23] and once again, the translator's role as interpreter is apparent. Paragraph markings are important to consider because they often signal shifts in genre, introduce new scenes, or mark changes in action. Sasson's excellent discussion on the scenes in chapter 4 does not need to be rehearsed here, but his warning is worth repeating since it addresses the issue at stake: "How we apportion Jonah into integral units is more critical on this occasion than previously; for it can influence our very understanding of Jonah's denouement."[24] All paragraph markings in the RSV and NRSV are identical in the first three chapters. By subdividing the RSV partition of 4:6–11 into two parts, the NRSV sets the *kikayon* episode off and also places the significant dialogue between Jonah and the Lord off into a separate scene.

9. Additional Critical Notes

a. (1:7)   no note in RSV
"the sailors;" note: "Heb *they*" (NRSV)

b. (1:17) note: "Ch 2.1 in Heb" (RSV)
note: "Ch 2.1 in Heb" (NRSV)

c. (2:4)   no note in RSV
"how;" note: "Theodotion: Heb *surely*" (NRSV)

d. (4:6)   "plant;" note: "Heb *qiqayon*, probably *the castor oil plant*" (4:6, 7, 9, 10; RSV)
"bush;" note: "Heb *qiqayon*, possibly *the castor bean plant*" (NRSV)

The RSV treats two different issues (b. and d.) in the footnotes to the book of Jonah (at 1:17 and 4:6 [6, 7, 9, 10]). The NRSV essentially duplicates these and adds two more (a.–d.). The NRSV translators supplied a subject ("sailors") to the initial clause in a.—perhaps because MT has a plural verb and a singular subject?—and provided an explanatory note to convey the Hebrew. Such a note is unnecessary in the RSV since its text reflects the Hebrew. The initial word of the second line in 2:4 has perhaps received more discussion than any other in the book. Both the RSV and the NRSV follow Theodotion's Greek translation (interrogative "how") here at c., but the RSV does not inform the reader that the Greek is followed. The NRSV does with a note. The *kikayon* referred to in 4:6, 6, 7, 9, 10 is translated as "plant" in the RSV and "bush" in the NRSV. Both translations provide a note (d.) The NRSV translates it as "bush" and then reports that it is possibly a plant.

10. New Punctuation

a. (1:1   "Amit'tai . . . Nin'eveh" (RSV)
 –2)   "Amittai . . . Nineveh" (NRSV)

b. (1:8) "'Tell us, on whose account this evil has come upon us?'" (RSV) [sailors]
"'Tell us why this calamity has come upon us.'" (NRSV)

c. (3:7 "And he made proclamation and published
-8) through Nineveh, 'By the decree of the king and his nobles: Let neither man nor beast, herd nor flock, taste anything; let them not feed, or drink water, but let man and beast be covered with sackcloth, and let them cry mightily to God; yea, let every one turn . . .'" (RSV) [king of Nineveh]

"Then he had a proclamation made in Nineveh: 'By the decree of the king and his nobles: No human being or animal, no herd or flock, shall taste anything. They shall not feed, nor shall they drink water. Human beings and animals shall be covered with sackcloth, and they shall cry mightily to God. All shall turn . . .'" (NRSV)

d. (3:9) "'Who knows, God may yet repent and turn . . . so that we perish not?'" (RSV) [king of Nineveh]
"'Who knows? God may relent and change his mind . . . so that we do not perish.'" (NRSV)

e. (4:6) "And the Lord God appointed a plant . . . to save him from his discomfort. So Jonah was exceedingly glad." (RSV)
"The Lord God appointed a bush . . . to save him from his discomfort; so Jonah was very happy." (NRSV)

The diacritical accentuation marks in Jonah (a.) have been purged from the RSV. The NRSV renders the initial sentence which the sailors put to Jonah (b.) as an imperative ("Tell us why!"); in the RSV they ask him a question ("Tell us, on whose account?"). The cluttered Hebrew in this verse has exercised many ancient and modern exegetes. Philological considerations aside, the question, "who is responsible?" is certainly unusual since Jonah's guilt has already been determined through the casting of lots in the preceding verse. Two recent commentators shed light on the Hebrew. After discussing the matter, Sasson offers an admittedly inelegant English translation: "(tell us) 'because (or: in as much as) to-whom—this evil is ours.'" He understands the purpose behind the phrases to be "'because it is you who are bringing this calamity upon us.'"[25] Wolff, claiming (unconvincingly) that part of the phrase is a "secondary interpolation," also translates as an imperative ("Just tell us why this evil has befallen us") and adds that it is "both clumsy and superfluous."[26] Thus the NRSV translators, perhaps aware of the problem of sailors asking a question in vs. 8 that had been answered in vs. 7, reflect the understanding of some of the best, recent exegesis on Jonah. The king's extended decree in c. is given in two sentences in the RSV. (This horrendous punctuation survives, with slight modification, from the KJV.) The king utters six sentences in the NRSV at this point of the narrative (3:7–8). After the publication of the RSV, the awkwardness of such long sentences was noticed by several commentators including Allen, Stuart, and Wolff.[27] The NRSV not only improves the punctuation; it also changes the character's words. The tone of the king's decree in the NRSV is harsh and exacting: "No human being . . . no herd or flock . . . They shall not feed." The RSV had implied a less demanding king: "Let neither man nor beast taste anything, let them not feed." At the end of the edict (d.), the king expresses the possibility that God may turn from being angry and spare the people. The punctuation of the RSV suggests that the force of the interrogative falls at the very end of the proclamation. However, the Hebrew expression, מִי יוֹדֵעַ ("who knows?"), which introduces the king's wishful thinking, is a question by itself. Further, the conclusion to the king's remarks, "God may relent . . . ," is not an interrogative. This change in punctuation in the NRSV more accurately reflects the tone of the Hebrew for it highlights the uncertainty: Does anyone on earth know? Once again, we observe that commentators have recently suggested such a change.[28] In e. two thoughts are conveyed: God's actions and the prophet's feelings. The RSV divides the images into two sentences. The NRSV separates the images with a semicolon thus incorporating both thoughts in a single sentence. By uniting the images in one sentence, the NRSV subtly connects the Lord's action with Jonah's response to it.

11. Translation and Hebrew Syntax

a. (1:9) "And he said to them, 'I am a Hebrew.'" (RSV) [narrator/Jonah]
   "'I am a Hebrew,' he replied." (NRSV) [Jonah/narrator]

b. (3:5) "They proclaimed a fast, and put on sackcloth, from the greatest of them to the least of them." (RSV)
   "They proclaimed a fast, and everyone, great and small, put on sackcloth." (NRSV)

c. (4:3) "'Therefore now, O Lord, take my life from me, I beseech thee.'" (RSV) [Jonah]
   "'And now, O Lord, please take my life from me.'" (NRSV)

Hebrew prose generally follows a particular word order (verb, subject [and modifiers], direct object [and modifiers], indirect object), which authors sometimes alter to emphasize thoughts, characters, and action. Since the NRSV departs from the RSV's word order on three separate occasions, it may be worthwhile to ask which translation more accurately reflects the Hebrew idiom. In the first instance (a.), the Hebrew word order is: "and he said to them, 'A Hebrew, I am.'" In conversation, Jonah is stressing the fact that he is a Hebrew. This kind of stress could be indicated in English by translating literally; however, a translation such as this would be awkward. The NRSV indicates the stress by placing Jonah's speech before the narrator's introduction. By contrast, the stress on the Hebrewness is lost in the RSV. I can find no evidence of a manuscript that supports the NRSV's omission of "to them" (אליהם). Is the Hebrew word omitted in translation because of the context? Jonah must, after all, be speaking to them. Or is it stylistically displeasing?[29] With respect to b., the RSV more accurately reflects the Hebrew word order. The qualifying phrase, "everyone, great and small" (NRSV), is not emphasized in the Hebrew. What motivated this change? Is anything stylistically awkward or unpleasant about the phrase coming just *after* "put on sackcloth" as the RSV has it? In the third instance (c.), the NRSV more accurately reflects the Hebrew word order where the particle of entreaty, "please" or "I beseech thee," is found *after* the address, "O Lord," and *before* the request for death. Finally, at 4:7, *neither* the RSV's nor the NRSV's word order accurately reflects the Hebrew syntax which is: "But God appointed a worm when the dawn came up the next day and it attacked the *kikayon* and it withered."

12. "Inconsistent" Translation of Hebrew Words in the NRSV

קוּם לֵךְ

a. (1:2)   "'Arise, go.'" (RSV) [Lord]
           "'Go at once.'" (NRSV)

b. (3:2)   "'Arise, go.'" (RSV) [Lord]
           "'Get up, go.'" (NRSV)

וַיָּקָם יוֹנָה

c. (1:3)   "But Jonah rose." (RSV)
           "But Jonah set out." (NRSV)

d. (3:3)   "So Jonah arose." (RSV)
           "So Jonah set out." (NRSV)

קוּם / וַיָּקָם

e. (1:6)   "'Arise.'" (RSV) [captain of the sailors]
           "'Get up.'" (NRSV)

f. (3:6)   "And he arose." (RSV)
           "He arose." (NRSV)

וַיְמַן

g. (2:1)   "And the Lord appointed a great fish." (RSV)
           "But the Lord provided a large fish." (NRSV)

h. (4:6)   "And the Lord God appointed a plant." (RSV)
           "The Lord God appointed a bush." (NRSV)

i. (4:7)   "God appointed a worm." (RSV)
           "God appointed a worm." (NRSV)

j. (4:8) "God appointed a sultry east wind." (RSV)
"God prepared a sultry east wind." (NRSV)

On several occasions a single Hebrew word is translated with multiple English words in the NRSV. We have already observed that ירא is translated in the NRSV both as "fear" and "worship." Other examples of one Hebrew word rendered with two different English words require extra consideration. First, קום in a.–f. is consistently translated as "arise" (or "rose," "arose") in the RSV. The NRSV translation of the Hebrew word is more fluid. In a.–b. the translation takes both קום and the accompanying imperative לך into account and produces something quite different: "go at once," "get up, go." In the remaining examples from the NRSV (c.–f.), other words are used to translate the single Hebrew word: "set out," "get up," "rose." If consistency is valued, it would appear at first glance that the RSV is to be preferred. The NRSV, again perhaps informed by recent commentators,[30] understands the two verbal forms, קום and הלך, as suggesting a coordinating complementary idea capable of being rendered in a variety of ways.

In similar fashion, the RSV consistently translates the Hebrew word מנה with one English word, "appointed," in g.–j. The NRSV offers some variety ("provided," "appointed," "prepared"). Sasson, after a careful consideration of the verb, concludes: "What these attestations suggest is that [מנה] is an act that generally needs a medium through which to be fulfilled. Applying this insight to Jonah 2:1, we can say that God is not so much keen to appoint a 'big fish' (nor, for that matter, in bringing forth plants, worms, or hot winds) than to set the most appropriate conditions for teaching Jonah the desired lessons."[31]

There is no question that this Hebrew verb found in the Piel (as it is in these four verses) may convey the sense of "provide," "appoint," "offer," "allot," "designate," and the like. What is less clear in this case is what motivates the translators to opt for different English words. Why not maintain the same translation once one of the English words has been settled upon? The RSV makes such repetition clear to the reader by translating מנה in a consistent manner. Indeed, such distinguished commentators as Allen, Lacocque-Lacocque, Sasson, Stuart, and Wolff also consistently translate מנה with one English word.[32]

13. Paratactic Style is Lost (Sometimes)

a. (1:5)   "And they threw" (RSV)
             "they threw" (NRSV)

b. (1:6)   "so the captain" (RSV)
             "the captain" (NRSV)

c. (1:7)   "and they said" (RSV)
             "the sailors said" (NRSV)

d. (1:14)   "'this man's life, and lay not on us innocent blood'"
             (RSV) [sailors]
             "'this man's life. Do not make us guilty of innocent
             blood'" (NRSV)

The issue of paratactic style (joining thoughts and speech with conjunctions) will be discussed in chapter 3. On numerous occasions, the NRSV does not retain the paratactic style, a common feature of biblical prose.[33] The RSV text of Jonah usually translates the Hebrew conjunction ו.[34] The advantage of the NRSV's frequent omission of the conjunction is that it is stylistically more pleasant than the frequent (and annoying) use of "and." In sum, with respect to paratactic style, the RSV more accurately reflects the Hebrew whereas the NRSV, in often omitting the conjunction, provides a translation which accords better with the modern conventions of English.

Conclusion

We have made observations about language, translation, and interpretation while focusing on the RSV and the NRSV translations of Jonah in this chapter. In addition to routine changes in the NRSV, such as the removal of archaic language and the introduction of inclusive language, this survey has also shown that some of the more substantive alterations reflect a new understanding of the original Hebrew. The large number of changes appearing in the new translation is surprising, particularly when we bear in mind that the RSV and NRSV are members of the same family of English Bibles. What general observations can be made to account for changes made to forty-seven of the forty-eight verses in Jonah, and more specifically, how will these modifications impact this present study?

Many of the changes reflected in the NRSV text of Jonah are the direct result of progress made in biblical scholarship. A comparison of several passages revealed that philologists and exegetes have clarified the meaning of some Hebrew words and phrases. For example, the NRSV translators, perhaps aware of the problem of sailors asking a question in 1:8 that had been answered by the lots in the preceding verse (as indeed Hans Walter Wolff and Jack Sasson are), changed the force of the interrogative from a who- to a why-question. Recent interpreters also understand מי יודע ("who knows"), which introduces the king's wishful thinking in 3:9, as a question. The NRSV translation is consistent with this view because it transforms the force of the king's asking from "God may relent" (RSV) to his initial words in vs. 9: "Who knows?" As such, the NRSV more accurately reflects the tone of the Hebrew where the king observes that God may (actually) relent. Another exegetical improvement was isolated with respect to the Hebrew word נחם, a term often translated as "repent." In Jonah, the NRSV translators, perhaps sensing the problem of God repenting (as the RSV translates it on three occasions), never render the Hebrew word as "repents" when God is the subject of the verb. The new translation improves upon the image of God who "repents of evil" (in the RSV) on three occasions (3:9; 3:10; 4:2). In these instances, the word is now translated as "change his mind" or "ready to relent" (as Jack Sasson, F. I. Anderson, and D. N. Freedman had recently suggested). The new translation also now calls Jonah's *right* to protest into question in 4:4 and 4:9. This understanding reflected in the NRSV of the Hebrew word ההיטב ("Is it right?") had recently been suggested by Leslie Allen.

We have also observed that translating from one language to another requires that interpretive decisions be made. A few examples illustrate this principle. ירא, an important word in the first chapter of Jonah, is consistently rendered as "fear" (or "afraid") in the RSV. The NRSV understands ירא in this fashion (1:5, 10, 16), but once renders the word as "worship" (1:9) to reflect the single word's shades of meaning. There is no question that the Hebrew verb מנה may convey the sense of "provide," "appoint," or "prepare" as the NRSV translates it in Jonah 2:1; 4:6, 7, 8. The RSV, however, maintains the repetition of the Hebrew word by consistently translating it as "appointed." קדמתי לברח in 4:2 is no longer understood as "made haste to flee" (RSV). The NRSV understands the verb קדמתי as an auxiliary to לברח, and thus translates it as a temporal qualifier ("in the beginning"). The implications of this statement, which emphasizes the antichronological nature of Jonah's speech, will be discussed in chapter 4 below. The translations offer different pictures of when news of the proclamation reaches the king of Nineveh. The NRSV's translation of "when the news reached the king" is more open-ended than the RSV's rendering, "then the news." Both are indefinite, yet a sense of immediacy ("then") is highlighted in the RSV. The implications of changes such as these on the temporal plane will be discussed in the final chapter of this study. And finally, even the NRSV's division of chapter 4 into three scenes (4:1–5; 4:6–8; 4:9–11) affects understanding.

The differences between the translations are nowhere more apparent and crucial for this study on Jonah than in the area of characterization. For example, we observed that the NRSV translation of וידעק ויאמר ("had a proclamation made") alters the RSV in two respects: The proclamation is no longer reported in the active voice, and, by combining the two verbal forms of the RSV, the king does not "publish" the proclamation through Nineveh. We also observed that the king is portrayed as more autocratic in the NRSV ("No human being . . . shall taste anything . . ." 3:7), whereas earlier in the story, by not translating the statement in 1:6 as a vocative, the NRSV gave a less accusing tone to the question that the captain asks Jonah. Changes in translation also affect the characterization of major characters. We observed that the NRSV highlights Jonah's response to the events in Nineveh in 4:1 with the translation, "this was very displeasing to Jonah, and he became angry." The causal connection between the outcome in Nineveh and Jonah's subsequent response, reflected in both translations, is highlighted in the NRSV, and this new translation sets a different stage for the events that follow. Characterization is an aspect of this study that warrants more attention, and it is to this topic that we turn in the next chapter.

Chapter 3

The Narrator and Characters

Wayne Booth refers to the narrator, who may be defined as the narrative voice or speaker of a text, as the "center of consciousness"[1] because he, she, or it[2] is the one who guides the reader through the projected world. The narrator may be dramatized or undramatized, and the more overt the narration, the stronger the addressee senses his presence. The narrator is intrusive as he interrupts the action and conversation to relay information to the audience. In Jonah, the narrator serves various functions as he describes action, introduces speakers, summarizes conversation, provides explanatory glosses, and tells us what various characters, including even the Lord, think and feel.

The narrator often records events in a neutral tone but sometimes provides evaluation by expressing a conceptual or ideological point of view. Consider three examples outside the book of Jonah:

a. And the Lord was sorry that he had made humankind on the earth, and it grieved him to his heart. (Gen. 6:6)
b. But the thing that David had done displeased the Lord. (2 Sam. 11:27b)
c. Judah did what was evil in the sight of the Lord. (1 Kings 14:22a)

These three passages, all revealing the Lord's displeasure with different individuals, suggest the breadth of the narrator's ability, but give little clue about his functional range in the Hebrew Bible.[3] In Jonah, when the narrator suspends a description of action and steps outside the spatio-temporal boundaries of the story to describe someone's appearance, to condemn or praise any of the characters, or to summarize a series of events in a single phrase, then he is doing what he frequently does: shaping the story *and* the audience. Since the narrator assumes such an important role, it is necessary to isolate comments to understand the function, point of view, and degree to which his presence is felt in each of the chapters. This analysis can best be accomplished by considering where one finds intrusions in the book of Jonah, but first, his vantage point should be considered.

Omniscient vs. Limited Perspectives

The narrator in Jonah, unlike the sailors, the Ninevites, and the prophet, has access to privileged information. He knows how the prophet feels ("and it displeased Jonah, a great evil, and he became hot with anger" [4:1]; "and Jonah was happy about the *kikayon*, extremely happy" [4:6b]) as well as what God perceives ("and God saw their deeds, how they turned from their evil ways, and God was sorry concerning the evil which he had said he would do to them . . ." [3:10]). Unlike the characters on earth who address each other (and us) from a limited perspective, the narrator speaks from an omniscient vantage point. But what exactly is the nature of this omniscience?

The knowledge the narrator possesses can only be inferred from, but should not be equated with, the information shared with the audience. The narrator in Jonah could, if he chose, undertake to tell us what any of the characters felt at *any* moment, but consistently conveys information at the moment that best suits his strategy. When the narrator devises ambiguity in the opening chapters (What motivates Jonah to disobey the Lord's command? What is the message he is to cry against the Ninevites? Does the prayer from the belly of the fish actually reflect the prophet's change of heart as his words in 2:10 suggest?), he perforce could, if he desired, devise lucidity instead. This distinction between the strategy selected among all the options available is a theoretical necessity, and only by recognizing it does the narrator's maneuvering emerge in its full light. Meir Sternberg provides a convincing argument for recognizing the biblical narrator's privileged position:

> The narrator's omniscience once postulated—and there is no escaping it—the consequences for the interpretation of dissonance logically follow. In the face of an omission or some other strange recounting on his part, it would be unthinkable to deny him the benefit of indeterminacy—between suppression and confusion—that he himself grants the characters. . . . If a narrator shows himself qualified to penetrate the mind of one of the characters and report his secret activities—a feat impossible in everyday life—he has established his competence to do so in regard to all other inaccessibles as well. The superhuman privilege is constant and only its exercise variable: it is precisely the distance between them that cries out for explanation. And what-

ever line the explanation takes, it always starts from the premise
that the narrator could do otherwise if he chose.[4]

The Narrator's Role by Chapters

If the narrator does in fact abstain from sharing some information
by choice, it will be worthwhile to notice how he exercises the options
in Jonah.

> (1:1) *And the word of the Lord was to Jonah, son of Amittai, saying,*
> (2) "Arise, go to Nineveh, the great city, and call to her, for
> her wickedness has come up before me." (3) *But Jonah arose to
> flee towards Tarshish away from the presence of the Lord, and he
> went down to Joppa and he found a ship going to Tarshish and he
> gave the fare and he went down in it to go with them towards
> Tarshish away from the presence of the Lord. (4) But the Lord hurled
> a great wind upon the sea and a great tempest was on the sea, and
> the ship thought about breaking up. (5) And the sailors were afraid
> and they cried out each to his god(s) and they hurled the cargo which
> was on the ship into the sea to be lightened from them, and Jonah
> had gone down into the inner recesses of the ship, and had lain down,
> and had fallen into a trance.*

The opening here, like all narrative beginnings, is crucial. These
words set the tone and with them the artist may align sympathy for
certain characters, adopt a neutral tone, set the stage for introducing
conflict, or even cause us to entertain questions that will only be
answered later (or never). In all biblical passages except Jonah, this
beginning ("And the word of the Lord was to . . .") occurs only when
circumstances about the prophet and the mission are established (as
for example, with Elijah in 1 Kings 17:2 and Jeremiah in Jer. 24:4).[5]
This departure from the norm is our first clue that something
different is in store. As the typographical distinction makes clear,
the narrator assumes a prominent role at the beginning conveying
information in all but one of the first six verses (i.e., vs. 2). Apart
from a brief allusion to Jonah's lineage in vs. 1, the focus is on
action. This introduction to the flurry of excitement contrasts with
other beginnings in the Hebrew Bible:

> a. *There was a man in Maon, whose property was in Carmel. The
> man was very rich; he had three thousand sheep and a thousand*

goats. He was shearing his sheep in Carmel. Now the name of the man was Nabal, and the name of his wife Abigail. The woman was clever and beautiful, but the man was surly and mean; he was a Calebite. (1 Sam. 25:2–3)

b. *Now Jephthah the Gileadite, the son of a prostitute, was a mighty warrior. Gilead was the father of Jephthah. Gilead's wife also bore him sons; and when his wife's sons grew up, they drove Jephthah away, saying to him,* "You shall not inherit anything in our father's house; for you are the son of another woman." *Then Jephthah fled from his brothers and lived in the land of Tob. Outlaws collected around Jephthah and went raiding with him.* (Judg. 11:1–3)

c. *There was once a man in the land of Uz whose name was Job. That man was blameless and upright, one who feared God and turned away from evil. There were born to him seven sons and three daughters. He had seven thousand sheep, three thousand camels, five hundred yoke of oxen, and five hundred donkeys, and very many servants; so that this man was the greatest of all the people of the east. His sons used to go and hold feasts in one another's houses in turn; and they would send and invite their three sisters to eat and drink with them. And when the feast days had run their course, Job would send and sanctify them, and he would rise early in the morning and offer burnt offerings according to the number of them all; for Job said,* "It may be that my sons have sinned, and cursed God in their hearts." *This is what Job always did.* (Job 1:1–5)

In a., the narrator provides a significant amount of background information before the story proper begins in vs. 4. The addressee learns not only Nabal's hometown, but also about his occupation and place of business; not only that he is rich, but also the source of his wealth; not only his and his wife's name, but also something about their physical appearance and disposition.[6] The introduction in b., like the Jonah beginning, also provides the reader with facts about the character's lineage ("the son of a prostitute"), but unlike Jonah, this detail has a specific and sustained bearing on the plot as the sons' direct speech soon reveals. The introduction to Job (c.) represents one of the best examples of extended exposition or background in the entire Hebrew Bible.[7] We learn Job's name, where he lives, exactly how many children he has, the inventory of his livestock and slaves, and something about the religious practices of his family. While it is true that the Hebrew Bible seldom gives full scale descriptions—Job, Goliath, and David being three marginal exceptions—the examples show that it sometimes provides the reader with background information, and although examples a.–c. contain varying amounts of background information, they do have a common denominator when compared to Jonah 1:1–5. The narrator functions initially in Jonah as he did in the first chapter of Genesis where no exposition was presented when God first came on stage. Who is God? Where does the Almighty come from? In the absence of explicit exposition, the reader has no choice but to piece the story together.

Another interesting aspect of narration in this opening scene may be observed at 1:4 where the ship is granted the faculty of thinking. I have intentionally translated the Hebrew literally (contra JB, NAB, NEB, NIV, NRSV, RSV). Thinking is, of course, normally associated with the animate world. Even at this early stage it appears the narrator wishes to draw us into the world of the fabulous. As Jack Sasson remarks, we can expect the unexpected.[8] The importance of this image is reinforced by the two Hebrew words (חשב, "think," and השבר, "break up")—remarkably similar in spelling and pronunciation—which appear side by side. The importance of sound and rhythm will emerge as a major concern when we turn to the prayers in chapter 2, but already we see how the author uses language to highlight certain phenomenon.

(6) *And the captain of the sailors came to him and he said to him,* "How can you fall into a trance?! Arise, call upon your god(s). Perhaps the god(s) will give a thought to us so that we will not perish." (7) *And they said each to the other,* "Come and let us cast lots so that we may know on whose account this evil has happened to us." *And they cast lots and the lot fell unto Jonah.* (8) *And they said to him,* "Tell us, we pray, on whose account has this evil happened to us? What is your occupation? And from where do you come? What is your country? And from what people are you?" (9) *And he said unto them,* "I am a Hebrew, and the Lord, the God of the heavens, I fear, who made the sea and the dry land." (10) *And the men were afraid, greatly afraid,*

and they said unto him, "What is this which you have done?" *for the men knew that he was fleeing from the presence of the Lord for he had told them.* (11) *And they said unto him,* "What shall we do to you so that the sea may quiet down for us, for the sea is storming tempestuously?" (12) *And he said to them,* "Lift me up and hurl me into the sea and the sea will quiet down for you, for I know that it is because of me that this great tempest is upon you." (13) *And the men rowed hard (trying) to return to the dry land but they could not, for the sea was storming tempestuously against them.* (14) *And they called unto the Lord and they said,* "We pray, O Lord, do not let us perish on account of this man's life, and may you not put innocent blood upon us, for you, Lord, as you have pleased you have done." (15) *And they lifted Jonah up and they hurled him into the sea and the sea ceased from its raging.* (16) *And the men were afraid, greatly fearing the Lord, and they slaughtered a slaughter-meal to the Lord and they vowed vows.*

The narrator's significant role in the opening verses is modified in this second pericope as he frequently suspends comments or observations and allows the characters to speak (vss. 6, 7, 8, 9, 10, 11, 12, and 14). The narrator also continues describing the action (the sailors cast lots [vs. 7], row hard in an attempt to return to the dry land [vs. 13a], lift up Jonah and hurl him into the sea [vs. 15a], and eventually offer a sacrifice [vs. 16b][9] while the sea storms tempestuously [vs. 13b] before it eventually ceases from its raging [vs. 15b]), providing spatial coordinates (Jonah *arises* to flee *toward* Tarshish *away from* the presence of the Lord, in vs. 3 for example), and accentuating the emotions of the sailors on three occasions (in vss. 5, 10, and 16).

The first chapter is characterized by a large number of conjunctions, and this paratactic style, common in biblical Hebrew narrative, is obvious at the beginning of each verse where the narrator speaks.[10] The lack of subordinate clauses or recurrent character-statement qualifiers highlights the quick pace of the story while concurrently de-emphasizing the nuances of thought and feeling. Here, the narrator focuses on the action by describing what Jonah, the Lord, and the sailors do.

(2:1) *And the Lord appointed a great fish to swallow Jonah, and Jonah was in the body of the fish three days and three nights.* (2) *And Jonah*

prayed to the Lord, his God, from the body of the fish. (3) And he said,
[Jonah's prayer is recorded as direct speech through vs. 10]. (11)
And the Lord spoke to the fish and it vomited up Jonah to the dry land.

The characterization of the Lord, which is well in place before
chapter 2 begins, continues in the prose frame of the poetic prayer.
The Lord "appoints" (מנה) a great fish in 2:1 and then "speaks"
(אמר) to the fish causing it to spew Jonah up to the dry land in
2:11. The picture drawn here is consistent with chapter 1: the Lord,
the creator God, appears to be in complete control. The Lord of
the sea in chapter 1 is now Lord of the creatures. The Lord, who
tosses the wind around to create a storm, summons a fish which,
like the water in chapter 1 and the plant in chapter 4, simply does
what it is told.

While the narrator's role in chapter 2 is less pronounced, the
emphasis on action which began in the opening scenes continues
here. In addition to describing action ("the Lord appoints" [vs. 1]),
the narrator also provides spatial coordinates ("in the body [מעה]
of the fish" [vss. 1–2] and "from the belly [בטן] of Sheol" [vs. 3];
"to the dry land" [vs. 11]), temporal coordinates ("three days and
three nights," [vs. 1]), and introduces speech ("and he said/spoke"
[vss. 3, 11]).

(3:1) *And the word of the Lord was to Jonah a second time, saying,*
(2) "Arise, go to Nineveh, the great city, and call to her the
message which I am speaking to you." (3) *And Jonah arose and
he went to Nineveh according to the Lord's word, and Nineveh was
an exceedingly great city, a journey of three days. (4) And Jonah
began to go into the city, a journey of one day, and he cried out and
he said,* "Yet in forty days and Nineveh will be overthrown!"
(5) *And the people of Nineveh believed in God, and they called a fast
and dressed themselves in sackcloth from the greatest to the least.
(6) And the word reached the king of Nineveh and he arose from his
throne and he removed his mantle from himself, and he covered
himself with sackcloth and he sat upon the ashes. (7) And he cried
out and he said throughout Nineveh by the decree of the king and
his great-ones, saying,* "Neither people nor cattle, herd nor flock,
shall taste anything; nor shall they pasture, and water they shall
not drink. (8) But they shall cover themselves with sackcloth,
people and animals, and they shall call to God with might, and
they shall turn each from their evil ways and from the wrong-

doing which is in their hands. (9) Who knows? God may turn and be sorry, and turn from the flaming of his anger so that we will not perish." (10) *And God saw their deeds, how they turned from their evil ways, and God was sorry concerning the evil which he had said he would do to them, and he did not do it.*

Parallels between chapters 1 and 3 (including the two commissions, role and presentation of the foreigners, and portrayal of the prophet) have frequently been noted.[11] To these observations one may add that the narrator's role in the first six verses of chapter 3 is similar to that in the initial chapter. In the scene at Nineveh, the narrator briefly suspends description of events (in 3:2, 4) allowing the Lord to speak to his prophet and then Jonah to address the Ninevites. In chapter 1 the narrator had conveyed all the material in the opening scene except for the Lord's direct speech in 1:2. Once again, in chapter 3, the major block of direct speech (vss. 7b–9) comes, not from either of the principal characters, but from a foreign king. The chapter ends with the first significant inside view of one of the characters, none other than of God.[12] Just as the praying sailors had been delivered from the fatal effect of the storm, the Ninevites are also spared by God. But more importantly in this study of the author's strategy, in describing the incredible actions of the Ninevites, the animals and then the Lord's response to their behavior, the narrator has once again passed over Jonah in misleading silence. No clues have been provided for the approaching, final storm.

(4:1) *And it displeased Jonah, a great evil, and he became hot with anger.* (2) *And he prayed unto the Lord and he said,* "I pray, Lord, was this not my word when I was in my country? This is why I made haste to flee towards Tarshish, for I knew that you are a gracious God, and compassionate, slow in coming to anger and great in *ḥesed* and repenting of evil. (3) And now Lord, take, I pray, my life from me, for I prefer death to life." (4) *And the Lord said,* "Is it right for you to become inflamed?" (5) *And Jonah went out from the city and he sat down east of the city, and he made for himself there a booth and he sat under it in the shade until he could see what would happen in the city.* (6) *And the Lord God appointed a kikayon, and it came up over Jonah to be a shade over his head to shade him from his evil, and Jonah was happy about the kikayon, extremely happy.* (7) *And God appointed a worm when the next dawn came up, and it struck the kikayon and it withered.* (8) *And it was as the sun rose and God appointed a cutting east wind and the sun struck upon the head of Jonah and he became faint, and he asked that his soul might die, and he said,* "I prefer death to life." (9) *And God said to Jonah,* "Is it right for you to become inflamed about the *kikayon?" And he said,* "It is right for me to become inflamed, even to the point of death." (10) *And the Lord said,* "You were concerned about the *kikayon* for which you did not labor nor cause to grow, which as a child of night came to be and as a child of night perished. (11) And may I not be concerned about Nineveh, the great city, where there are more than 120,000 people who do not know their right hand from their left and many cattle?"

The narrative voice, apparent once more at the beginning of the chapter (as it has been in each of the previous three), provides the first inside view of the prophet. No sooner has the reader recovered from the surprise in learning how Jonah feels about God's compassion for the Ninevites (4:1) than she or he discovers from Jonah himself why he anxiously fled from the Lord's presence (4:2–3).

The narrator's most important role in the fourth chapter is found in the *kikayon* scene (vss. 5–8). The initial verse of the scene (vs. 5) has proven to be enigmatic. Many scholars (including Sellin, Robinson, Weiser, and Trible, all following Winckler) have suggested that 4:5 should be moved to a more "logical" position (i.e. just after 3:4) since is appears to be "out of place" in chapter 4.[13] Others have stressed that 4:5 should be retained in its present position and viewed as a flashback.[14] In the light of unanimous textual evidence and unconvincing arguments on *how* and *why* 4:5 was "moved," MT's ordering should be retained, but other reasons can be found supporting MT.[15]

Deformation in chronological ordering in the Bible, so long considered a sign of sloppy or accidental integration work, may actually signal artistic genius, and it is worth recalling that the true chronological order has been rearranged at several points of the text continuum before 4:5. For example, (*a*) the indirect speech reported at 1:10b does not follow the true chronological pattern; (*b*) the narrator's description of the great fish that swallows Jonah in 2:1 may also be out of its true order (cf. the description of the sailors in 1:16 who remain on the ship after Jonah has been hurled into the sea); (*c*) the two prayers in chapter 2 also show that the author has altered the true temporal sequence (see "The Prayers of Chapter 2" section in chapter 5); and (*d*), most obviously, the antichronological statement which comes in 4:2 ("was this not my word . . .") is another example of the author's manipulation of temporal order to suit his purpose. Thus, altering the sequence once again at 4:5, the author emphasizes that the prophet clings to the hope the Ninevites will be destroyed. In the light of these observations on how the author has misdirected us on several occasions, it seems likely that the spatial indication at 4:5 was *purposefully* displaced.

The narrator describes all the (re)action in the *kikayon* scene before allowing Jonah and God to resume their dialogue in the final three verses of the book. While the book of Kings, for example, often prefers explicit condemnation or praise coming from the narrator ("[Baasha] did what was evil in the sight of the Lord, walking in the way of Jeroboam and in the sin that he caused Israel to commit" [1 Kings 15:34]; "Now Obadiah revered the Lord greatly" [1 Kings 18:3b]; "Jehoash did what was right in the sight of the Lord all his days" [2 Kings 12:3, Ev 2]; Amon "served the idols that his father served, and worshiped them; he abandoned the Lord . . . and did not walk in the way of the Lord" [2 Kings 21:21b–22]), we see in Jonah that the author prefers a more sophisticated strategy. It is Jonah himself who cries out lamenting his situation and suggesting to us that this is a story *about* a prophet, more than a story about prophecies or oracles. It is the Lord who poses the important question to the prophet at the end, which, as a rhetorical question, invites a response from the audience. In retrospect, we see that the narrator never gives any moral evaluation in the entire story, not because he lacks fervor but because he prefers a more sophisticated course.

The Characteristics of Narration in Jonah

Now that the narrator's technique has been considered in the isolated chapters, what general course or strategy emerges when the book is considered as a whole? A few scholars have recently discussed the close relationship between dialogue and narration, and their findings are confirmed when one considers the narrator's role in Jonah. Robert Alter has called attention to narrative statements that often mirror "elements of dialogue which precede them or which they introduce," a phenomenon he describes as "dialogue-bound narration," and Robert Polzin, in a provocative book on 1 Samuel, has recently confirmed Alter's findings.[16] As the isolated examples below will suggest, this trend, where the narrator's words reinforce the characters' own patterns of speech (or vice versa), turns out to be true for Jonah as well. They fall into three categories:

    a. Narration Confirming Dialogue. On at least four occasions, the narrator, speaking the words of the characters, calls attention to their speech through repetition. In the first two examples (1:7a/1:7b and 1:12a/1:15a) the narrator's comments closely parallel the words of the sailors and Jonah. The verb שוב ("turn") in the third example (3:9a/3:10a) is repeated with a different object: the king hopes that *God* will turn; God sees how *they* turn. In the fourth example, the three commands ("arise," "go," "call") are repeated as past indicatives ("arose," "went," "called"), as the narrator expands the initial description of Nineveh ("the great city"→ "an exceedingly great city, a journey of three days").

SAILORS: "And let us cast lots." (1:7a)
NARRATOR: "And they cast lots." (1:7b)

ונפילה גורלות

ויפלו גורלות

JONAH: "Lift me up and hurl me into the sea." (1:12a)
NARRATOR: "And they lifted Jonah up, and they hurled him into the sea." (1:15a)

שאוני והטילני אל הים

וישאו את יונה ויטלהו אל הים

KING: "God may turn and be sorry." (3:9a)
NARRATOR: "and God saw . . . how they turned . . . and was sorry." (3:10a)

ישוב ונחם האלהים

וירא האלהים . . . כי שבו . . . וינחם

LORD: "Arise, go to Nineveh, the great city, and call to her." (3:2)
NARRATOR: "And Jonah arose and he went to Nineveh . . . and Nineveh was an exceedingly great city, a journey of three days . . . and he cried out." (3:3–4a)

קום לך אל נינוה העיר הגדולה וקרא אליה

56   A Poetics of Jonah

ויקם יונה וילך אל נינוה...וננוה היתה
עיר גדולה לאלהים מהלך שלשת ימים...ויקרא

b. Dialogue Confirming Narration. Sometimes key words of the
narrative appear on the lips of the characters. In the isolated examples
above, it was shown that the narrator adopts the words of the
characters. In the following examples, one notices a greater variety
in the dialogue parallels that confirm narration. The first example
is interesting because it may be an instance of characters using each
other's words. A translation of the final clause in 1:11 ("for the sea
is storming tempestuously") requires, once again, an interpretative
decision. While I have incorporated the phrase as part of the sailors'
speech, it could be the narrator's comment. Jack Sasson acknowledges that both options may be defended. He assigns the words to
the sailors and makes the astute observation that "it [is] potentially
more dramatic that Jonah should practically borrow the mariner's
vocabulary [in vs. 12] as he acknowledges his own responsibility."[17]

NARRATOR: "a great tempest was on the sea."(1:4)
JONAH: "the sea is storming tempestuously." (1:11b)

ויהי סער גדול בים
הים הולך וסער

NARRATOR: "He asked that his soul might die." (4:8b)
JONAH: "I prefer death to life." (4:8b)

וישאל את נפשו למות
טוב מותי מחיי

NARRATOR: "The people . . . dressed themselves in sackcloth."
(3:5)
KING: "But they shall cover themselves with sackcloth." (3:8a)

אנשי[ם]...ילבשו שקים
ויתכסו שקים

c. Chapter 4. The thesis that chapter 4 represents the high point
of the story is suggested in the concentrated "dialogue-bound narration" at the end.[18] Unlike any pattern observed in the first three
chapters, key words from the narrator's statement at the beginning
of chapter 4 are repeated on three separate occasions.

NARRATOR: "And he became inflamed." (4:1)

LORD: "Is it right for you to become inflamed?" (4:4b)

LORD: "Is it right for you to become inflamed about the *kikayon*? (4:9a)

JONAH: "It is right for me to become inflamed." (4:9b)

וייחר לו
ההיטב חרה לך
ההיטב חרה לך על הקיקיון
היטב חרה לי

With these four blows, the writer throws the climax into bold relief. The intensifying element accomplishes the desired goal: Jonah is now seen as the one who needs the lesson about God's compassion.

Another characteristic of narration in Jonah may be described as syntax-vocabulary-image reversal. The technique of highlighting causal chains and stirring sentiments for or against characters is sometimes achieved by altering the usual Hebrew sentence order (verb, subject, object). English and other languages do, of course, have their own standard patterns for meaning as the words, "time, how precious it is," would suggest. In Jonah 1:4, emphasis falls upon *the Lord* who hurls the powerful wind upon the sea (subject, verb, object in the Hebrew). In 1:9, the name of Jonah's God is stressed by an atypical word order once again: "the Lord, the God of the heavens, I fear" (direct object, subject, verbal adjective). As Jonah finally approaches Nineveh (3:3a), the narrator chooses to call attention to the city. The emphasis is made by altering the expected or usual word order: "and *Nineveh* was an exceedingly great city" (subject, verb, nominative).[19] Sometimes reversals are observed when unexpected words are used. The word יבשה "dry land" (instead of the more common ארץ, "earth") is unusual. This word Jonah uses in 1:9 suggests the dryness or solid features of the earth, a felicitous word based on the events at sea! The word חום ("concern") also stands out in this regard and is discussed in chapter 6. Sometimes stock images are altered for dramatic effect. The sequence of nouns Jonah uses in his panegyric to God in 1:9 is unusual. In the Hebrew there are many instances of the cosmos being described as having three major components, and the progression is typically heavens— earth—waters or the reverse, with earth always in the middle. Jack Sasson concludes that the sequence in Jonah (heavens—waters— earth) is not accidental. In fact, "Jonah is not relying simply on words to convey God's omnipotence; rather, he is cleverly using these terms to appeal to the less sophisticated instincts of the sailors."[20]

The Characters

The popularity of the book of Jonah rests heavily on the characters who inhabit the narrative world. What sort of characters are in this book? What (dis)advantages does the reader have over the characters thanks to the narrator's sharing or withholding of privileged information? How do they relate to each other? In this section the focus will be on the characters, their speech patterns, and on the manner characterization is achieved through dialogue.

Portrayal is accomplished through what the narrator chooses to reveal about characters, by the way some are perceived by other characters, and by the manner they speak to each other and to themselves. In the book of Genesis, for example, a character's thoughts are revealed (exclusively) to the reader by means of interior monologue on five occasions. The biblical idiom, "speaking in the heart" (אמר בלב) is used three times and is translated literally in the following examples: "And when the Lord smelled the pleasing odor, the Lord said in his heart, 'I will never again curse the ground because of humankind, for the imagination of the human heart is evil from youth; nor will I ever again destroy every living creature as I have done'" (8:21). "Then Abraham fell on his face and laughed, and said in his heart, 'Shall a child be borne to a man who is a hundred years old? Shall Sarah, who is ninety years old, bear a child?'" (17:17, RSV). "Now Esau hated Jacob because of the blessing with which his father had blessed him, and Esau said in his heart, 'The days of mourning for my father are approaching; then I will kill my brother Jacob'" (27:41, RSV).[21] From the reader's side, this rich interplay results in delight and concomitant frustration as the narrative world is reconstructed through plot linkage, causal chains, and proleptic portraits.

Before proceeding, perhaps it is worth asking how the foreigners and Jonah understand each other since this issue has interested several interpreters.[22] At first glance, one might assume that Jonah is understood either because the foreigners know Hebrew or because the prophet is familiar with their local dialect. Ezekiel appears to provide a better approach, however, to this either/or possibility:

He said to me: Mortal, go to the house of Israel and speak my very words to them. For you are not sent to a people of obscure speech and difficult language, but to the house of Israel—not to many peoples of obscure speech and difficult language, whose words you cannot understand. Surely, if I sent you to them, they would listen to you. But the house of Israel will not listen to you, for they are not willing to listen to me; because all the house of Israel have a hard forehead and a stubborn heart. (Ezek. 3:4–7)

The issue for Ezekiel, and by extension for the prophets who speak for God, concerns *obedience* much more than understanding the oracle. If the resolution in Ezekiel can be applied generally, foreigners do not need a translator to understand a prophet's message.

In Jonah the narrator focuses on two characters or on one character and a group of characters: the Lord ↔ Jonah; Jonah ↔ sailors/captain of the sailors; Jonah ↔ Ninevites/king of Nineveh; the Lord ↔ Ninevites. Occasionally, the presence of a third character is suggested by the action and conversation of two characters in the foreground. For example, in 1:1–4, the Lord and Jonah are the principal characters. In 1:5–16 the scene shifts, and the emphasis is on the sailors and Jonah, with the Lord's presence being suggested periodically (vss. 9, 10, 14, 16). In 2:1–11 the emphasis is on the Lord and the prophet. While Jonah is the only character whose direct speech is recorded in chapter 2, the Lord's presence is reflected throughout the scene in the prophet's speech. Before the reader learns that Jonah prays to *the Lord*, the Lord appoints a great fish. When Jonah speaks, he says, "*you* heard my voice" (vs. 3); "*you* cast me" (vs. 4); "*your* breakers and *your* waves" (vs. 4); "I was cast away from *your* sight yet I will again look upon *your* holy temple" (vs. 5); "*you* brought my life up from the Pit, O *Lord*, my God" (vs. 7); "I remembered *the Lord*" (vs. 8); "my prayer came . . . unto *your* holy temple" (vs. 8); "I will sacrifice to *you* . . . Salvation is of *the Lord!*" (vs. 10). While no direct speech from the Lord is recorded in chapter 2, the prophet's speech highlights the important symbiotic relationship between the Lord and the prophet.

Chapter 3 begins with the scene limited to the Lord and Jonah (vss. 1–3). In 3:5–10 the focus shifts to God and the Ninevites while Jonah fades into the background. During this scene (3:5–10), the only one in the book where Jonah is absent, the reader may conclude that the story has reached its conclusion: the prophet has finally delivered the message, the Ninevites have turned from their evil ways and the Lord has repented of the evil which he had said he would do to them. But the narrator quickly draws Jonah back into the picture as chapter 4 begins with the first in a series of surprises: "and it displeased Jonah, a great evil, and he became hot with anger" (4:1).

Throughout chapter 4, the Lord and Jonah emerge as the principal characters just as they did at the very beginning (1:1–4), and once again in this final scene, characters in the background (this time the Ninevites) are also suggested in the statements made by the characters in the foreground:

> a. And Jonah went out from the city and he sat down east of the city, and he made for himself there a booth and he sat under it in the shade until he could see what would happen in the city. (4:5)
> b. "And may I not be concerned about Nineveh, the great city, where there are more than 120,000 people who do not know their right hand from their left and many cattle?" (4:11)

What are the implications of the technique of focusing on two characters (or a character and a group) with only occasional explicit references to others in the background? This strategy allows the author to emphasize one of the *dramatis personae* over others thus highlighting and allowing the reader to notice any departure from expected norms. For example, in 1:5 "the sailors are afraid" (וייראו המלחים). They cry out to their god(s) and hurl the cargo into the sea. Jonah, on the other hand, is certainly aloof as he goes down into the ship (vs. 3) until he eventually reaches the "inner recesses of the ship" (ירכתי הספינה) where "he lies down and falls into a trance" (וישכב וירדם). Throughout the scene the sailors act; Jonah reacts. At the very end of the scene, *they* "slaughter a slaughter-meal to the Lord" (ויזבחו זבח ליהוה) "and they vow vows" (וידרו נדרים).

Portrayal by contrast is not limited to the characters in Jonah. Jonah's behavior throughout chapter 1 also contrasts with prophets such as Moses, Isaiah, and Jeremiah (see "Jonah and the Hindsight Fallacy" in chapter 4) who are all only *momentarily* hesitant in accepting the Lord's commission. Amos' words call attention to the contrast in Jonah 1: "The Lord God has spoken; who can but prophesy?" (Amos 3:8b).

The difference between the pagans and Jonah is even more pronounced in chapters 3 and 4. After the prophet's brief proclamation in 3:4b (עוד ארבעים יום ונינוה נהפכת, "yet in forty days and Nineveh will be overthrown"), the people believe in God; they call a fast; they dress in sackcloth; and the king removes his mantle, covers himself with sackcloth, and sits on the ash-heap. Before issuing a proclamation calling for sweeping reforms throughout Nineveh which include even the cattle, this collective behavior contrasts once again with the prophet's actions in chapter 4. The Ninevites, fearing death, perform actions so that they might live. Jonah, seeing that *they* have been spared, twice asks that his life might be taken from him (4:3, 8).

The contrast that is apparent among characters within and outside the book is also noticeable in Jonah's shifting attitude throughout chapter 4. The prophet asks to die in 4:3 but then three verses later is "happy" (וישמח) about the *kikayon*, "extremely happy" (שמחה גדולה). And two verses later, just after he experiences the cutting east wind and the heat of the sun on his head, he asks once again to die (4:8). Jonah's joy about the shade withers as quickly as the *kikayon* itself. The most significant example of characterization by contrast occurs in the final two verses of the chapter where the Lord points out that Jonah's concern is for the *kikayon* which he did not even labor, nor cause to grow (אתה חסת על הקיקיון אשר לא עמלת בו ולא גדלתו). The artistic gives way to the ideological dimension as the narrator allows the Lord to question Jonah's actions. Jonah is concerned, not about the *kikayon*, but for himself, and his self-pity is overshadowed by the Lord's concern for all of creation.

Contrast also occurs at the linguistic level. Jonathan Magonet has called attention to the way in which characterization is achieved by opposing actions developed around key words.[23] Consider, for example, the various actions all relating to "arising" and then the contrasting movements of "arising" and "sitting." A contrast between the commission and its realization begins in 1:2 where Jonah is first commanded to "arise" (קום) and go to Nineveh but then "arises" (ויקם) in 1:3 to flee towards Tarshish. In 1:6, the captain approaches the prophet and commands him "to arise" (קום) and to call upon his god(s). In 3:3 Jonah does finally "arise" (קום) and go to Nineveh. In 3:6, after the king learns of the prophet's proclamation, he "arises"

(ויקם) from his throne. Jonah, on the other hand, "sits" (וישב) under the booth in 4:5 as he anxiously awaits to see what will happen to the city.

Thus one is able to recognize the author's technique in using both opposite and identical verb forms with different subjects to focus attention on the contrasting actions (i.e. Jonah's response to the Lord's command, the king's response to the prophet's prediction, and so forth). The contrast at the linguistic level between the king's standing and Jonah's sitting underscores the disparity in attitude: the king is concerned that the Ninevites be spared at considerable discomfort to all, including even the animals; Jonah, on the other hand, hopes the city will be destroyed while he enjoys the luxury of the shade.

Additionally, Magonet has pointed out that the difference in action and attitude among characters also centers around the word דבר.[24] The "word" of the Lord comes to Jonah in the opening verse of the book and then a second time in 3:1. The emphasis on the "word" is repeated in 3:2. In 3:3 Jonah arises and goes to Nineveh according to the Lord's "word." The "word" which the prophet delivers on behalf of the Lord reaches the king in 3:6, and then in 3:10 God "sees their deeds" and "is sorry concerning the evil which he had said (דבר) he would do to them." With the fulfillment of God's "word" in chapter 3, the prophet is now able to express his thoughts which he does by saying, "was this not my word (דברי)?" (4:2). Jonah, appointing himself religious adviser to the Lord, rails against the Lord emphasizing the irreconcilable difference between the divine and prophetic word.

Perhaps the most interesting and complex inconsistency that is achieved by the repeated use of a single word occurs with רעה ("wickedness," "evil"). The word רעה is not only applied *to* each of the *dramatis personae*, but is also found on the lips of each character or character group.[25] The word refers to the Lord in 4:2, to Jonah in 4:1, 6, to the sailors in 1:7 and to the Ninevites in 1:2, 3:8, 10. The word רעה is also spoken *by* the Lord in 1:2, the narrator in 3:10; 4:1, 6, the king in 3:8, the sailors in 1:7, and the prophet in 4:2. But it is not until the final scene that the reader understands the significance of this play. The audience learns of the evil deeds of the Ninevites in the opening scene when the Lord says "for their wickedness (רעתם) has come up before me" (1:2b). Only at the very end of the path to enlightenment does the reader discover that Jonah is the appalling one after all, the one more concerned with his self-image than with the good news that God's grace is extended to the Ninevites after they turned "from their evil ways" (מדרכם הרעה) in 3:10.[26]

Jonah and the Lord. The story's principal characters, Jonah and the Lord, are the only ones who have a name and thus an identity. Apart from them, the captain of the sailors does stand out from the unnamed crew on the ship, the image of each sailor sacrificing to his own god(s) does individualize the fright, and the Ninevite king is also portrayed more prominently than are the citizens. But neither the captain nor the king receives a name. Meir Sternberg calls attention to the important relationship between the bestowing of names and forward movement of the plot: "If for a biblical agent to come on stage nameless is to be declared faceless, then to bear a name is to assume an identity: to become a singular existent, with an assured place in history and a future in the story ... All ... epithets are implicitly proleptic within the dynamics of action. Not even the most idiosyncratic trait fails to cohere, sooner or later."[27] Jonah soon becomes a living incarnation of his name running from Nineveh, swimming in the sea, before finally fleeing from Nineveh so that he might see what will become of the city.

Jonah and the Lord both come on stage with a complete absence of preliminaries, much like God in the very first chapter of Genesis. Who is the Lord and who is Jonah, the son of Amittai? Without any overt exposition, the reader can only piece it together based on the action and conversation itself, as, for example, in 1:9 where the prophet reveals ironically that he is a Hebrew, fearing the Lord, the God of the heavens. Likewise, the Lord does eventually emerge as the creator God who apparently controls the natural order—hurling a great wind upon the sea (1:4),[28] appointing a great fish to swallow Jonah (2:1), later commanding the fish to spew the prophet up to the dry land (2:11), causing a *kikayon* plant to grow and to shade Jonah's head (4:6), and then finally appointing a worm to kill the plant (4:7) and a cutting east wind to strike Jonah's head (4:8). Our knowledge about Jonah will also increase as the story develops, but, to anticipate my argument in small measure, vital information has not been evenly distributed. We are told very little about Jonah in this first chapter. Even the best of commentators reach conclusions that the text does not support. Hans Walter Wolff, commenting on the cost of the voyage, concludes that "Jonah had to pay the price of the whole ship,"[29] and Jack Sasson asserts that "Jonah hired the ship and its crew."[30] The author of Jonah implies that anyone who fishes for answers to questions like these will not bring home a catch.

Once again Jonathan Magonet, working at the linguistic level, has pointed out that acts performed by humans and introduced by the infinitive turn out to be unsuccessful; however, the infinitive, when used to refer to an act by the Lord, continually refers to an act which succeeds.[31] Thus the picture throughout and at various levels is of the Lord acting and of the creation, including even the stubborn prophet, responding. Animals and plants function as obedient servants of the Lord who uses them to carry out the divine purposes. It is the Lord, unlike Jonah in chapter 4, who shows a special concern for all of creation. At the end of the story, "much cattle" (בהמה רבה) are placed alongside the people "who do not know their right hand from their left" (4:11), but yet evoke divine compassion on the city.

The Sailors and Ninevites. The faceless and anonymous sailors and Ninevites serve largely to illuminate the prophet and the Lord. They function, much like Duncan in *Macbeth*, as a foil as they help carry the action forward. At the level of plot, their (re)actions are inextricably linked to the drama that is being acted out between the Lord and Jonah. Their activity in chapters 1 and 3 follows a threefold pattern: threatened disaster→actions associated with contrition or repentance→resulting deliverance.[32] This order is highlighted by means of contrast in the final scene outside Nineveh where Jonah experiences discomfort in 4:8 (but his life is certainly not threatened)→shows *no* sign of repentance or remorse→before finally asking to be delivered from his suffering by means of death (4:4b, 8b).

Thus the sailors and Ninevites have two primary functions: (1) as individuals with whom Jonah can interact, they draw out various aspects of the prophet's character, and (2) they provide the reader with images that contrast with the prophet's stubborn and ultimately self-serving attitude.

Dialogue

The observations above have suggested that there is a particular logic to the assigning not only of specific actions but also of words to characters. In Jonah, the author establishes a particular rhythm that begins with narration (1:1), moves quickly to dialogue (1:2), is interrupted as the narrator resumes the description of events (1:3–6a), and so forth. The emphasis in each of the chapters is on the verbal interaction among the characters themselves who reveal thoughts, describe actions, and even suggest scenery through the power of language. But *why* is dialogue introduced at specific points along the text continuum?

Any or all of the speech-events throughout the book could have been summarized by the narrator. This type of summary is accomplished in 1:10b ("for the men knew that he was fleeing from the presence of the Lord for he had told them"), but the author almost always prefers to render speech directly making dialogue a narrative event itself. The distinction between the author's choice of direct over indirect speech is important to recognize because the option he usually chooses foregrounds the speech-event making us aware of each of the characters as people addressing each other, defining relationships, revealing through speech much (though certainly not all) of what we need to know.

Robert Alter has emphasized the importance of direct over indirect speech in Hebrew biblical narrative: "Spoken language is the substratum of everything human and divine that transpires in the Bible, and the Hebrew tendency to transpose what is . . . nonverbal into speech is finally a technique for getting at the essence of things . . . The biblical scene, in other words, is conceived almost entirely as verbal intercourse, with the assumption that what is significant about a character, at least for a particular narrative juncture, can be manifested almost entirely in the character's speech."[33] The narrator enjoys the privilege of omniscience while the characters' speech reveals their limited perspective. The foreigners use the voluntative mood in the first and third chapters. In 1:6 the captain of the sailors says, "Perhaps the gods will give a thought to us," and in 1:14b the sailors cry out to the Lord, "May you not put innocent blood upon us." The king of Nineveh issues a decree stating, "Who knows? God may turn and be sorry" (3:9a).[34] The shift from narration proper to direct speech throughout the book of Jonah highlights the dramatic actions while calling attention to the different points of view.

An interesting feature of the dialogue in Jonah is the representation of scenery and setting by means of the characters' speech. Obviously, pictures or images of the setting are suggested by the narrator who tells us that the Lord hurls a great wind (1:4); appoints a great fish

(2:1); appoints a worm to strike the *kikayon* (3:7), and so forth. Characters also render setting through speech. Consider the following statements of the foreigners:

a. "How can you fall into a trance?!" (1:6)
b. "Come and let us cast lots." (1:7)
c. "Neither people nor cattle, herd nor flock, shall taste anything; nor shall they pasture, and water they shall not drink. But they shall cover themselves with sackcloth, people and animals, and they shall call to God with might, and they shall turn each from their evil ways and from the wrongdoing which is in their hands." (3:7–8)

And the words of the Lord:

d. "for her wickedness has come up before me." (1:2)
e. "Nineveh, the great city." (3:2)
f. "Is it right for you to become inflamed?" (4:4)
g. "Is it right for you to become inflamed about the *kikayon?*" (4:9)
h. "You were concerned about the *kikayon* for which you did not labor nor cause to grow, which as a child of night came to be and as a child of night perished. And may I not be concerned about Nineveh, the great city, where there are more than 120,000 people who do not know their right hand from their left and many cattle?" (4:10–11)

This direct speech functions at two levels. First, it serves to advance the plot. The captain's exclamatory question a. arouses the prophet so that a hurried trial can be held; the talk about casting lots b. reveals that Jonah is responsible for their misfortune here, etc. Second, from the reader's perspective, these short and extended quotations also suggest the scene: Nineveh is a large city e. where, if the people and animals heed the king's command, one can imagine many frantic actions taking place c.

Characterization through Dialogue

In the light of these observations about characterization and dialogue, it is now possible to consider how characterization is achieved through dialogue. To what extent do speech patterns themselves reveal thoughts and shifts in attitude? Are they part of the author's strategy? What can be said about the absence of dialogue where one might expect it?

With respect to dialogue, the author's strategy is important to notice because it relates to rhetoric. Meir Sternberg has called attention to the antididactic moves of Hebrew biblical narrative: "if biblical narrative is didactic, then it has chosen the strangest way to go about its business."[35] His observation that the Bible's rhetoric is quite different from that of the heavy-handed preacher is certainly true for Jonah 4 where both the prophet and the Lord reveal their feelings through speech while the narrator has little to say. In line with the view that chapter 4, and not 3, represents the high point in the story,[36] one may note the way in which characterization is achieved through dialogue.

Major Characters: Jonah and the Lord. While the foreigners appear on the literary stage just long enough to fulfill their role in the portrayal of the prophet, the Lord and Jonah are multidimensional characters. The Lord's direct speech in the final verses is significant not only because of the comparatively large number of words but also because they show how art serves ideology. The story about a prophet's apprehension, struggles, and fear turns out to be about God's own hurt as well.[37]

The narrator allows the Lord, like Jonah, to reveal himself through speech at the very end. The Lord's rhetorical question seeks to differentiate the "concern" (חוס) the prophet feels for the *kikayon* (4:10) from the divine "concern" (חוס) the Lord feels for Nineveh (4:11). The Lord seeks to educate Jonah by calling attention both to the prophet's response to the shade and subsequent loss of the *kikayon* and to the tragedy of God's own hurt. With the sense of disproportion accentuated, the audience gains a perspective on the folly of human disappointment when compared with divine sorrow.

The theme of the prophet's self-love represented by his response to the loss of the *kikayon* shade is matched by the picture of a God who suffers. The intimidating, thundering God of the opening chapters turns out at the end of the "tortuous route to enlightenment"[38] to be not only commanding and compassionate but also a God subject to distress, disappointment, and suffering at the thought of losing 120,000 Ninevites and much cattle. The Lord, who had only issued commands in the first and third chapters (three imperatives in 1:2 and three in 3:2: קרא "call," לך "go," קום "arise") and whose speech had not been recorded at all in chapter 2, only asks questions in chapter 4. The Lord begins the attempt to persuade the prophet by issuing nothing but commands yet ends up trying to convince him (and us) by consistently asking short, compelling questions:

a. "Is it right for you to become inflamed?" (4:4)
b. "Is it right for you to become inflamed about the *kikayon?*" (4:9a)
c. "May I not be concerned about Nineveh . . . ?" (4:11)

This *reversal in portrayal through dialogue* of the angry God who practically stops at nothing—a ship load of sailors were placed in danger because of the error of one—in pursuing his prophet, but who finally emerges as one truly compassionate, also applies to Jonah.[39] Throughout the first three chapters, the prophet's personality is shrouded in mystery. In the first and third chapters, Jonah has had little to say. In chapter 1, his direct speech is recorded only when questions are addressed to him (1:9, 12), and in chapter 3, he only speaks the five-word proclamation (3:4b). The poetic language in chapter 2 serves to ambiguate while actually hinting that the prophet has willingly accepted the commission (esp. 2:9–10). But, by comparison, the taciturn prophet speaks verbosely and unambiguously in chapter 4:

a. "I pray, Lord, was this not my word when I was in my country? This is why I made haste to flee towards Tarshish, for I knew that you are a gracious God, and compassionate, slow in coming to anger and great in *ḥesed* and repenting of evil. And now Lord, take, I pray, my life from me, for I prefer death to life." (4:2–3)
b. "I prefer death to life." (4:8b)
c. "It is right for me to become inflamed, even to the point of death." (4:9b)

Hans Walter Wolff calls attention to Jonah's preoccupation with his self-image evident at the beginning of the final chapter by noting the prophet's references to himself in his speech in 4:2–3: "kommt allein in V. 2 fünfmal ein Ausdruck der 1. Person vor ('Das ist's ja, was *ich* dachte, als *ich* noch in *meinem* Lande war, weshalb *ich* auch eilends fliehen wollte; denn *ich* wusste . . .') und in dem kurzen V. 3 viermal ('Nimm, Herr, *meine* Seele von *mir*; denn *mein* Sterben ist besser als *mein* Leben')."[40] To this observation one may add that

Jonah's speech also characterizes the Lord—and only at this late stage of the story!—as "a gracious God" (אל חנון), "compassionate" (רחום), "slow in coming to anger" (ארך אפים), "great in *ḥesed*" (רב חסד), and "repenting of evil" (נחם על הרעה).

That these dialogue patterns reflect part of the author's strategy may also be seen in the words of the Lord, who throughout most of the story has had conspicuously little to say. A command, reported as direct speech in 1:2, is repeated almost verbatim in 3:2. Jack Sasson is correct, I believe, in suggesting that the interchange of prepositions (על and אל, "to" and/or "unto") in the two verses affects interpretation. Essentially, the LXX, Targum, and most commentators do not maintain any distinction between the two occurrences, קרא עליה ("call to her") and קרא אליה ("call to her"). Hebrew, especially late Hebrew, does interchange the two prepositions, but Sasson suggests that one needs to establish whether or not the two phrases, imperative plus preposition, are equivalent. After examining the occurrences of קרא על (1:2) and קרא אל (1:6, 14; 2:3; 3:2, 8) in Jonah as well as other biblical passages, Aramaic syntax, Elephantine texts, and a number of modern commentaries, Sasson concludes that קרא על suggests the notion of "imposing an (unpleasant) fate upon something." Thus the artist wishes to show that Jonah's purpose before the Ninevites is to pronounce impending doom rather than to lead them to repentance. In the first instance, Nineveh is "being served with a death warrant." When God commissions Jonah with קרא אל in 3:2 "Nineveh, therefore, will receive a specific message from Israel's god."[41] A brief question to the prophet in 4:4 is repeated (again, almost verbatim) in 4:9a. Yet at the very end and for the first time, the crucial question is part of the extended speech:

> "You had concern for the *kikayon* for which you did not labor nor cause to grow, which as a child of night came to be and as a child of night perished. And may I not be concerned about Nineveh, the great city, where there are more than 120,000 people who do not know their right hand from their left and many cattle?" (4:10–11)

Most experts agree that the qal impf. verb in 4:11 (לא אחום, rendered here as "may I not be concerned?") should be understood in a modal sense, and a majority translate it as "should I not be concerned?" The implication is that at the end of the story, the

Lord's action has a kind of inevitable and binding quality about it. At first glance, a translation such as this appears to be signalled by Jonah's action and attitude in the previous episode: Jonah, incapable of creating the plant, is able to "concern" (חום) it when it withers. Should not God "concern" (חום) the Ninevites whom he has created? Terence E. Fretheim has made the astute observation that this verb in 4:11 should be translated in a different modal sense. He asserts that the preceding actions in the story point not so much to human (re)action as to God's sovereign freedom.[42] God's repentance, which abrogates the forecast of 3:4 ("Yet in forty days and Nineveh will be overthrown"), comes *after* the Ninevites "turn from their evil ways" (3:10). At the end of the scene, we do learn that God pities the Ninevites and pardons them because of their action, but the decision to spare them rests ultimately with God. The human change of heart should therefore be understood as a necessary condition, but not the basis, for God's delivering compassion. Fretheim's view gains added significance when art's central role is considered. That is, if the translation of לא אחום as "may I not be concerned" is correct and if the words suggest that God's sovereign freedom is a motif which gains in rhetorical force at the book's terminus, such language reveals one of the author's typical moves. This writer delights in drawing our attention, even tugging at our emotions, at one moment only to align our ideological perspective with his at the most opportune time.

Minor Characters: The Sailors and Ninevites. Characterization of the foreigners is also achieved through dialogue. In chapter 1 the rapid exchange of brief questions (vs. 8) accentuates the quick pace of the story and highlights the sailors' confused state of mind. The piling up of questions contrasts with a different strategy which is apparent in the more placid interchange between Jacob and "the people of the east" (בני קדם) in Gen. 29:4–8:

> Jacob said to them, "My brothers, where do you come from?" They said, "We are from Haran." He said to them, "Do you know Laban son of Nahor?" They said, "We do." He said to them, "Is it well with him?" "Yes," they replied, "and here is his daughter Rachel, coming with the sheep." He said, "Look, it is still broad daylight, it is not time for the animals to be gathered together. Water the sheep, and go, pasture them." But

they said, "We cannot until all the flocks are gathered together, and the stone is rolled from the mouth of the well; then we water the sheep."

In this excerpt from the extended narrative of Jacob's sojourn with Laban, one notices the almost stately progression as the story moves from Jacob's ignorance ("Where do you come from? . . . Do you know Laban? . . . Is it well with him?") to enlightenment ("here is *his daughter* Rachel, coming with the sheep"). With Jacob and the "people of the east," the dialogue follows an orderly design in these four verses ("Jacob said . . . They said . . . He said . . . They said . . . He said . . . they replied . . . He said . . . But they said . . .") whereas in Jonah 1:8 the prophet has a series of questions put to him and only responds fully to the fifth and final one: "from what people are you?" (מזה עם אתה).[43]

The sailors' words in 1:14 ("may you not put innocent blood upon us") is a phrase from Israelite tradition. In Deuteronomy 21 instructions are given regarding the practice for the community to observe in the event a murderer is not found. When the question arises—could the community ever rid itself of the "blood-guilt"?—the elders of the city are instructed to testify, "absolve, O Lord, your people Israel, whom you redeem; do not let the guilt of innocent blood (דם נקי) remain in the midst of your people Israel" (Deut. 21:8). In Jeremiah's temple sermon (Jer. 26), when the priests, prophets, and all the people hear the prophet declare that the house of the Lord shall be like Shiloh and that Jerusalem will become a city without inhabitants, the people threaten to kill Jeremiah. He responds saying, "Do with me as seems good and right to you. Only know for certain that if you put me to death, you will be bringing innocent blood (דם נקי) upon yourselves and upon this city and its inhabitants" (26:14b–15).

In Jeremiah, the *obedient* prophet warns the people that if they listen to the priests and the prophets who call for his death (26:11), innocent blood will fall upon everyone in the city. In Jonah, the innocent sailors, when confronted by the *disobedient* prophet, cry out asking that his innocent blood be spared. Their words are charged with irony because they perceive (incorrectly) that Jonah is innocent. What their words put forth (correctly) is that the Lord does not want a dead but a live Jonah for the mission to Nineveh.[44]

Conclusion

For convenience of discussion, this chapter on portrayal has been presented in ordered segments. Of course, characterization emerges as a rich interplay of combined principles, and the arrangement is what makes the book such exciting reading. The words of the characters and the narrator have been blended and distributed in a specific way to reveal a basic ideological perspective. Several aspects of the narrator's strategy have emerged. First, he avoids explicit praise or condemnation of any of the characters. This neutral tone is similar to what one finds elsewhere in the Hebrew Bible, as for example in portions of the Deuteronomic History. Robert Polzin's point about strategy in the book of Samuel applies for Jonah as well: "the narrator's style is to point rather than to say, reflect rather than project."[45]

At the level of plot, the narrator performs various functions without hesitating to intrude for a purpose. He introduces dialogue, describes action, reveals thoughts and attitudes (including the Lord's), summarizes speech, indicates the passing of time, and describes spatial coordinates. He conveys actions and thoughts both essential and ancillary to the unfolding plot. It has also been suggested that every strategy the narrator follows is calculated and deliberate. He does not show his cards in the first three chapters because of his artistic aims and ideological goals. That the narrator is a master at the art of indirection becomes clear in the final, climactic chapter where he eventually assumes a secondary role as Jonah and the Lord both reveal their sorrow and disappointment. After surveying the role the characters play, we see that the sailors, Ninevites, and all of creation serve primarily as foils to Jonah and the Lord. By calling attention to certain speech patterns, it becomes clear that characterization is achieved through dialogue. Finally, the direct speech of Jonah and the Lord in chapter 4 stands out because the author has provided few clues in chapters 1–3 for the drastic turn of events that take place in the scene outside Nineveh. But most of all, we have seen how art serves ideology.

Chapter 4

Jonah and the Reading Process

In a significant article, published more than twenty years ago, George Landes addressed the question of the originality and relationship of the prayer in Jonah 2:3–10 (Evv 2–9) to the surrounding prose narrative.[1] He concluded his discussion of the psalm with these words: "Thus, although we must grant the possibility that the Jonah psalm attained its present position in the book of Jonah through the work of a scribe who was not the author of the prose stories, our study surely suggests that if this is so he was no less sensitive to the form, structure, and content of the book than the original writer himself. When, as we think, it is just as plausible that the initial author of Jonah knew of and used the psalm, this raises the question whether it is even necessary to introduce the figure of a secondary interpolator."[2] Landes, in his careful and extended exegesis, paid particular attention to each verse of the psalm as well as to other biblical material and nonbiblical sources. I wish to acknowledge my general agreement with his position without referring to the details of his article. His argument for the contextual interpretation of the psalm based on the book's form, structure and content can be supported, I believe, by a completely different route. My purpose here is to suggest that the *extended poetic prayer is part of a major pattern in the book overarching all of the action, including the crucial, final scene outside Nineveh.* But first, a few general comments about the reading process will serve to introduce the discussion in this chapter.

The Reading Process

Few who have seriously studied the Bible would deny that the stories customarily invite readers into a world of unexpected twists and turns. Anyone wishing to understand the narrative field of reality must, at least to some extent, reconstruct the projected world. Plot structure, shifts in perspective, repetition, metaphor, and a variety of expositional modes all require the reader to shape and reshape numerous questions related to the action: What is happening and why is it happening? What is the connection between past and present actions? Is there any connection at all? Why do characters act the way they do, especially in the light of what may occur in the future?

My attempt to establish the poetic prayer in 2:3–10 as part of a well-designed pattern is based on the premise that all stories, from the simplest to the most complex, offer readers opportunities to construct a framework for establishing connections. At specific points throughout the Jonah story a certain instability in the framework exists, and the reader must attempt to stabilize the story as it unfolds. This instability, as we will see, is not unique to Jonah's prayer in chapter 2, but rather becomes apparent in the opening lines of the story.

It is an inherent feature of texts, ancient or modern, that they produce uncertainty in the mind of the reader by providing insufficient or misleading information at key points. The reader is forced into insecurity (or misled into security) and frequently called upon later to change his or her viewpoint. The reading process may in fact be described as ranging from making "simple linkage of elements, which the reader performs automatically, to [constructing] intricate networks that are figured out consciously, laboriously, hesitantly, and with constant modifications in the light of additional information disclosed in later stages of the reading."[3] Elements of indeterminacy invite the reader to search for meaning, and it is precisely these indeterminate elements that require the reader's most active attention in the reading process.[4] Informational suppression is not only "the most common, problematic, and instructively variable, but also the most crucial"[5] issue related to exposition. Various names have been associated with this highly complex feature: vacancies, gaps, lacunae, hiatus, blanks, and, in the words of Martin Price, "moments of oblivion and transcendence."[6] The present discussion will describe the stimulating interplay between the text of the Jonah story and the reader, define temporary gaps which surface early in the reading, and also suggest that much of the attention given the book has overlooked the complex way in which readers reconstruct its narrative world. Gaps, which refer to a "lack of information about the world—an event, motive, causal link, character trait, plot structure, law of probability—contrived by a temporal displacement,"[7] may be temporary (i.e. "[opened] at some point upon the continuum of the text only to [be filled] in explicitly and satisfactorily . . . at a subsequent stage") or permanent (i.e. producing "questions or sets of questions to which no single, fully explicit and authoritative answer is made by the text from beginning to end").[8]

With respect to the book of Jonah, gaps are formulated in the mind of the reader as questions, and since these questions are elicited all along the text continuum, different readers formulate various questions in an attempt to make sense of the action.[9] This range of possibilities in the gap-filling process is certainly endless and not unique to Jonah. One might think of the shifts in the reader's attitude as the action unfolds in other, equally famous, biblical stories: the two women before Solomon (1 Kings 3:16–28); the extended Joseph narrative (Gen. 37–50); or the drama that reaches a climax as Haman is finally brought to justice (Esther 8:3–8). In each of these stories and throughout the Bible, the reader draws and redraws mental pictures or images to explain character action, shapes and reshapes ideas to understand plot development, and forms various hypotheses in an attempt to comprehend the projected world. Of particular importance is the fact that none of the various questions that customarily arise in the process of reading offers itself as totally relevant or irrelevant; instead, it is left to the reader to make sense of the action by supplying a multiple system of gap-fillers for the purpose of actualizing the story. Whenever the reader's curiosity is tapped, the author may provide the conditions for establishing causal connections. This ever-changing network does allow for a certain free play of interpretation, but should not be equated with randomness or chance since the play is regulated in a variety of ways by the narrator, the characters, and the plot as perceived by the reader. If the reader of the book of Jonah is to reach an understanding of the narrative, organize the material according to exposition,[10] arrange events of the narrative past in relation to events in the present within a web of probabilities,[11] and relate thoughts to action, then she or he cannot avoid filling in the gaps as they present themselves or making distinctions between relevancies and irrelevancies.

Jonah and the Hindsight Fallacy

For the moment, let us assume that the following question, central to Landes's article mentioned above, cannot be answered satisfactorily: Did two (or more) authors compose the material the Massoretes preserved as the Jonah story? The question is not, be it noted, whether the prayer is an *addition*; for writing, like reading, is a time-art, and Jonah's first prayer was certainly added to existing material—as were chapters 3 and 4—if in fact chapter 1 was composed first. The writing process requires in principle that additions be made—a chain of words is needed to form a sentence, sentences to form paragraphs, and so forth. Of course, the discussion about the psalm or prayer addition has focused more on the time of the addition than on the fact of the addition itself. What many have argued is that rather than having been added moments, days, or a few weeks later, the prayer in chapter 2 was added decades or possibly centuries after the first author composed the prose story. Three quotations illustrate this position:

> So this [Jonah's prayer] cannot be the prayer which Jonah prayed, or which the author of the story would have put into Jonah's mouth, while he was inside the fish, for it does not fit into the situation.[12]

> [The] inclusion or omission [of the prayer] makes no difference to the point of the narrative.[13]

> The prayer is of some beauty but scarcely congruous with Jonah's situation.[14]

To these positions one might add that Jonah never asks God to deliver him from his distress while in the fish's belly.[15] The argument has many variations and continues to be made despite recent trends in biblical scholarship.[16]

There is, however, a better question with respect to Jonah's first prayer, and there are scholars who have raised it also: Is the poetic prayer an appropriate addition? That is, was the author or later redactor sensitive to the structure and content of the surrounding prose framework when the prayer was inserted? Thus posed, the question acknowledges that someone, though not necessarily someone else, added the poetic prayer while simultaneously shifting the spotlight from the author(s) to his/their creation. Several have addressed the "appropriateness" issue with respect to the prophet's prayer in chapter 2 and concluded that the psalm is in fact closely tied to the rest of the story both in terms of theme or motifs (descent and ascent, repentance or turning, and especially divine sovereignty) and in terminology (fainting, calling out, steadfast love).[17] However, the discussions of the poetic prayer, whether focusing on questions of origin or "appropriateness," are consistently made in the light of the book's final chapter.[18] Little attention has been given to the text continuum, particularly in terms of the action and discourse that precede the prayer. I wish to emphasize that the "appropriateness" question is best answered when the text is viewed as a continuum and when the "hindsight fallacy" is considered.[19]

Stated succinctly, hindsight reading derives from the all too common disregard of a story's potential as a time-art. While the ending of any story affects interpretation, reading—even subsequent re-readings—is not carried out exclusively or even predominantly with the terminus in mind. The view that compositional dynamics shape the reading all along the path to enlightenment is perhaps illustrated best by the reading (or viewing) of the murder mystery. Knowledge of the resolution does little to dispel tension or to slow an accelerating heart and breathing even if one knows that the mystery solver will deliver once again. While the reader's inability to escape the effects of the work's strong measures to produce multiple hypotheses is perhaps most apparent with the mystery genre, calculated distribution and ordering of events induce readers to formulate conclusions from beginning to end with respect to other literary types as well. The process of constructing such a network cannot be separated from the linear movement of the text, and the fact that conjectures may turn out to be partially or entirely true (or completely false) is an understanding that author and audience share. Because of the temporal nature of reading, readers can look back upon the work, but only as the compositional parts have been pieced together throughout the reading process. To discuss chapter 2 predominantly in the light of events outside Nineveh is to disregard the literary text's other misleading traps that have been laid along the way.

The insertion of Jonah's words from the fish's belly—a brief speech when compared to the lengthy journey to Nineveh—emerges as part and parcel of the author's overall strategy: the words spoken inside the belly of the fish, like the events on board ship, create a need for more information about the prophet. Nowhere in the first three chapters has the reader been told why Jonah flees, and what is more, the work does its utmost to misdirect its audience. Upon completion, it is difficult to imagine why a reader would suspend knowledge of past events with the *actual* knowledge derived by the trial and error experiences encouraged by the contours of the tale.

To claim, therefore, that "the inclusion or omission of the prayer makes no difference to the point of the narrative" is to discount the author's ability to manipulate narrative interest. The consequences of this kind of hindsight fallacy are instructive for they lead to a distortion of developments in the reader's understanding of the plot.

When reading is understood as a time-art, one begins to understand that meaning is equated not only with what happens in the final chapter or verse in the Jonah story, but, instead, with all that happens in the mind of the reader as impressions are drawn and redrawn throughout each of the chapters. This approach to reading might be dismissed as merely a reflection of modern trends or theories associated with narrative technique, but any objection of this kind appears to be countered by the Jonah story itself. For if the author(s) of the initial chapters of the story was/were not concerned with creating narrative interest, then why has vital information been withheld from the reader? Jonah's astonishing testimony explaining his reasons for fleeing comes toward the end of the story (4:2), and his true character is revealed only subsequently. By focusing on the sequence of events and by exploring the gaps that result in the reading process, the "hindsight fallacy" may be corrected. Two gaps emerge early, and they both relate to the story's central characters: (a) What motivates Jonah to disobey the Lord's command ("Arise, go to Nineveh," 1:2a), and (b) What is the message the prophet is "to call to her" (1:2b)? Ultimately, the reader will find answers to both of these questions but only after considerable plot development. The gap which relates to Jonah's attempt to flee is not closed until 4:2 when the reader finally learns what the author has kept from us all along:

> And he prayed unto the Lord and he said, "I pray, Lord, was this not my word when I was in my country? This is why I made haste to flee towards Tarshish, for I knew that you are a gracious God, and compassionate, slow in coming to anger and great in *ḥesed* and repenting of evil." (4:2)

Jonah's response to the call narrative at the beginning of the story is unique. He is shown protesting with actions rather than with words, but his attitude does reflect the prophetic pattern. Moses offers two reasons why he is not equipped to carry out the Lord's work. He fears that Pharaoh will not listen to him (Exod. 4:1) and then says, "O my Lord, I have never been eloquent, neither in the past nor even now that you have spoken to your servant; but I am slow of speech and slow of tongue" (Exod. 4:10). Jeremiah expresses a similar protest with fewer words when he proclaims, "I do not know how to speak for I am only a boy" (Jer. 1:6b), while Isaiah admits, "I am a man of unclean lips, and I live among a people of unclean lips" (Isa. 6:5). The picture of the reluctant prophet is certainly among the Bible's most famous portraits, and when their reluctance surfaces, the gaps—if they arise at all in the mind of the reader—are quickly closed. When Moses admits that he would prefer not to appear before Pharaoh (Exod. 4:1), the Lord promptly offers two signs to reassure his spokesman (4:2–9); and when the prophet mentions that his speech is bad (4:10), the Lord immediately offers a solution (4:11–17). Table 1 demonstrates the similarity among the narratives in Exodus, Jeremiah, and Isaiah, and also illustrates the unique extended gap, represented by the horizontal line, in the Jonah story.

Since Jonah registers his protest in the first chapter by acting ("But Jonah arose to flee towards Tarshish away from the presence of the Lord" [1:3]) and not with words, and since such actions as sleeping (1:5), offering to be hurled overboard (1:12), and praying (2:3–10) provide no decisive means for the gap to be closed, attempts to close it will remain unsuccessful until the prophet finally answers the reader's question. While considering these various call narratives and the "hindsight fallacy," one may begin to see that the gap remains open in the Jonah story not only because all the action which contributes to plot development in 1:1–2:2 and 2:11–4:1 has been added but because the poetic prayer (2:3–10) has been inserted as well. In contrast to the other call narratives, the gap in the Jonah

Table 1
Closure in Prophetic Call Narratives

Prophet	Call	// Verbal Response which Leads to Closure
Moses	Exod. 4:1	// 4:2–9
	Exod. 4:10	// 4:11–17
Isaiah	Isa. 6:5	// —6:7
Jeremiah	Jer. 1:6	// 1:7
Jonah	Jon. 1:2	// —————————————— 4:2–3

story remains open for an extended period of time because the telling, and hence the reading, strategy differs.

The second gap also emerges early in the reading. What is Jonah to cry against Nineveh? When Jonah is commissioned to go to Nineveh the second time, the command begins as it did before but ends differently. Initially, the Lord says to Jonah:

> Arise, go to Nineveh, the great city, and call to her for her wickedness has come up before me. (1:2)

Subsequently,

> Arise, go to Nineveh, the great city, and call to her *the message which I am speaking to you.* (3:2)

The second command redirects the prophet and reminds us, however subtly, that this message remains known only to the Lord and his spokesman for the moment. We understand the significance of the prophet's cry against Nineveh only when the gap is finally closed. Not only does Jonah have much less to say than prophets who speak about foreign nations and to foreign nations, the content of his message is also unique.[20] No biblical parallel exists for the prophet's brief message in 3:4a: "Yet in forty days and Nineveh will be overturned." Why forty days? Are we to assume, as the king obviously does (3:9), that the Ninevites might be spared? Readers realize now that none of the Lord's actions or words to his prophet has prepared them for this particular message. In fact, the action in chapter 1 suggested just the opposite—a God of wrath in active pursuit of his prophet, a God whom we thought would *not* be likely to "repent from the evil which he said he would do to them" (3:10).

In view of the present thesis, namely, that the extended poetic prayer is part of this major pattern in the book, overarching all of the action until the crucial, final scene outside Nineveh, a general trend may also be observed that links chapter 2 with chapters 1 and 3 and that distinguishes these three from the final chapter. A dialogue pattern is established between the Lord and the prophet in the first chapter and is repeated in the second and third. In the first three chapters, Jonah's recorded direct speech to the Lord is found only at 2:3–10. The Lord addresses Jonah in direct speech twice in the first three chapters (1:2; 3:2). Consistently, in each of these first three chapters, when the Lord speaks to Jonah or when Jonah speaks to the Lord, the addressee does not offer a verbal response. The pattern is particularly important because Jonah and God emerge, as the story develops, as the primary characters. This dialogue pattern is so well in place that the reader can hardly help noticing the reversal in chapter 4. With the sailors and Ninevites clearly in the background, the stage is set for further revelations.

In 4:2–4 the Lord and prophet finally respond *verbally* to each other. Next, the narrator describes Jonah's actions just outside of Nineveh (4:5–8a) and then allows God and Jonah to resume their dialogue in the closing verses (4:8b–11). In the final conversation between God and Jonah, the dialogue becomes packed with emotion and excitement as both characters continue to address each other: "And God said to Jonah, 'Is it right for you to become inflamed about the *kikayon?*' And [Jonah] said, 'It is right for me to become inflamed, even to the point of death'" (4:9). The direct speech between Jonah and God in chapter 4 serves as a contrast to the silence, ambiguity, and indirection of the initial three chapters. Characterization in the Bible is sometimes achieved by the narrator's direct statements. For example, at the end of the David and Bathsheba story, the narrator concludes the scene by implicating David: "But the thing that David had done displeased the Lord" (2 Sam. 11:27b). Here in the fourth chapter of Jonah, characterization is achieved through the character's own speech and action. Jonah's prayer in 4:2 certainly suggests that he is too concerned with his self-image, and this impression is reinforced in the subsequent *kikayon* episode where Jonah is "happy, . . . extremely happy" (4:6) when God's mercy is extended to him. At the very end, and after many turns, we are able to perceive the merits of God's love and mercy as we see human self-love contrasted with divine compassion:

> And the Lord said, "You were concerned about the *kikayon* for which you did not labor nor cause to grow, which as a child of night came to be and as a child of night perished. And may I not be concerned about Nineveh, the great city, where there are more than 120,000 people who do not know their right hand from their left and many cattle?" (4:10–11)

Conclusion

This brief discussion of the reading process has intentionally avoided focusing on the psalm in an attempt to highlight the text continuum and to suggest the importance of a reading strategy that corrects the "hindsight fallacy." In providing insufficient, even misleading, information at key points of the Jonah story, the author invites the reader to stabilize the action as it unfolds. Reconstructing the projected world is essential for understanding the narrative field of reality, and informational suppression proves to be a distinguishing feature of the narrative. Discussions about the poetic prayer (2:3–10) have too often been made exclusively in the light of the book's final chapter, and little attention has been given to the text continuum, particularly in terms of the action and discourse that precede the prayer. Meaning is equated not only with what happens at the book's terminus but also with all that develops in the mind of the reader as thoughts and impressions are drawn, then redrawn, throughout.

As mentioned above, Landes and an increasing number of scholars have in fact examined the prayer of chapter 2 and concluded that it fits quite harmoniously with the surrounding prose narrative, both in terms of physical-psychological portrayal and in terms of symmetry. So much attention had been paid to the differences between the poetic prayer in 2:3–10 and the prose frame before Landes's article in 1967 that it is not surprising that some of the similarities and points of contact had completely been overlooked until recently. Leslie Allen, for example, observed for the first time and as recently as 1976 that Jonah's two verbal formulations of prayer (2:3–10 and 4:2–3) share three key words: חסדם, "their *ḥesed*" / חסד, "*ḥesed*" (2:9 [Ev 8] and 4:2), חיי, "my life" (2:7 [Ev 6] and 4:3), נפשי, "my soul" or "my life" (2:8 [Ev 7] and 4:3).[21] I have endeavored to supplement the arguments for a contextual interpretation of the poetic prayer by suggesting that the first three chapters reveal part of an integrated and highly sophisticated narrative strategy which becomes apparent in the scene outside Nineveh. With reading understood as a process, chapters 1, 2, and 3 display common features: they (a) prolong gaps which surface early in chapter 1, and (b) establish a dialogue pattern between the two principal characters that will be altered in the final, crucial scene.

Chapter 5

The Multiple Reports of
Prayer in Jonah

Interpreters of the book of Jonah during the post-Enlightenment period have consistently focused on the psalm in 2:3–10 (Evv 2–9), often producing significant, though not unambiguous, results.[1] The reasons for the focused discussion are obvious: these verses are almost always read as the only poetic section in the entire book; they contain a verbal formulation of prayer which is at least twice the length of the prayers that precede and follow it; the extraordinary images drawn from the Psalter are unlike any other material in the book; and the meaning is not readily apparent because the psychological portrayal of the prophet is mixed (Does Jonah lament his situation in the belly of the fish or is he expressing gratitude for being rescued from drowning?).

The focused research on the poetic prayer has unfortunately left the wrong impression. There are no less than seven references to prayers in the four chapters of Jonah (see Table 2 below). On four occasions, distinct prayer events (or possible prayer events) are reported with the body of prayer left unrecorded: (1) 1:5, (2) 1:6b, (3) 2:3=2:6–8,[2] and (4) 3:8. Three verbal formulations of prayer are given after being introduced in different ways at: (5) 1:14, (6) 2:3–10, and (7) 4:2–3. The initial group of prayers is found in the first, second, and third chapters and are given by the sailors, Jonah, and the Ninevites respectively. The investigations about the reports of prayer in the book of Jonah are so convoluted that the first portion of this chapter will serve to isolate and describe what is obviously one of the author's primary concerns before turning to the more complex, functional side of the coin. A series of questions will be addressed: Why are these prayers or reports of prayer here? In what way do they shed light on the ideological perspectives and interests of the author?[3] And in the light of these answers: Why does the writer modulate from prose into poetry and vice versa? Is the traditional generic designation of 2:3–10 as poetry accurate or appropriate? And does biblical verse follow its own logic or poetics, thus providing a unique design for making connections with distinctive semantic thrusts following the curve of its habits of expression?

The first request for prayer is found in the opening scene. After several actions by the men on the ship, the chief sailor approaches Jonah and asks the prophet to call (קְרָא) to his god. The sailors' hope, which will be reinforced in the verbal formulation of their prayer which follows (1:14), is that they will not perish (1:6). With plot exigencies already established, the account of Jonah's specific response to this request is not reported. The author immediately shifts attention away from the disobedient prophet to relate the actions of the sailors ("And they said each to the other, 'Come and let us cast lots . . .'" [1:7]). Unlike the request for prayer which the "king" will make in Nineveh, the events here imply that Jonah does not obey the chief sailor's request. In fact, the impression the reader has in the opening scene is that Jonah does not wish to speak to anyone, including God, for in chapter 1 the prophet is portrayed not only as disobedient but also as reticent, speaking only when spoken to. When the prophet finally addresses the sailors in vs. 9, he is responding to a series of questions which had just been addressed to him in vs. 8; and in vs. 12, the only other verse containing Jonah's direct speech in the opening chapter, the prophet once again responds to a question which he had just been asked. In the books of Obadiah and Micah, which surround the Jonah story, the prophets speak on behalf of the Lord, and their words occupy almost every verse of the combined eight chapters! Because the Hebrew Bible routinely achieves characterization through dialogue, Jonah's speech in the initial chapter is surprisingly and significantly meager even when compared to non-prophetical books. The prophet's solution to the raging storm that threatens to kill them all, appears to be a deliberate affront to the possibility of communion with God. Jonah's answer to their pointed question, "What shall we do . . . ? (1:11) is not "allow me, God's prophet, to intercede on your behalf" or "I will call to God so that the storm will not destroy you," but instead, "lift me up and hurl me into the sea and the sea will quiet down for you" (1:12).

The second request for prayer appears in a different context. In the subsequent scene of chapter 3, the Ninevites, not Jonah, are asked to pray, and although neither a prayer nor a report of prayer is recorded, the multiple actions of the foreigners in this scene certainly suggest that this command is in fact carried out. After Jonah delivers the message in Nineveh that the Lord had spoken to him, the "king" of Nineveh issues a decree containing various specific instructions, one of which is "they shall call to God with might" (3:8). Once again, the report of a prayer (or of a refusal to pray) from the foreigners is passed over as it was in the opening scene, but the future actions of God ("And God saw their deeds, how they turned from their evil ways, and God was sorry concerning the evil which he had said he would do to them, and he did not do it" [3:10]) suggest that their combined efforts (believing, fasting, putting on sackcloth [3:5], and probably also prayer) produced a favorable divine response.

The Prayers of Chapter 2

The second chapter contains references to two separate prayers, a distinction frequently overlooked. A prayer whose verbal formulation is not given, but is signalled at 2:3 and 2:6–8, requires explanation. At the beginning of 2:3, the prophet expresses his feelings through prayer and the words are shared with us: "I called from my distress." The form of the verb קראתי ("I called") is a perfect, signalling a previous action. So while the verb יתפלל ("he prayed") in vs. 2 refers to the subsequent recorded prayer in 2:3–10, the beginning of the prayer itself (vs. 3) as well as some of the description in the following verses (6–8) refers to an unrecorded formulation of prayer *before* Jonah was swallowed by the fish. The two separate reports of petition in chapter 2 are frequently obscured in translation when קראתי is not rendered in the past tense. The position of several scholars who do not perceive the two prayers in chapter 2 or who suggest that קראתי *may* be translated as a present tense verb are given below.

Jerome noted that the opening verses of the psalm were for a previous rescue, but the "anomaly" confused the translator so much that he altered the past tenses of the Hebrew.[4] According to Calvin, Jonah "relates here, as it appears from the preceding, 'and he said,' the prayer he offered when in the fish's bowels, and not a prayer offered after his deliverance. Some have entertained the latter opinion, because some of the verbs here are in the past tense: but this circumstance only shows that he continued to pray from the time when he was swallowed by the fish to the time when he was delivered. It was a continual act. It is the same as though he said, 'I have called, *and do call* on Jehovah'" (my emphasis).[5] Ibn Ezra interpreted the past verbs of deliverance in the song as "prophetic perfects" thus ensuring the interpretation that Jonah was looking forward to deliverance when he was in the belly of the fish.[6] Jerome T. Walsh, a contemporary scholar, overlooks the references to the distinct prayers. He writes: "The couplet in v. 3 stands as an introduction to the whole poem. It presents the drama of distress, entreaty, and salvation of which the entire psalm is an artful elaboration."[7]

In the laments of the individual found in the Psalter (the parallels in form between this psalm type and Jonah 2:3–10 are frequently noted), the verbs employed in the address are not in the pf. but in the impf. or one of the derivational forms (cohortative or impv.), referring to distress that has not been overcome presently.[8] Ps. 120 does appear to be an exception to the trend where the verbs are preterit, in the unmodified pf. or the vav-consecutive impf. tense forms. George Landes has correctly pointed out that when the perfect tense form is used in the lament genre to signal present durative action, associated verb forms in the cohortative, impv., or unmodified impf. are also employed instead of accompanying vav-consecutive impf. verb forms as in Jonah 2:3 (ויענני, "and he answered me").[9] For example, the perfect form קראתי ("I cry") in Ps. 130:1 may be translated present durative ("Out of the depths, I *cry*") because it is followed by an impv. שמעה ("hear it") and an unmodified impf. תהיינה ("let be attentive"), unlike the verb form sequence in Jonah 2:3. Of course, a vav-consecutive impf. verb form may occasionally be rendered in the present tense, but the translator's decision depends ultimately on such contextual clues as mentioned above.[10] Thus the initial verbs of Jonah 2:3 should *both* be translated as preterits: "I *called* . . . and he *answered* me."

A feature of the psalm in Jonah 2 that is frequently overlooked is the relationship it bears to the "thanksgiving" or "praise of the individual" psalm type. In Ps. 40, for example, a previous appeal appears in the opening verse ("I waited patiently for the Lord") which has been answered ("He brought me up out of the Pit" [vs. 2]). In the Jonah story, the prophet's earlier prayer which is signalled by קראתי ("I called") has been answered. The fish, at least from Jonah's perspective, is a vehicle of deliverance. Therefore, the opening verses of the prayer that begins at 2:3 do not describe the prophet's state in the belly of the fish but a previous condition and attitude that occurred after the sailors hurled him into the sea and before he was swallowed by the fish. They also suggest that the author has combined the elements of both the "thanksgiving" and the "lament of the individual" psalm types to produce a prayer entirely consistent with the psychological portrayal of this prophet fleeing from the Lord—lamenting his situation as the reeds wrap around his head and thankful for the deliverance from drowning which he had previously experienced.

When considered separately, these two prayers derive from distinct moments after Jonah has been hurled into the sea and allow us to understand that Jonah had in fact lamented his experiences as he was drowning ("I called from my distress; . . . From the belly of Sheol[11] I cried out; . . . Waters encompassed my neck; The deep swirled around me; Reeds were wrapped around my head . . ." [2:3; 2:6–7a]) and *before* he expressed gratitude for his deliverance or rescue by means of the fish. James Ackerman has made the astute observation that (בלע) "swallow" is not used in the Hebrew Bible with a beneficent goal in mind. In fact, it always carries a negative meaning.[12] Therefore, if the interpretation that *Jonah* views the fish as a vehicle of divine rescue is correct, it appears the author has included this motif to highlight Jonah's *mis*understanding of the swallowing. The author seems to delight in creating discrepancy in awareness both among characters on the one hand and characters and the audience on the other. Questions worth considering which will eventually be answered are: Does the author bring everyone into line, and, if so, how and when?

The view that Jonah perceives the sea as his enemy and the fish as his friend does not rest on grammatical distinctions alone. The Hebrew Bible and extrabiblical sources also shed light on this issue. The Hebrew Bible does not contain references to fish in any other contexts that might serve either as a friend or enemy to a prophet, and conclusions can only be drawn tentatively. André Feuillet has considered the possibilities and concludes his discussion with these words: "le poisson de Jonas, c'est, tout comme les corbeaux d'Élie ou l'ânesse de Balaam, le monde animal mis par Dieu au service de la cause prophétique. . . . le poisson ne soit présenté comme une punition."[13] Evidence from extrabiblical sources provides clearer signs of deliverance effected by means of a fish, especially from the Greek or Aegean world, and from India.[14] For example, Heracles was swallowed by a sea creature after his ship sank, and when Arion, a Greek poet from the seventh century B.C.E., jumped into the sea, a dolphin returned him to land.[15] The absence of parallels to the fish motif in the Hebrew Bible may indicate its non-Israelite origin and suggests the author freely adapted material for his purposes.

Prayers without Verbal Formulations

The author's choice not to include the words of characters when they pray is also apparent outside of chapter 2. In the first four verses of chapter 1, several actions and one speech event are reported. After a quick reference to the prophet's lineage ("Jonah, son of Amittai" [vs. 1] which serves as an obvious link to the eighth century prophet from the northern kingdom [1 Kings 14:25]), the command to "arise, go to Nineveh" (vs. 2) causes Jonah to flee in the opposite direction, towards Tarshish. The sailors are first introduced, indirectly, in vs. 3 as Jonah's flight from the Lord is being described: "and [Jonah] went down in [the ship] to go with *them* towards Tarshish" (my emphasis). The narration continues with a description of the Lord's actions which obviously pertain to the prophet's disobedience ("but the Lord hurled a great wind" [vs. 4]) which causes the sea to become tempestuous. When the narrator chooses to suspend the description of the rebellious prophet's actions, he begins with a quick view of the sailors from within ("and the sailors were afraid") in vs. 5 which is immediately followed by a description of their calling out "each to his god(s)." This initial sketch of their outward activity will gain its true rhetorical weight only as the story unfolds. Already the reader or listener is struck by the fact that even more spontaneous than a concerted effort to throw their cargo overboard to lighten their load (vs. 5), a casting of lots to determine the cause of the storm (vs. 7), or even desperate attempts to row back to dry land to save their lives from the raging storm (vs. 13) is this natural response, a kind of reflex action, to call out to a higher power hoping that something beyond their own efforts will save them.

The second reported prayer without verbal formulation in the book occurs at the beginning of 2:3 with "I called" קראתי and is referred to once again at 2:6–8. As explained above, these references to prayer apply to a previous invocation that was made sometime after the sailors hurled Jonah into the sea and before the fish swallowed him.

Prayers with Verbal Formulations

Of the three reports of prayer that include verbal formulations [(a) 1:14, (b) 2:3–10, (c) 4:2–3], the one by Jonah in chapter 2 is certainly the longest, and, as mentioned in the introduction, the most complex in terms of psychological portrayal. It is preceded by a supplication attributed to the collective voice of sailors in 1:14, and then followed by a subsequent prayer, also from Jonah, in 4:2–3. These three prayers, which will serve as the focal point in the discussion that follows, are introduced in different ways, but share certain words. For example, the sailors "called (ויקראו) unto the Lord (יהוה) and they said (ויאמרו)"; Jonah's prayers in 2:3–10 and 4:2–3 are introduced with identical verb forms: "and Jonah prayed (ויתפלל) . . . and he said (ויאמר)"; and in all three instances, the sailors and prophet pray or call "unto the Lord" (אל יהוה). The fact that the sailors had previously called each "unto his god(s)" (אל אלהיו, vs. 5), and then later call unto the Lord (יהוה) indicates subtly that Jonah's confession ("the Lord [יהוה] the God of the heavens, I fear" [1:9]) has caused them to recognize Jonah's God as the author of their present suffering.

   a. 1:14. The sailors pray a second time in the initial scene, and this time the content of their supplication is shared with us:

   We pray, O Lord, do not let us perish on account of this man's life, and may you not put innocent blood upon us, for you, Lord, as you have pleased you have done.

This prayer comes after considerable plot development in the first scene. Between the opening prayer in vs. 5 and this one, several events have occurred, with the author focusing primarily on the sailors throughout. In addition to their two prayers, the sailors also "hurl the cargo . . . into the sea" (vs. 5). The chief of the sailors (רב החבל) interrogates the prophet, and in the Hebrew the questioner's excitement and fear is accentuated: מה לך נרדם "How can you fall into a trance!?" He commands Jonah to call upon his gods—or god, the Hebrew may be translated in either the singular or plural—hoping they will consider the sailors and save them from perishing. Attention turns again to the group of sailors who begin throwing lots in an attempt to isolate the cause of the storm (vs. 7). After the lots fall to Jonah, they ask him a series of five questions in vs. 8 before allowing him an opportunity to respond: "On whose account has this evil happened to us? What is your occupation? And from where do you come? What is your country? And from what people are you?" The content of the questions highlights for the reader what is already obvious: their confused state of mind and desperate attempts to prolong life. The last three questions are essentially the same, and in this context highlight the sailors' thoughts and attitudes while the narrator passes over Jonah's mental state altogether. The frightening scene continues. They ask Jonah for his opinion about the solution to the problem (vs. 11), and he responds by volunteering to be hurled overboard (vs. 12). In a final effort to avoid casting him into the sea, they pray a second time. The frame formed by the prayers in vss. 5 and 14 surrounds the various and desperate attempts of the sailors to prevent what appears to be imminent death, and the author suggests that spoken prayer is the substratum of everything human. In a different context, Moses appeals for the people whom God had just promised to destroy in Exod. 32:10 for worshiping the calf. In this context and in contradistinction to the taciturn prophet in Jonah 1, Moses intercedes for the sake of *the people*. Moses, after being promised not only that he would not be destroyed but would also be the progenitor of a great nation (32:10), says to the Lord, "Turn from your fierce wrath; change your mind and do not bring disaster on your people" (32:12b).

A careful look at Jonah 1:14 reveals that the sailors' supplication includes an address, a double petition, and a motivation (i.e. a persuasive reason intended to induce compliance):

Address:	"We pray,[16] O Lord!
Petition:	Do not let us perish on account of this man's life, and may you not put innocent blood upon us,
Motivation:	for you, Lord, as you have pleased you have done."[17]

The pattern is worth considering. How common is this prayer outline? A quick glance at prayers outside the book of Jonah reveals interesting results. For example, after Abraham's servant arrives in Nahor in pursuit of a wife for Isaac, he prays to the Lord:

Address:	"O Lord, God of my master Abraham,
Petition:	please grant me success today, and show steadfast love to my master Abraham.
Motivation:	I am here by the spring of the water, and the daughters of the townspeople are coming out to draw water. Let the girl to whom I shall say,

'Please offer your jar that I may drink,' and who
shall say 'Drink, and I will water your camels'—
let her be the one whom you have appointed
for your servant Isaac. By this I shall know that
you have shown steadfast love to my master."
(Gen. 24:12–14)[18]

In Exod. 32:11–13, Moses, while on the mountain, pleads with the
Lord after the people have built a molten calf.

Address:	"O Lord,
Motivation:	Why does your wrath burn hot against your people, whom you brought out from the land of Egypt with great power and with a mighty hand? Why should the Egyptians say, 'It was with evil intent that he brought them out to kill them in the mountains, and to consume them from the face of the earth?'
Petition:	Turn from your fierce wrath; change your mind and do not bring disaster on your people."

In Num. 14, the people express their frustration as they wander in
the wilderness: "Oh that we had died in the land of Egypt! Or that
we had died in this wilderness" (vs.2). The Lord then asks Moses
how long his people will spurn him (vs. 11), and Moses, in an attempt
to placate the Lord, responds:

Address:	"You, O Lord . . .
Petition:	Let the power of the Lord be great in the way that you promised when you spoke, saying,
Motivation:	'The Lord is slow to anger and abounding in steadfast love, forgiving iniquity and transgression. . . .'" (vs. 14–19)

In Deut. 3:24–25, an account of Moses' request to cross over with
the people to the promised land is given.

Address:	"O Lord, God,
Motivation:	You have only begun to show your servant your greatness and your might; what god in heaven or on earth can perform deeds and mighty acts like yours!

Petition: Let me cross over to see the good land beyond
                   the Jordan, that good hill country and the
                   Lebanon."

Though the arrangement sometimes varies, the components can be
found in four of the five books of the Torah and in the Psalter.[19]
The pattern is also found, though less frequently, in the prophetic
literature:

Address: "O Lord, God of Abraham, Isaac, and Israel,
Petition: let it be known this day that you are God in
                   Israel, that I am your servant, and that I have
                   done all these things at your bidding. Answer
                   me, O Lord,
Motivation: so that this people may know that you, O Lord,
                   are God, and that you have turned their hearts
                   back." (1 Kings 18:36–37)[20]

And also in the Writings:

Address: "O our God
Petition: ... turn their taunt back on their own heads,
                   and give them over as plunder in a land of
                   captivity. Do not cover their guilt, and do not
                   let their sin be blotted out from your sight;
Motivation: for they have hurled insults in the face of the
                   builders."[21]

The fact that the petition of the heathen sailors is rendered in
the form of an Israelite prayer is certainly significant and suggests
that the design of extemporized prayer was not understood by the
narrator to be uniquely an Israelite practice. Thus the author is able
to make the ideological point as he testifies to the universal capacity
of prayer without respect to time, place, or even persons.

Moshe Greenberg has pointed out that extrabiblical evidence of
extemporized lay prayer is meager, too sparse in fact to draw conclusions about the pattern of such prayers or their prevalence among
sailors or kings outside Israel.[22] Two of the few examples of nonbiblical extemporized prayer in ancient literature are found in "The
Story of the Two Brothers" and *The Epic of Gilgamesh*. After the
elders of Uruk attempt to dissuade Gilgamesh from travelling to the

Cedar Forest where Huwawa resides, Gilgamesh kneels and prays to Shamash:

Address:	"I go, O Shamash, my hands [raised up in prayer].
Motivation:	May it henceforth be well with my soul.
Petition:	Bring me back to the landing-place at [Uruk]; Establish [over me] (thy) protection!"[23]

In "The Story of the Two Brothers," the younger brother prays to Re-Harakhti as the elder brother attempts to kill him, saying, "O my good lord, thou art he who judges the wicked from the just." This prayer consists only of an extended address (though perhaps an implicit motivation and petition as well) which is followed by the narrator's report of the requests: "thereupon the Re heard all his pleas."[24]

Therefore, we may conclude that the collection of petitions in the book of Jonah testifies to the efficacious nature of prayer in a universal context. Along with such heroes as Moses, Jeremiah, and Elijah, we learn that the Lord also responds to the supplications of the sailors, in this case with a nonverbal reply. When the sea ceases from its raging (1:15), this answer to prayer brings forth a specific response from the sailors. The narrator reveals that they fear the Lord and that they sacrifice to the Lord. Even the prophet's disobedient behavior has produced welcome results: the "fear" and "sacrifices" in vs. 16 are responses to an answered prayer.

b. 2:3–10. The second verbal formulation of prayer in the book of Jonah is signalled at the beginning of 2:2: "and Jonah prayed to the Lord, his God, from the body of the fish.[25] (3) And he said, . . ."

Several issues that relate to this prayer will be discussed in the next chapter, but a few comments are in order here.[26] The distinguishing feature of the Jonah psalm is that it is spoken by one person in a specific context; with these words it establishes that Jonah is in fact a Hebrew who fears the Lord who made the dry land and sea (as the prophet had indicated to the sailors back in 1:9). Jonah is, we now know, a *worshiping* Hebrew. A significant number of parallels exist between this prayer and particular psalms. In fact, the prayer that Jonah offers from the belly of the fish consists almost entirely of phrases from the Psalter.[27] This pastiche highlights the prophet's frenzied mental state. Because of the variety of short phrases drawn from different parts of the Psalter, its rhetorical function is quite unlike that of David's prayer of deliverance in 2 Samuel 22, an extended prayer which he quotes from Psalm 18. The prayer uttered from the belly of the fish shows other thematic similarities to the action and words of the previous chapter. Initially, Jonah's going down had been reiterated several times in the opening scene beginning with his descent to Joppa. While this first image may not denote a specific downward movement—Hebrew merely refers to setting out to sea by means of such an idiom (see, for example, Ps. 107:26 and Isa. 42:10)—Jonah does go down into the ship (1:3), and then continues to descend into its recesses (1:5).[28] Even the sailors' activity is characterized by similar actions. They cast lots which "fall" to Jonah (1:7) and then finally throw him overboard as they attempt to save their lives. This descent motif continues especially in the first half of the psalm, and then the movement is reversed in 2:7b as Jonah recounts that the Lord brought him up from the Pit.

The prophet's concluding remark at the end of the prayer ("I will sacrifice to you; what I have vowed, I will pay" [vs. 10]) reminds the reader of the sailors' action at the end of the previous scene (1:16). From the ideological plane, we see that the author begins to align the action of the stubborn (Hebrew) prophet with those of the desperate (foreign) sailors. However, their deeds were an unambiguous response to the Lord's deliverance. How does Jonah's expression of thanksgiving relate to the opening commission from the Lord to go to Nineveh and prophesy against her? A certain indeterminacy of meaning, especially with regard to motive and psychology, is evident at the end of chapter 2. The conclusion to Jonah's prayer thus serves to ambiguate, whereas the sailors' prayer had functioned earlier to elucidate, character.

c. 4:2–3. The final prayer in the book is found at the beginning of chapter 4. The formulaic pattern is present once again, but here the petition comes last:[29]

Address:	"I pray,[30] Lord,
Motivation:	was this not my word when I was in my country? This is why I made haste to flee towards Tarshish, for I knew that you are a gracious God, and compassionate, slow in coming to anger and great in *ḥesed* and repenting of evil.

Petition: And now Lord, take, I pray, my life from me
for I prefer death to life." (4:2–3)

The two verbal formulations of Jonah's prayers (2:3–10) and (4:2–3) both contain certain key words in close combination to each other: חיי "my life"; נפשי "my soul"; and חסד "*ḥesed*" appear in 2:7b; 2:8, 2:9b and again in 4:2b and 4:3, a feature that reinforced the argument for contextual appropriateness in "Jonah and the Reading Process" (in chapter 4).[31] While the prayer of the foreign sailors in 1:14 followed the Israelite pattern, only Jonah's prayers contain traditional phrases. Again, we notice the author's ideological concern: the prayers of the sailors and Jonah do share a common feature, namely a dialogue pattern, but Jonah's prayers bear witness to his claim that he *is* a Hebrew (1:9). André Feuillet, focusing on the author's use of sources throughout the Jonah story, isolated four biblical books: (1) Kings, (2) Jeremiah, (3) Ezekiel, and (4) Psalms.[32] In addition to the remarkable number of phrases from the Psalter that appear in Jonah 2:3–10, passages from 1 Kings 19:4, as well as from Exod. 34:6 and Joel 2:13, contain some of the words the author incorporates in Jonah's subsequent prayer at 4:2–3.[33]

In the scene from Kings, Ahab reports to Jezebel that Elijah had killed all of the false prophets of Baal at the river Kishon. Jezebel sends a messenger to Elijah to tell him that she promises to seek revenge. The prophet becomes afraid, flees past Beersheba to the wilderness where he sits under a juniper tree, and finally requests to die, saying, "It is enough; now, O Lord, take away my life for I am no better than my ancestors" (1 Kings 19:4). In the scene from Exodus, the Lord speaks to Moses and provides specific details about what the prophet is to do now that the tablets have been shattered (Exod. 34:1–5). Moses rises early in the morning, follows the Lord's instructions carrying two tablets of stone to the top of Mt. Sinai. Then the Lord passes in front of the prophet and says, "the Lord, a God merciful and gracious, slow to anger, and abounding in steadfast love and faithfulness" (34:6b). The traditional words appear in Joel as part of an extended exhortation: "Return to the Lord, your God, for he is gracious and merciful, slow to anger, and abounding in steadfast love, and relents from punishing" (Joel 2:13).

The context of these passages has been established to show how different the circumstances are in the Jonah story. For example, both

prophets, Elijah and Jonah, ask to die just after saying, "now" (עתה),
a word that typically introduces the essential point of a speech in
the Hebrew Bible, but give different reasons.[34] Elijah claims, "for I
am no better than my ancestors"; Jonah, "for I prefer death to life."
Elijah, obviously weary after the long and dramatic struggle with
Baalism, begins to feel that he will fail as his fathers had and now
asks to be united with them in death. Jonah reveals, and what a
surprise it is to us, that he longs for death because of the very success
of his mission. While Jonah is as successful as the prophet who had
requested to die shortly after the events on Mt. Carmel, he is no
Elijah. What kind of prophet is this, despising the grace that had
earlier saved him? Thus a close reading of the parallel biblical passages and the points of contact between 2:3–10 and 4:2–3 in the
book of Jonah suggest that the author fashioned the material in a
way to define motives and to anchor the theme of God's saving
power, an aspect of his artistry that will be discussed in the "Analogy
along Generic Lines" section below. The prayers are highly conventional, yet have few formal constraints.

What effect does the mixture of prayers in the book of Jonah
have on the reader? Why does the author sometimes choose to
report the words of some supplications and withhold them on other
occasions? Both forms do share certain characteristics. Each report
of prayer in Jonah is plaintive, quite unlike Samuel's crying (זעק)
unto the Lord which lasts all night (כל הלילה) in 1 Sam. 15:11.
The ejaculatory prayers in the initial three chapters of Jonah occur
when life is threatened, and the high numbers of prayers reported
aids dramatization. Table 2 represents the major points of the
discussion above, and contains the designations a,b,c for the verbal
reports of prayer that will be used in the discussion that follows.

A few general observations may be drawn based on this information: Jonah and the sailors pray. The king commands the Ninevites
to call on God, but their response to the command is not given. (In-
terestingly, the king's proclamation detailing specific instructions
comes *after* the citizens have already begun believing in God, calling
for a fast, and wearing sackcloth.) The royal proclamation—a series
of short and specific commands (3:7–8)—reminds the reader of the
pithy questions of the sailors in the opening chapter (1:8). At least
one report of prayer appears in each chapter, and two of the three
verbal formulations come from the prophet's mouth.

Analogy along Generic Lines: Poetry and Prose in Jonah

As in real life, repetition is common in literature, and the authors of the Hebrew Bible were keenly aware of its function as a unifying factor for blending themes and highlighting points of view. However, unlike scenes from real life, repetition in literature is always managed and ultimately controlled by an implied author who selects and arranges the sequence of events, effecting psychological portrayal and producing dramatic complications and tensions as he or she chooses. In the Hebrew Bible, messages are sometimes passed from one person to another with interesting omissions and additions. For example in 1 Kings 1, Bathsheba not only repeats (almost) verbatim what Nathan had earlier instructed her to say to the ailing King David about an alleged promise to make Solomon the next king, but also expands the message giving it considerable, persuasive force.[35]

From the reader's side, repetition takes the form of informational redundancy.[36] For example, in Exod. 25, the Lord gives Moses specific instructions about how the ark of the covenant is to be built ("They shall make an ark of acacia wood; it shall be two and a half

Table 2
Reports of Prayer in Jonah

Location	Pray-er(s)	Description	Designation
1:5	sailors	report without verbal formulation	
1:6b	Jonah(?)	request	
1:14	sailors	report with verbal formulation	a
2:3 = 2:6–8	Jonah	report without verbal formulation	
2:3–10	Jonah	report with verbal formulation	b
3:8	Ninevites(?)	request	
4:2–3	Jonah	report with verbal formulation	c

cubits long, a cubit and a half wide, and a cubit and a half high. You shall overlay it with pure gold, . . ." a command that continues for 30 verses [vss. 10–39], according to traditional enumeration). As the reader moves from forecast to enactment, a formulaic summary would be sufficient, but he or she is *not* told that Bezalel, the craftsman appointed for the task, "followed the instructions which the Lord commanded Moses." Instead, the specifications are repeated in the enactment scene ("Bezalel made the ark of acacia wood; it was two and a half cubits long, a cubit and a half wide, and a cubit and a half high. He overlaid it with pure gold . . ." which continues for 25 verses [Exod. 37:1–24]).

Commentators, with eyes on the structure of the book of Jonah, have frequently called attention to the importance of repetition. Not only do certain words keep emerging ("great" appears fourteen times; "call," seven; "arise," six, etc.); they also function in a dynamic fashion and might be compared to a motif of a symphony. The high frequency of certain key words has allowed many commentators to make comparisons, and the events in the chapters also encourage this kind of analysis.[37] The book of Jonah is only one of many, and certainly one of the most symmetrical, stories from the Hebrew Bible where parallel situations and themes are established for the purpose of providing psychological commentary on its characters. The parallel structures in this book often produce a kind of crescendo in development where certain images or motifs are produced in the first part of the story and then brought to a climax in a subsequent scene. For example, the action in chapters 1 and 3 follows this pattern: divine commission→ prophet in the midst of foreigners→ life is threatened→ the foreigners' (and not Jonah's!) desperate, quick attempts to placate God→ resolution of the problem for foreigners→ further conflict for the prophet. In the Nineveh episode, and in contrast to the scene of the sailors, an inside view of God is given toward the end of the sequence: "And God saw their deeds, how they turned from their evil ways, and God was sorry concerning the evil which he had said he would do to them, and he did not do it" (3:10).[38]

These seven references to prayer signal a need for special attentiveness for readers or listeners, and one can think of several questions about the way they emerge and develop. Why does the writer choose on many occasions to reveal his characters through speech instead

of summary, and why is the speech often a prayer? Just how do
these events and speech patterns of the pray-ers themselves—the
syntax, tone, brevity, lengthiness, and imagery—serve to delineate
character and to establish points of contact for the reader? In looking
for answers, it should be noted that biblical writers consistently
organize the speech of their characters not in terms of regional or
class dialects, as Faulkner or Salinger would in the modern era, but
along contrastive principles—simple versus complex, perceptive versus obtuse, accurate versus deceptive, crude versus eloquent, symmetrical versus unbalanced, short versus long, and so forth. Yet in
putting "normative" Hebrew in the mouths of men as different as
a prophet, the chief of sailors, and the "king" of Nineveh, the author
is able to delineate a character.

The seven references to prayer in the book of Jonah do not belong
to the forecast→ enactment→ report pattern which is apparent elsewhere in the Hebrew Bible, as, for example, in 1 Sam. 15 when
Samuel, speaking for the Lord, commands Saul to utterly destroy
Amalek (forecast)→ which is followed by Saul's capturing of the
Amalekite king (enactment)→ which is then followed by Saul's multiple reports of his actions including (finally!) his confession of sin
(vs. 24). Instead, the prayers in Jonah are separate events of the plot
related to the characters' psychological portrayal and the activity of
God, and are best discussed under the rubric of analogy which is
"essentially [a] spatial pattern, composed of at least two elements
(two characters, events, strands of action, etc.) between which there
is at least one point of similarity and one of dissimilarity."[39] Recourse
to the principle of analogy is certainly not unique to biblical literature. One might think, for example, of the play within a play in
Midsummer Night's Dream where Bottom and his friends perform
Pyramus and Thisbe at the court or the recurring scenes at the Althing
in *Njal's Saga* where desires for revenge blend with assembly pro-
cedures. In more ancient literature, such as "The Story of the Two
Brothers," an elder brother's wife turns out to be a liar as well as a
thief when she steals some of the younger brother's words and
ideas: "But I wouldn't listen to him: 'Aren't I your mother?—for
your elder brother is like a father to you!'"[40] And in *The Gilgamesh
Epic*, multiple dream reports play important functions in the development of the plot.[41] In each of these cases, diverse as they are,
a kind of rhythm is established that has thematic significance, and

in Jonah, where explicit evaluation of characters' thoughts is frequently avoided, such analogies play an especially critical role for the reader.

In the first three chapters of Jonah, reports of prayer are given when life is threatened. The men on the ship call on God twice, and a similar action and frequency of praying are repeated in the second chapter, with two prayers coming from the prophet. The cyclical plot pattern of crisis→ prayer→ deliverance is well in place at the end of the second chapter when the Lord speaks to the fish which "vomits up Jonah to the dry land" (2:11). Although the reference to prayer in the subsequent Nineveh scene is less explicit because the response to the king's command in 3:8 ("they shall call") is not given, the pattern is repeated once more: (a) death appears imminent ("Yet in forty days, and Nineveh will be overthrown" [3:4]) which leads to (b) a call for prayer ("people and animals . . . shall call [קרא] to God" [3:8]) which in turn is followed by (c) deliverance ("and God saw their deeds, how they turned from their evil ways, and God was sorry concerning the evil which he had said he would do to them, and he did not do it" [3:10]).

Following the designations of Table 2, in (a) the idol-worshiping sailors forsook their gods—if only temporarily—when they learned that Jonah's God had power over the sea. While both of Jonah's prayers, (b) and (c), refer to earlier distress (the former to drowning; the latter to the prophet's reason for disobeying the divine commission), the final prayer in the book, (c), serves to represent character in a crucially different way. Instead of the expected pattern of crisis→ prayer→ deliverance, the reader may be surprised to learn that Jonah now longs for death. (C) comes at a time when Jonah has apparently just witnessed deliverance, the preserving of life, and now offers the first prayer which is a request for death! With the petition drawn out to the end, a departure from the biblical norm, the reader experiences the surprise (deliverance→ crisis→ prayer for death!) at the last possible moment.

Generic considerations aside, connections between (b) and (c) are established by a sophisticated and integrated system of situations producing actual recurrence of thematic words or *Leitworter* linked to the plot and images of the narrative world. Some of the very words which came in the form of praise in (b) are now used in (c) to express Jonah's grief over the preservation of life.[42]

The points of similarity and dissimilarity also reveal how the author is able to achieve a sense of depth in characterization through what appears by modern standards to be meager and rudimentary means. As discussed in chapter 3 ("The Narrator and Characters"), the author has ensured that Jonah and God emerge as the two characters of central interest. Unlike the foreigners, Jonah prays when no one else is around. The prophet's solo voice both in the fish's belly and in the scene outside Nineveh contrasts with the prayers of the sailors which are offered as a collective expression. Further, when the sailors pray in a collective voice, the Lord's attributes are rendered in general terms: "For you, Lord, as you have pleased you have done" (1:14b), but when Jonah says specifically, "I called from my distress . . . and he answered me" (2:3a); "you brought my life up from the Pit" (2:7b); and "I knew that you are a gracious God . . ." (4:2), the relationship between God and the prophet is highlighted. In addition, only one prayer in the book elicits a verbal response from the Lord. When Jonah asks to die (c), the Lord responds immediately, "Is it right for you to become inflamed?" (4:3). Only now does Jonah emerge as the true center of interest, and only now do we realize what the storyteller has strategically passed over all along: judgment is not just for the Ninevites whose wickedness had come up before the Lord (1:2), but, as chapter 4 will show, for Jonah as well.

Chapter 6

Jonah and Poetry

What difference would it make if Jonah's prayer within the belly of the fish were delivered not as poetry but as prose, or, conversely, what if either of the two prose prayers had been delivered as poetry? Since the thesis has recently been advanced, most forcefully by James Kugel, that no true distinction existed between poetry and prose in ancient Israel, we will first ask if the traditional designation of 2:3–10 as poetry is justifiable? More explicit genre distinctions in other literary traditions highlight part of the problem. For example, the translators of Icelandic sagas frequently provide formal clues in the prose narrative, quite unlike anything in the Hebrew Bible, that indicate a shift from prose to poetry: "This is what Throkel Elfara-Poet said about his defence . . ."; or "He chanted a verse so loudly that they could have heard it clearly from much farther away . . ."; or "It was then that he uttered this couplet, which has been remembered ever since . . ."[1] With Shakespeare, genre differences are as obvious as class distinction where nobles and leading characters typically speak in poetry, peasants and comedians in prose. In the Hebrew Bible itself, where there is a large number of genre or genre-like classifications within the text—speeches, oracles, orations (of rebuke or consolation), genealogies, curses and blessings, prayers and proverbs—no word exists for "poetry" or for "prose."

James Kugel's Thesis. The appearance of James L. Kugel's *The Idea of Biblical Poetry: Parallelism and Its History* in 1981 caused quite a stir among biblical scholars. He asserts that the distinction between poetry and prose is foreign to Hebrew biblical material; it is a Hellenistic imposition instead based on the faulty notion that some verses were written in meter. The words below, drawn from several parts of his book, are intended as a fair representation of his thesis advanced in the first section of his discussion (chapters 1–2) and will serve as a point of departure for the prose/poetry discussion in Jonah.

> We have discussed "seconding" as essentially an emphatic form, and as such it is hardly limited to the normal purview of poetry. It seems to be something far more basic, a "reflex of language," which turns up in every conceivable context . . . The same traits that seem to characterize Hebrew "poetry" also crop up in what

is clearly not poetry. . . . Thus, to speak of "poetry" at all in the Bible will be in some measure to impose a concept foreign to the biblical world. . . . To see biblical style through the split lens of prose or poetry is to distort the view; then even an awareness of parallelism will not much improve things, for it too will be distorted in the process. . . . In sum, what is called biblical "poetry" is a complex of heightening effects used in combinations and intensities that vary widely from composition to composition even within a single "genre." No great service is rendered here by the concept of biblical poetry.[2]

Despite voices of protest,[3] it is especially clear that Kugel's challenge to accepted ideas has highlighted the way in which social and intellectual history has conditioned our reading of biblical material—prose or poetry, or, as Kugel argues, "the continuum." His reformulation and discussion of the parallel line as "A, and what's more, B" is certainly a significant achievement in biblical scholarship, but I agree with those who are not convinced by the other portion of his thesis. A "continuum" certainly exists in the Hebrew Bible, as it does in all literary traditions where poetry and prose are found, but this does not mean that the genre distinction is anachronistic.

Kugel is able to argue as he does because he has driven a wedge between terseness (that is, compression or concision of expression) and parallelism. He concludes, "So it is evident that terseness ought to be treated on its own as a heightening feature of biblical style, separable (and often separate) from parallelism."[4] By placing the prayer that Jonah offers from the belly of the fish at the center of the discussion and by shifting the investigation from the levels of plot and theme to the levels of genre and sound, one may attempt to explain why the wedge which Kugel has driven between terseness and parallelism is illusory. For heuristic purposes, the three verbal formulations of prayer are labeled (a) for 1:14, (b) for 2:3–10, and (c) for 4:2–3 in the discussion below (see Table 2 in the preceding chapter).

By focusing on the work of three scholars who have recently grappled with the complex issues of biblical prosody, conclusions will be drawn that relate to the author's strategy in the Jonah story and that may also have implications in the larger area of biblical poetry. The two articles and one monograph from a collection of essays, summarized briefly below, were published within a period of four years (1982–85), and each relates to the prayer which Jonah offers from the belly of the fish.[5]

Jerome T. Walsh. According to Walsh, the Jonah psalm is a fifteen-line poem written in a 3 plus 2 (the *qina* or lament) pattern with slight variations at vs. 4a (4 plus 2) and vss. 5a and 7aβ (both 2 plus 3). The "meter" (in this case, stress is measured in terms of word clusters rather than syllables) is more consistent than in other comparable examples of Hebrew poetry. He claims that the poem is arranged chiastically (A–B–B'–A') with the B (vss. 4–5) and B' (vss. 6–8) sections being twice as long as the surrounding frame. The "B" groups are designated as "stanzas" which are inset with verbal indicators:

ונהר יסבבני . . . אל היכל קדשך / תהום יסבבני . . . אל
היכל קדשך.

"and a river encircled me . . . upon your holy temple" / "the deep swirled around me . . . unto your holy temple."

The surrounding "A" sections are described as "unit[s] half [their] length." Walsh does not emend MT "because it presents a version of that psalm that is available for study, without prejudice to arguments for potential textual emendations" and because "rhetorical criticism . . . prefers to accept the received text as given, rather than attempt reconstruction of an earlier reading, no matter how probable." He acknowledges the lack of scholarly consensus on the nature of biblical Hebrew meter and adopts "an entirely pragmatic" option of counting stress groupings based on Massoretic accentuation (the disjunctive accents) because "syllable count does not seem to yield useful results."[6]

Duane L. Christensen. On the other hand, Christensen incorporates what is generally regarded as the prose framework (2:1–2 and 2:11) in his attempt to further the discussion. He approaches all of chapter 2 by counting morae, that is, "the length of time required to say the simplest syllable from a phonetic point of view."[7] This approach to scanning Hebrew poetry apparently began in the seventeenth century and was articulated by J. Alting and J. A. Danz. Other advocates of this approach, which has not been considered in biblical scholarship until recent years, included B. Spinoza, J. W. Meiner, and H. Grimme. Christensen writes that James Hoard introduced this approach to him pointing out that it is also used in scanning modern Japanese poetry.[8]

Christensen's analysis of Jonah 2:1–11 rests completely upon the morae counting system. Like Walsh, he accepts MT as the working text, but, unlike Walsh, does make one emendation at the end of vs. 4 (עברו, "they passed over") to accommodate his organizational scheme. Syntactic-accentual units, corresponding with only a few exceptions to the Massoretic accentual system, are also incorporated in the discussion. After counting morae, he discovers two equal sections between vss. 1–5 (213 morae) and vss. 6–11 (210 morae) which are then subdivided into neat symmetrical blocks with vss. 1–3 (127 morae) corresponding to vss. 6–11 (123 morae) and vss. 4–5 (86 morae) to vss. 9–11 (87 morae). Christensen detects six strands in the chiasm of the "poetic section" (vss. 3–10), which differs from Walsh's chiastic arrangement of four. Both scholars find a different center, the most critical point, in the chiasm: 2:6–7 (Christensen); 2:4–8 (Walsh).

Frank M. Cross. Unlike the two scholars mentioned above, Cross does not adopt MT as the working text in his discussion of the verse form of the Jonah psalm. He emends MT frequently (particularly in vs. 4 where each of the initial five words has either been altered or deleted, and at times without any support from ancient versions).[9] He refers to cola by *l* (*longum*) and *b* (*breve*) and discovers a quatrain-couplet-quatrain structure in vss. 3–7 with numerous, small chiastic structures (vs. 3, for example) which are altogether unlike those which Walsh and Christensen have proposed. Cross "reconstructs" early pronunciation of the "original" Hebrew vowel system and counts syllables to determine the verse structure. In his view, the initial four bicola, vss. 3–4 (which he labels a "quatrain"), are followed by a pair of bicola (which he calls a "couplet") represented by vs. 5 and then another quatrain represented by vss. 6–7. The fourth section (vss. 8–10) yields a pattern "far less sophisticated and intricate"[10] in its makeup.

The result is a third scheme, completely different in scope from what was observed above. Walsh's "groupings," Christensen's elaborate mathematical system based on morae, and Cross's reconstruction of the early vowel system produce radically different pictures of biblical prosody which go far beyond the nomenclature problem ("hemistich"="colon"="line-half"). Regardless of the merits that any scholar might attach to any of these approaches, the fact that *no two* agree on such fundamental issues as the criteria for emendation, the frequency of chiasms, the chiasmic center points, or strophe divisions, sheds as much light on the present state of research as on Jonah's prayer from the belly of the fish.

The incompatability and conflicting interpretations throw into bold relief a problem related to the study of biblical prosody: once the green light is given, once complex methods of scansion involving intricate mathematical systems are spelled out as foundational to any particular argument, then conflicting interpretations will result. The systems, especially Cross's and Christensen's, quickly reach the point of diminishing returns in view of the elaborate mathematical schemes required, and they overlook the fact that poets from numerous cultures and time periods notoriously bend the rules to achieve their purposes. The inadequacy of the approaches may be compensated for if (a) semantic and grammatical relationships in parallel lines are reconsidered, (b) one's understanding of rhythm (which is the basic point of disagreement in the three articles surveyed above) is isolated, and (c) the search for a nonexistent strict metrical scheme is abandoned.

The Proposals of Benjamin Hrushovski and Adele Berlin: Better Alternatives

Benjamin Hrushovski, in a review article on the history of Hebrew prosody published in *Encyclopedia Judaica*, provides a better alternative when he suggests that where the rhythm of biblical poetry is concerned, strict numerical regularity is *not* an imperative.[11] In line with traditional biblical scholarship, Hrushovski affirms that the fundamental principle of biblical poetry is parallelism with parallel lines consisting of two, three, or occasionally four versets.[12] He departs from traditional scholarship in asserting that the basis of biblical verse is a "semantic-syntactic-accentual" rhythm which is fundamentally a "free rhythm" with quantitative limits regulated by the logic of its poetics. Thus the parallelisms of meaning, accent, and syntax are constantly shifting, always possible, but never obligatory. Therefore, it is conceivable that the rhythm established by major stresses is the primary or only supporter of the two versets in a parallel line where no repetition of meaning or syntax can be found. On the other hand, syntactic or semantic parallelism may dominate in the line. This fluid and rich orchestration of biblical verse suggests that rhythm is not based on strict numerical regularity and provides a starting point for a new look at Jonah's prayer from the belly of the fish.

In an attempt to understand just how an overlapping of heterogeneous parallelisms ("semantic-syntactic-accentual") operate in Jonah 2:3–10, the poet's style will be described in a rather wooden fashion. The Massoretic accentual system, serving as an approximate index of the original stress system, reveals a basic 3 plus 2 pattern, with variations at lines 3 (4 plus 2), 5 and 9 (both 2 plus 3).[13] But this pattern is not the key that unlocks the parallel system. While it is true that this structure often dominates the parallel line where short phrases and basic syntactic units exist, there is almost no evidence that the counting of stresses was what set poetry apart from prose. Robert Alter, who advocates abandoning the term "meter" for biblical verse, concludes, from a lack of evidence, that the ancient Hebrews did not view stress as the governing standard for poetry, certainly not as the Greeks or Romans did.[14]

When Robert Lowth, in the middle of the eighteenth century, recognized the presence of parallelism in biblical poetry, he distinguished three broad types: synonymous, antithetical, and synthetic. A weakness of his scheme was recognized early in the twentieth century. George Buchanan Gray, in *The Forms of Hebrew Poetry*, pointed out that the "synthetic" category was too broadly defined, but Lowth's categories continued to be used widely.[15] Kugel's thesis that the B clause (or verset) *carries the A clause further* by echoing it, defining it, contrasting it, or rephrasing it, certainly represents a major reformulation of Lowth's position. What needs to be emphasized in the present context is that Lowth's scheme, which has been widely followed until recent times, has consistently gravitated towards discussions of semantic parallelism alone, the first part of Hrushovski's semantic-syntactic-accentual triad.

Parallelism, certainly since Lowth, has been established as the most conspicuous phenomenon of biblical poetry. But to perceive parallelism is not necessarily to understand what effect it has upon the reader or listener. Most readers would readily admit that Jonah 2:3–10 consists of parallel units, but since the arrangements include a network of equivalences and contrasts involving many aspects of language (not just semantic), Hrushovski's account of the biblical verse system will be adopted (and slightly adapted) for a discussion of semantical, grammatical (syntactic and morphological), and phonological parallelisms. The semantic parallelisms will be discussed in English, since the meaning is apparent in translation, and the grammatical and phonological aspects will be considered with reference to the Hebrew.

Semantic Parallelism. Semantic parallelism refers to the relationship of meaning that exists between versets. The significance of Lowth's contribution in this area, both conceptually and terminologically, has not been equalled, at least not until the appearance of James Kugel's, *The Idea of Biblical Poetry.* The Psalter, which the author of Jonah 2:3–10 obviously knew, was composed during a span of hundreds of years, and reveals that basic differences existed among poets of different generations with respect to their preference for static versus accentuated semantic parallelism. For example, Ps. 145 consists almost entirely of static lines, that is, versets that complement, but do not accent, heighten, or amplify, each other. The tendency is apparent in vss. 10, 11, and 17:

> All your works shall give thanks to you, O Lord,
>> And all your faithful shall bless you.
> They shall speak of the glory of your kingdom,
>> And tell of your power.
> The Lord is just in all his ways,
>> And kind in all his doings.

But static parallelism does not always prevail. Indeed, Ps. 3 moves in the other direction, with many B versets heightening what was said or sung earlier. For example, in three consecutive lines one finds this tendency where focusing or heightening is apparent in consecutive B versets:

> I cry aloud to the Lord,
>> And he answers me from his holy hill.
> I lie down and sleep;
>> I wake again, for the Lord sustains me.
> I am not afraid of ten thousands of people
>> Who have set themselves against me all around.
>> (vss. 5–7; Evv 4–6)

Both tendencies, toward static and heightened parallelism, can be recognized in the Psalter and at times one predilection is dominant. In places, the Book of Job, for example, the preference for height-

ening is so strong that only a few examples of static parallelism can
be found. In the third chapter, just after Eliphaz, Bildad, and Zophar
arrive in the land of Uz, Job curses the day of his birth:

> Why did I not die at birth,
>   Come forth from the womb and expire?
> Why were there knees to receive me,
>   Or breasts for me to suck?
> Now I would be lying down and quiet;
>   I would be asleep; then I would be at rest. . . .
>
> (vss. 11–13)

In each of these three lines, the second versets serve to advance
the initial thought, to heighten or in some way to expand the image
or concept of the first. As should already be apparent from these
isolated examples, the system of versification itself encourages an
interplay, where images, thoughts, and feelings in the A verset are
either matched with equivalent expressions in the B verset or carried
forward by means of a heightened or sharpened image.

In an attempt to establish the interplay of semantic relations between versets in the Jonah psalm, typographical symbols will serve
to highlight the alliance. Static relationships are indicated by: = synonymity; {} complementary. Dynamic relations by: > focusing,
heightening; < focusing, heightening reversed; → narrative moments. The "∣" mark refers to a distinct interlinear relationship.[16]

The poem, eight verses according to traditional enumeration,
consists of fifteen lines.

1		"I called from my distress;
	>	Unto the Lord and he answered me.
2		From the belly of Sheol I cried out;
	>	You heard my voice.
3		And you cast me to deep, into the heart of the seas,
	<	And a river encircled me.
4		All your breakers and your waves
	{}	Passed over me.
5		And I said,
	→	'I was cast away from your sight.
6		Yet I will again look
	→	Upon your holy temple.'

7		Waters encompassed (my) neck;
	>	(The) deep swirled around me.
8		Reeds were wrapped around my head
|	>	To/At the roots of the mountains,
9		I descended to the underworld;
	{}	Bars were upon me forever.
10		Yet you brought my life up from the Pit,
	{>}	O Lord, my God.
11		My soul fainted within me;
	>	I remembered the Lord.
12		And my prayer came unto you,
	>	Unto your holy temple.
13		Those who regard vain idols,
	=	Abandon their *ḥesed*.
14		But I, in a voice of thanksgiving,
|	→	I will sacrifice to you.
15		What I have vowed, I will pay.
	>	Salvation is of the Lord!"

A few observations may be made about the typographical marks. Parallel lines in the body of the poem tend to be dynamic rather than static. One line is characterized by synonymity and two by complementariness. If the interlinear relationships and overlap of semantic types are considered, there are three synonymous and three complementary lines. The frequency of heightened parallel lines is much higher. Eight lines are characterized by focusing, heightening, or intensification (nine considering the overlap at line 10) and three by narrative moments (four considering the interlinear relationship between lines 8 and 9). Thus the logic of intensification, the norm in biblical poetry, gains rhetorical strength here as Jonah cries out in this distressing situation.

Since there is no reason that semantic relationships cannot overlap, two symbols have been superimposed at line 10 where both a static and dynamic union exist. The reference to "you" in the first verset of line 10 is certainly more specific than the associated "O Lord, my God," but unlike most other lines where the second verset relates more specifically to the meaning of the first (as, for example, in line 1 where "I called" is matched with "unto the Lord" in the accompanying verset, or conversely, "he answered me" with the previous "from my distress"), the epithet "O Lord my God" in the second verset of line 10 complements as well as focuses the initial image, "Yet you brought my life up from the Pit."

It is interesting to note that at line 3 the pattern of intensification is actually reversed. The initial verset, "and you cast me to the deep, into the heart of the seas," is more intense and more specific than its counterpart, "and a river encircled me." This kind of movement along the syntagmatic axis is rare in biblical poetry.

At times the relationship is best described as specification, as, for example, in line 12 "and my prayer came unto you" (where, specifically?) / / "Unto your holy temple." At other times "intensification" serves as a more accurate description. In line 7, "waters" of the first verset corresponds to "the deep" in the second; they "encompass" the pray-er's neck, and then "swirl" around him.

Another feature, which the typographical marks highlight, is the way in which some lines overlap. This interlinear relationship, a much neglected aspect in many discussions on biblical poetry, is especially obvious at lines 8 and 9 and lines 14 and 15. Particularly at these lines a striking feature links the artistry of the poem to the prose narrative. Even after the modulation to poetry, the main burden of the story continues to be carried by dialogue, a tool of characterization used to advance the thematic argument. Thus, the shift from prose to poetry should not lead to the conclusion that verse is essentially an eloquent or dramatic way of representing thoughts and feelings that might be expressed otherwise, nor a poetry of assertion and reassertion lacking narrative elements. This narrative impulse (so obvious throughout the prose sections[17]) rears its head in the poem, occasionally from verset to verset and even from line to line, but only momentarily. The prophet's promise to sacrifice (line 14b) and his reference to making vows (line 15a) obviously parallel the action of the sailors, which Jonah did not witness, at the end of chapter 1. Semantic parallelism in line-pairs is sometimes carried by way of contrast: "I descended to the underworld" (line 9); "Yet you brought my life up from the Pit" (line 10). In addition to the terseness or compact nature of the structuring between versets and occasionally between lines, certain phrases are repeated in the poem and function as a motif: "Yet I will again look / *upon your holy temple*" (line 6) recurs six lines later: "And my prayer came unto you / *unto your holy temple*" (line 12). In Jonah's verse prayer, the swerve

away from semantic parallelism has the effect of approaching the
curve of the plot, but the narrative impulse never dominates the
poem. Even where the narrative impulse is absent, the steady progression of image and theme continues.

It will become clearer in the discussion below that the poetry is
characterized by shifts within the semantic-grammatic-phonological
framework as one aspect tends to dominate at one line while another
is prevalent elsewhere. At other times, the semantic and grammatic
levels work together, as for example, in line 13 where two polar
attitudes ("regard"/"abandon") surround two abstractions ("idols"
or "vain nothings"/"ḥeseḏ") and are reinforced grammatically with
two verbal forms enveloping two nominal forms.

Grammatical Parallelism. Grammatical parallelism relates both to
morphology (the description of grammatical forms and function
within the distribution of larger stretches of speech) and syntax (the
arrangement or sequence of words in phrases or sentences). True
grammatical identity between versets, that is, exact morphological
correspondence between the constituent elements in the verset pair
does not exist in Jonah 2:3–10. A noun-verb-preposition-noun sequence, to mention only one possibility, being paralleled with the
same grammatical distribution in the accompanying verset is rare
outside of the book of Jonah.[18] Grammatical parallelism, where it
exists in the Jonah psalm, consists either of equivalence with the
versets containing different, though equivalent, morphological parallels (a noun in the first verset corresponds to an equivalent pronoun
in the second) or morphological contrasts (a noun paired with a
verb). The relationship between the verset pair may also be syntac-
tically paralleled by equivalence or contrast in a similar fashion. For
example, the syntax of the initial verset may be indicative with the
accompanying verset in either the same, or, in a contrasting mood,
such as the interrogative.

A few grammatical parallels will be isolated below. It is worthwhile
to recall that Lowth's discussion of parallelism was semantically
oriented, not grammatically oriented. The grammatical parallelisms
isolated below are just as parallel as the lines which are semantically
parallel—but the former are of an entirely different nature than the
latter.

a. Morphological pairing of words from different classes.

Pronoun / / Noun

line 10   ותעל משחת חיי
                               יהוה אלהי

Yet *you* brought my life up from the Pit,
O *Lord* my God.

The pronominal subject "you" is incorporated in the verbal root
(עלה, "bring up") in the A verset and corresponds to the more
specific and reiterated proper name, "Lord, God" in the B verset.
This morphological pairing coalesces with the intensification or
specification trend of the second verset which was observed in the
discussion above on semantic parallelism.

   *b. Morphological parallelism by equivalence and contrast in definiteness
or indefiniteness.* A noun is made definite in biblical Hebrew in one
of two ways: (a) by a prefixed definite article or (b) by being put in
the construct state with either an adjoined pronominal suffix or with
an independent substantive. Jonah's prayer in chapter 2 is characterized by a high number of equivalences in definiteness between
versets:

Contrasts.
line 3   ותשליכני מצולה בלבב ימים   definite
                              ונהר יסבבני   indefinite

You cast me to (the) deep, to *the* heart of *the*
   seas,
And *a* river encircled me.

Equivalence.
line 7   אפפוני מים עד נפש   indefinite
                          תהום יסבבני   indefinite

Waters encompassed neck;
Deep swirled around me.

line 9   ירדתי הארץ   definite
                       ברחיה בעדי לעולם   definite

I descended to *the underworld*
Her bars were upon me forever.

line 12   ותבוא אליך תפלתי   definite
                        אל היכל קדשך   definite

And *my prayer* came unto you,
Unto *your* holy *temple*.

line 13   משמרים הבלי שוא   definite
                                חסדם יעזבו   definite

Those who regard *vain idols*,
Abandon *their ḥesed*.

c. Contrasts in person. Shifts in grammatical person are a feature of
the declarative psalms of praise more than of any other psalm type,
and a traditional explanation for this feature is that the divine name
is employed in the third person when the pray-er describes for the
benefit of assembled worshipers his or her understanding of deliverance gained from personal experience. The psalmist initially addresses an audience, then, at the moments when the pray-er speaks
intimately of the Lord's response to his or her supplication, addresses
God in the second person.[19] The shifts in person can also be found
on rare occasions outside the Psalter, as, for example, in Song of
Songs 1:2, Eccl. 5:1 and Lev. 23:42.

line 1   קראתי מצרה לי
                                אל יהוה ויענני

line 2   מבטן שאול שועתי
                                שמעת קולי   [shift]

I called from my distress;
Unto the Lord and he answered me.

From the belly of Sheol I cried out;
You heard my voice.   [shift]

line 11   בהתעטף עלי נפשי
                                את יהוה זכרתי

line 12   ותבוא אליך תפלתי   [shift]
                                אל היכל קדשך

My soul fainted within me;
I remembered the Lord.

And my prayer came unto you,   [shift]
Unto your holy temple.

In the present context, where there are obviously no worshipers
present, how are the two shifts from third to second person to be
explained? At least three conjectures are possible. First, the shift
gives the impression that, on occasion, Jonah is speaking to himself.
The prophet who did not speak to God in the first chapter and who

spoke to the sailors only when they asked him questions, now addresses himself before speaking to God. A second possibility is that a sense of divine presence is suggested by certain ejaculatory phrases: "You heard my voice" (line 2); "Unto your holy temple" (lines 6 and 12), and so forth. With this explanation, the mood of immediacy is accentuated. A third possibility is that the shifts in person highlight misunderstood causal connections. In the opening verse of the prayer, references in the first person are made five times: *I* called; *my* distress; answered *me*; *I* cried out; *my* voice, and exceed second and third person references (three times combined). The pattern is reversed in the following verse where five second and third person references correspond to two first person references. In the midst of the shifts in person, Jonah's misunderstanding of causal connections is thus highlighted. The attribution of the breakers and waves to God (line 4) is certainly correct, but the prophet's statement "you cast me . . ." is inaccurate. These three explanations [(a) Jonah speaks to himself; (b) the mood of immediacy is highlighted; (c) a misunderstanding of causal connections is revealed] are not mutually exclusive, and each appears to be possible here.[20]

d. Contrasts in tense. No morphological pairing of verbs from the same stem and different tenses (*qtl, yqtl*) exists in the psalm, but two lines contain contrasts in verbs from different roots.

line 1	קראתי מצרה לי	pf.
	אל יהוה ויענני	impf.

I called from my distress;
Unto the Lord and he answered me.

line 7	אפפוני מים עד נפש	pf.
	תהום יסבבני	impf.

Waters encompassed (my) neck;
The (deep) swirled around me.

e. Contrasts in conjugation.

(line 2	מבטן שאול שועתי	pi.
	שמעת קולי	qal

From the belly of Sheol I cried out;
You heard my voice.)

line 3	ותשליכני מצולה בלבב ימים	hi.
	ונהר יסבבני	pol.

You cast me to (the) deep, to the heart of
  the seas,
And a river encircled me.

| line 5 | ואני אמרתי | qal |
| | נגרשתי מנגד עיניך | ni. |

And I said,
"I was cast away from your sight."

| line 11 | בהתעטף עלי נפשי | hit. |
| | את יהוה זכרתי | qal |

My soul fainted within me;
I remembered the Lord.

Since the verb שועתי ("I cried out") in the A verset of line 2
occurs only in the pi., no morphological contrast (pi./qal) exists here.
On the other hand, lack of morphological equivalence is noticeable
in the other three lines since יסבבני ("it encircled me," line 3),
נגרשתי ("I was cast away," line 5), and התעטף ("fainted," line 11)
regularly occur in multiple conjugations.

   f. Syntactical parallelism: contrasts in grammatical mood. We now turn
to consider syntactical parallelism that has been included in the
discussion with morphological parallelism, since both are tradition-
ally subsumed under the rubric of grammar. Of the fifteen lines in
the psalm, all but one consist of versets in the indicative mood. The
shift in mood occurs at line 10:

| ותעל משחת חיי | indicative |
| יהוה אלהי | vocative |

Yet you brought my life up from the Pit,
O Lord, my God.

   g. Grammar and interlinear relationships. In the discussion of semantic parallelism above, a few comments were made about the
interlinear relationship of meaning between lines. At the grammatical
level, an interlinear relationship is also apparent at lines 8 and 9.
The preposition ל ("to," "at") serves a double function and is probably best translated into English with two separate prepositions since
the prepositional phrase functions adverbially for two distinct verbs,
"wrapped" and "descended." This common configuration of ellipsis,
which occurs more frequently with the verb, may be rendered as
"reeds were wrapped around my head / *at* the roots of the moun-

tains . . ." *and* "*to* the roots of the mountains, / I descended . . ." The
verb ירדתי "I descended" in line 9 also functions elliptically, governing both "at/to the roots" of line 8 and "to the underworld" in
line 9.

The weight of these isolated examples of parallelisms indicates
that the poet uses grammar as a whole, morphology and syntax, to
convey meaning and images that are particularly relevant to the
action narrated in chapter 1. The opening verb of the psalm, "I
called," is one that Jonah has heard on two occasions, once from
the Lord [1:2] and once from the chief of the sailors [1:6], and
Jonah's vow at the end of the prayer ("I will sacrifice to you / what
I have vowed, I will pay" [2:10]) also mirrors the sailors' action at
the end of chapter 1. The investigation of parallel versets in Jonah
2:3–10 has suggested how grammar is used in the construction of
tight, formally organized lines. Grammar serves the poetic function
in prose and poetry, and in distinct ways allows for the imaging of
characters and events in their shifting and relevatory connections.

Phonological Parallelism. In addition to semantical and grammatical
parallelism, biblical poetry is also organized phonologically. Unlike
the rhymed Piyyut which was developed in Israel between the fourth
and sixth centuries C.E., biblical poetry rhymes only on occasion.
The small poem of chapter 2 exhibits "rhymes" (i.e. several words
end with first person pronominal or verbal suffixes and thus sound
alike) in two distinct places: at lines 1 and 2 each of the versets end
with the same sound and the versets at line 5 rhyme internally (גרשתי
"—tee" sound / אמרתי "—tee" sound). Equivalences and contrasts
in sound are often noticeable in the parallel versets, and, of course,
sound is also important in prose. However, the systematic arrangement of sound elements in prose is less noticeable because correspondence is more sporadic. There our attention is drawn instead
to the larger units.

Correspondence in sound is found in all of the lines of the Jonah
psalm except line 6. Without attempting to discuss all of the sound
patterns, table 3 will represent the arrangements from verset to verset
and from line to line. Since there are only twenty-two consonants,
some repetition is inevitable; thus in an attempt to control the
discussion the following constraint is imposed: the relationships must
be in close proximity, within consecutive versets or lines. Alliteration
refers to the recurrence of the same initial sounds in a number of
successive words, (as, for example, "When to the sessions of sweet

Table 3
Sound Patterns in the Jonah Psalm

---

1 קראתי מצרה לי   אל יהוה ויענני

2 מבטן שאול שועתי   שמעת קולי

assonance —"ee" sound at the end of each of the versets; "ol" sound (line 2)

alliteration —ש (line 2)

---

3 ותשליכני מצולה בלבב ימים   ונהר יסבבני

assonance —"ee" sound

consonance —צ, ס

---

4 כל משבריך וגליך   עלי עברו

consonance —ך

alliteration —ע

---

5 ואני אמרתי   נגרשתי מנגד עיניך

consonance —תי (internal rhyme)

---

7 אפפוני מים עד נפש   תהום יסבבני

8 סוף חבוש לראשי   לקצבי הרים

9 ירדתי הארץ   בריחה בעדי לעולם

alliteration and consonance of sibilants—ש, ס, צ (lines 7–8). These two lines contain many nasals and labials (ב, פ, מ, נ).

consonance —ר (lines 8b and 9a)

alliteration and consonance—ל, ב, ע (line 9b)

assonance —"oo" sound (lines 7a and 8a)

---

10 ותעל משחת חיי   יהוה אלהי

assonance —"ah" sound

---

11 בהתעטף עלי נפשי   את יהוה זכרתי

12 ותבוא אליך תפלתי   אל היכל קדשך

consonance —ת (ties first three versets together)

---

13 משמרים הבלי שוא   חסדם יעזבו

consonance —ש, ס, ז

---

14 ואני בקול תודה   אזבחה לך

15 אשר נדרתי אשלמה   ישועתה ליהוה

consonance —אש, אז

---

silent thought . . ." [Shakespeare]). Assonance applies to the repetition of identical vowel sounds ("The rain in Spain stays mainly in the plain") and consonance to identical final consonant sounds of closed syllables in a series of words (*dash* and *fish*).[21] A translation of these lines is given at the "semantic parallelisms" section above.

How do these sounds function? The repetition of parallel sounds within adjoining versets or lines forges a union. The interlinear relationship, which was noted in the previous sections, appears once again and is marked by line groupings of single units (lines 7, 8, and 9, for example). As observed in the discussion of the grammatical parallelisms, the parallel (as well as perpendicular and vertical) phonological structures lead once again to a perception of correspondence in meaning. Roman Jakobson's observation about sound and meaning, made in a different context, has implications here: "In a sequence, where similarity is superimposed on contiguity, two similar phonemic sequences near to each other are prone to assume a paronomastic function. *Words similar in sound are drawn together in meaning*" (my emphasis).[22]

In the instances mentioned above, the first two lines indicate the way in which phonological parallelism forges and enhances the semantic parallelism, as for example in lines 1 and 2 where each of the first four versets end in a distinct "ee" sound and then again at lines 10, 11, 12A.

Prayers (a) and (c) as Poetry?

Throughout this discussion, I have separated for heuristic purposes the semantic-grammatic-phonological parallelisms to highlight the way they work. But of course this isolation leaves the wrong impression—just as listening to the first violin, then to the oboe, and then to the cello might if one were attempting to comprehend Beethoven's bold departure from classical form with his Third Symphony. It is the interaction of all of these types of parallelism which contributes to a special unity of frequently balanced, emphatic, and elevated lines. Of course, prose also employs grammatical constructions, has semantic parallels, and is characterized by sound, so, in the light of the discussion, one might ask how prayers (a) and (c) would read if scanned as poetry. With the disjunctive Massoretic accentual marks as a guide, the lines would look like this:

(a)

אנה יהוה אל נא נאברה בנפש האיש הזה /
ואל תתן עלינו רם נקיא //

כי אתה יהוה /
כאשר חפצת עשית //

(c)

אנה יהוה הלוא זה דברי עד היותי על ארמתי /
על כן קדמתי לברח תרשישה //

כי ידעתי כי אתה אל חנון ורחום /
ארך אפים ורב חסד /

ונחם על הרעה /
ועתה יהוה /

קח נא את נפשי ממני //
כי טוב מותי מחיי //

(a)
We pray, O Lord, do not let us perish on account of this man's
   life,
And may you not put innocent blood upon us,

For you, Lord,
As you have pleased you have done.

(c)
I pray, Lord, was this not my word when I was in my country?
This is why I made haste to flee towards Tarshish,

For I knew that you are a gracious God, and compassionate,
Slow in coming to anger and great in ḥesed

And repenting of evil.
And now Lord,

Take, I pray, my life from me,
For I prefer death to life.

The strictly observed principle of parallelism in prayer (b), where linguistic equivalences and contrasts are established with adjacent words and versets, is obviously lacking here. The binary lines of (a) and (c) are characterized by terseness or concision, but only on occasion, as for example, ארך אפים ורב חסר / ונחם על הרעה ("slow in coming to anger and great in *ḥesed*" / "and repenting of evil") in (c).

The detour through linguisic analysis underscores the way the rhetorical resources of formal verse at (b) create for the reader or listener an experience quite different in kind than the surrounding prose frame, at least at the other two formulations of prayers, (a) and (c). It will not do to argue as Kugel has that this analysis only reveals patterns which are part of "a continuum." Both poetry and prose are ways of using language and both employ parallelisms, but with verse, an obvious terseness of expression is observed at the semantic-grammatic-phonological levels giving the compactness of the versets conspicuous force. Finally, the modulations to and from poetry can also be observed in light of the author's use of imagery.

Imagery

By isolating these three verbal formulations of prayer, one is able to distinguish the uniqueness of (b) in terms of one other figure, its suggestive interplay between literal and figurative elements. The extraordinary gifts of the poets from ancient Israel have frequently been noted, and are well articulated in James Muilenburg's concise description. "The most striking characteristic of biblical poetry, the feature more than any other that makes it the supreme lyrical literature that it is, are the images and figures which the poet employs to embody his feelings and thoughts. There is scarcely a poem within the entire corpus of Old Testament literature which does not bear witness to Israel's genius for imagery."[23]

A few observations highlight the poet's use of images which is essentially organized around two figures: temple and sea. The image of the temple appears twice (lines 6 and 12), and scholars arguing against the contextual appropriateness of Jonah 2:3–10 sometimes call attention to perceived incongruities in these verses.[24] If Jonah is attempting to escape God's cultic presence, they argue, why does he express a desire twice to look again to God's earthly temple? But once the generic gears have shifted, the laws of genre apply. Jonah's reference to the temple is to be understood figuratively instead of in a more explicit fashion as in Ps. 11:4 ("The Lord is in his holy temple; the Lord's throne is in heaven").

In the first four lines of the poem, reference is made to "the belly of Sheol," coupled with water and pit imagery, especially in lines 3, 4, 7, 8, 9, and 10. Each of these are conventional images which may reflect a cosmology common in Hebrew and Canaanite descriptions of death.[25] In the discussion above, Pss. 30, 69, 142, and 143 were shown to share specific words and phrases with prayer (b) in the book of Jonah, and the highest concentration of sea imagery in these prayers from the Psalter is found in Ps. 69. Seen alongside such a magnificent and imposing poem as Ps. 69, the prayer in Jonah exhibits a substantially higher concentration of sea imagery and provides yet another indicator of the way the author uses traditional material in an innovative fashion. With Jonah, intensity of ordeal is matched by intensity of expression.

Conclusion

The discussion above has suggested that seeing the biblical style, at least in the book of Jonah, through the "split lens of poetry or prose" does not distort the view, as Kugel has asserted, and a count of "prose particles" (ה ,אשר, ,את)—used in a different approach for distinguishing prose from poetry than the approach described above—also supports the idea that the biblical writers discriminated between the two modes.[26] Other issues have been considered as well. While in the finished product, each of the reports of prayer gives weight to the ideological argument, they also testify to the author's aesthetic perspective. The structure of intensification and the crescendo development in the parallel lines where conventional images are used innovatively have confirmed that there is a formal system of biblical versification, distinct from prose. With a slight modification of Benjamin Hrushovski's formula, this investigation has shown that parallelisms of equivalence or contrast are found at semantic-grammatic-phonological levels, and that the innovative imagery at (b) is characterized by action, simplicity, and concreteness. There are certain elements of repetition and parallelisms in the prose frame, but set next to the tight and formally organized lines in 2:3–10, the surrounding narrative text is perceived by the reader or listener as prose discourse. The formulation of prayer (b), working through a complex system of images, linkages of sound, and distinct syntax, proves to be an instrument for transferring densely patterned meanings, even contradictory meanings, that are most readily conveyed as poetry.

Ultimately, the relatively high frequency of prayers in the forty-eight verses gives depth to the characters and sets this story apart from others in the Hebrew Bible where the absence of prayer gives a secular impression.[27] For example, and by way of contrast, in the action which follows the rape of Dinah (Gen. 34:3–31), no mention is made of crying out to God. Dinah's reactions or attitudes before and after the rape are completely passed over while Jacob "keeps silent," החרש (vs. 5). The narrator does inform us that Jacob's sons are grieved (vs. 7) and that Simeon and Levi eventually take revenge by killing all the males of Hamor's city (vs. 25). Thus, in a scene which provides numerous opportunities for laments, their absence gives the story a secular quality with Shechem, Hamor, Jacob, Simeon, and Levi all being motivated by their passions and desires. By contrast, recourse to prayer in Jonah testifes to an author's perspective of God's saving power and to the efficacy of human speech in the form of prayer. The combined effect leaves no doubt that the central authority figure in this narrative is God, and it is the author's "ultimate semantic authority,"[28] as Bakhtin puts it, which has kept everything in balance. Art has once again served ideology.

Chapter 7

Representation of the Inner Life: A Case for Inside Views

Nous avons insisté sur le fait que l'auteur du livre de Jonas poursuit un seul but: raconter l'histoire d'un prophète.
—Carl A. Keller, "Jonas. Le portrait d'un prophète"

So reading a character becomes a process of discovery, attended by all the biblical hallmarks: progressive reconstruction, tentative closure of discontinuities, frequent and sometimes painful reshaping in face of the unexpected, and intractable pockets of darkness to the very end.
—Meir Sternberg, *The Poetics of Biblical Narrative*

The most important single privilege is that of obtaining an inside view of another character.
—Wayne Booth, *The Rhetoric of Fiction*

While numerous conflicting views have been offered on the book of Jonah, its popularity has never been questioned either in ancient or modern times. Elias Bickerman points out that as early as the second century B.C.E. Jonah and Daniel were considered outstanding examples of deliverance, and early Christians viewed Jonah's return from the depths of the sea as a prefiguration of the Resurrection.[1] In modern times, the book continues to receive a considerable amount of attention. Zalman Shazar's remark captures the essence, even as an understatement, of the book's popularity:

היה מפרש אחר שאמר. שמספר הספרים והפירושים
שנכתבו על הספר הקטן הזה. ספר יונה. עולה על
מספר הכתובים שבתוך הספר עצמו.[2]

As an artistic expression of human and divine experiences and as a book that devotes more attention to the prophet than to his message, Jonah stands alone when compared with other prophets, including his closest neighbors within the Book of the Twelve. The views of a few scholars express the general consensus.[3] James Ackerman concludes that the Major and Minor Prophets are essentially collections

124

of oracles, whereas Jonah is an account of the adventures of a prophet in conflict, struggling against God's commission,[4] and Adele Berlin that Jonah differs from the other books of classical prophecy because it is "theoretical—it presents a hypothetical case—whereas the others are historical."[5] Carl A. Keller, in his fine analysis of the author's strategy, finds various thematic and stylistic similarities between the book of Jonah and other portions of the Hebrew Bible without mentioning any of the prophets from the Book of the Twelve.[6] André Feuillet does not discover the sources of the Jonah story among the Minor Prophets but in Jeremiah and Ezekiel as well as in Kings and Psalms.[7]

Each of these commentators calls attention to some of the unique features of the book: a prophecy of only five words (עוד ארבעים יום ונינוה נהפכת, "Yet in forty days and Nineveh will be overthrown"), the absence of כה אמר יהוה ("thus says the Lord"), an account of the prophet's adventures, and the most radical, if not unbelievable, repentance and fasting (which includes the cattle) recorded in the Bible. Seen against such a background, Jonah is certainly an unforgettable character, but one of the book's claims to originality—constant focus on the inner life—has escaped notice. This overlooked aspect is of particular importance because it highlights a narrative strategy while affirming the view that this is primarily a story *about* a prophet.

Before turning to the book of Jonah, a few remarks may be made about characterization. Portraits of biblical characters are achieved by a number of techniques, many similar to those of nonbiblical narrative. For example, characterization may be accomplished through: (a) a description of action ("So David and his men went to Keilah, fought with the Philistines, brought away their livestock, and dealt them a heavy defeat" [1 Sam. 23:5]); (b) exposition presented by an omniscient narrator ("There was once a man in the land of Uz whose name was Job. That man was blameless and upright, one who feared God and turned away from evil" [Job 1:1]); (c) by a series of epithets ("I have seen a son of Jesse the Bethlehemite who is skillful in playing, a man of valor, a warrior, prudent in speech, and a man of good presence; and the Lord is with him" [1 Sam. 16:18]); (d) interior monologue ("Saul thought, 'Let me give her to [David] that she may be a snare for him and that the hand of the Philistines may be against him'" [1 Sam. 18:21]); or (e) through dialogue ("Then [Jeremiah] said, 'Ah, Lord, God! Truly I do not know how to speak, for I am only a boy.' But the Lord said to me, 'Do not say, "I am only a boy"; for you shall go to all to whom I send you, and you shall speak whatever I command you'" [Jer. 1:6–7]). The Hebrew Bible's repertoire of portrayal, diverse as it is, inevitably centers on one of two possibilities: representation of the outer life where the world of action is described, or representation of the inner where feelings and thoughts are revealed.

Representation of the inner life, the focus in this chapter, may be made in one of three ways: through (a) direct narrative statement, (b) direct discourse, or (c) through interior monologue. The book of Jonah contains narrative statements that sometimes continue in an uninterrupted fashion for several verses (for example, 1:3–5 and 4:5–8) as well as direct speech (which is found in all four chapters). While it might be argued that the prayer in chapter 2 is interior monologue, strictly speaking, it is rendered as direct discourse ("and he said, . . ." [2:3]) without any of the Hebrew Bible's signals of interior speech. Therefore, the present discussion will be limited to character and direct narrative statements.

A question that should be raised first of all relates to why it is important that the external and internal worlds be divided. The representation of any biblical character's inner life (thoughts, aspirations, anxieties, sexual desires, general state of mind) as compared to the outer (talking, killing, traveling) is important to consider because, as in real life, *characters* obtain certainty of no one's inner thoughts but their own. On the other hand, with the help of the biblical narrator, the reader is allowed to peer into the mind of a character and is thus guaranteed a certain privilege. For example, when Joseph's brothers stand before him in Egypt (Gen. 42:3–26), he knows more than they do, and the narrator through a double inside view ensures that the reader shares this privilege: "Although Joseph had recognized his brothers, they did not recognize him" (Gen. 42:8). The positions vary significantly throughout the Hebrew Bible, and one can think of numerous examples where the reader knows more than the characters and times when some characters know more and some less than others: Esther conceals her racial identity during her first days at the royal palace in Susa in accord with Mordecai's instructions (Esth. 2:9), and David's discovery that the Lord has sent Nathan comes *after* the king condemns himself (2 Sam. 12:7). Carl A. Keller does not mention the reader's elevated position as he discusses the book of Jonah, but he does highlight the way the prophet enjoys a distinct privilege over the other characters:

> Là, il [Jonas] jouit d'un statut privilégié. Les marins prient avec ferveur et ils offrent des sacrifices—mais Dieu reste muet. Les habitants de Ninive "croient" et ils se livrent à toutes les manifestations de l'angoisse, de la soumission, d'une espérance contenue—Dieu les voit, mais il ne se révèle pas. Jonas prie— et Dieu lui répond. Jonas désire mourir—Dieu fait pousser une plante qui le console. Jonas est exaspéré par la disparition de la plante—Dieu lui parle, longuement, avec une inlassable sollicitude. Jonas seul peut entendre Dieu, Jonas seul est initié aux mystères de l'amour divin: Jonas est l'unique intermédiaire entre Dieu et les hommes. Jonas seul "connaît" Dieu parce que c'est à lui seul que Dieu se fait connaître.[8]

In works such as Henry James's *The Turn of the Screw* or J. D. Salinger's *The Catcher in the Rye*, where the narrator is unreliable, this privilege must be qualified because the reader is often misled. However, the biblical narrator is not only all-knowing but reliable.[9]

A central question for this discussion is: How much and in what way does the biblical artist choose to focus on a mind tormented by a dilemma in this, the only canonical book where every human character senses that death is imminent. Theoretically, anyone's mind in the Jonah story could be opened at a given moment and his or her inner thoughts revealed, and often the withholding of an inside view proves to be as significant as the sharing of one.

Certainly part of the reason that the inner life as represented by inside views has been overlooked in the book of Jonah relates to the widespread misconception that the Hebrew Bible does not convey the inner life of its characters. Robert Scholes and Robert Kellogg contend that the inner life is not presented in Hebraic literature but is instead a Christian development. They allude to Jesus' revision of the commandment

> "Ye have heard that it was said of them of old time, Thou shalt not commit adultery: But I say unto you, That whosoever looketh on a woman to lust after hath committed adultery with her already in his heart"[10]

as one of the earliest signs of a culture which was beginning to become less concerned with external actions and more aware of the inner life. This trend, according to Scholes and Kellogg, was further developed by Ovid, then by Augustine through allegorical and auto-biographical representation, until it eventually reached a peak in modern psychological narration. Their position about the inner life in Hebraic literature, represented below, will serve as a point of reference as we consider inside views in the book of Jonah.

> Homer and other composers of primitive heroic narrative do not aspire to certain complexities of characterization which we find in later narratives and which we sometimes think of as essential elements in the creation of characterizations of interest. . . . The concept of the developing character who changes inwardly is quite a late arrival in narrative. . . . But the character whose inward development is of crucial importance is primarily a Christian element in our narrative literature. . . . The inward life is assumed but not presented in primitive narrative literature, whether Hebraic or Hellenic. . . . The notion of peering directly into the mind and dramatizing or analyzing thoughts instead of words and deeds seems to arise quite late in most literatures. . . . It may be that the technique of such presentation was simply not available to primitive narrators.[11]

While Hebrew narrative—and recent studies have certainly shown that "primitive" is an inappropriate adjective here—frequently avoids rendering the inner life of characters, especially among the prophets (What were Hosea's thoughts when he was commanded to take a wife of harlotry? [Hos. 1:2] or Ezekiel's when his wife died? [Ezek. 24:10]), Scholes's and Kellogg's conclusion, given in such general terms, is certainly far from the truth. 1 Sam. 18 contains no less than twenty inside views of the characters, and the book of Jonah also shows all of its characters from within, some more than once.

Inside Views in Jonah:
Degree, Reliability, Duration

Of course, by modern standards the Hebrew Bible does not linger on mental processes. Movement within the consciousness of individuals is more obvious in nineteenth and twentieth century literature where almost everything stated appears in relationship to the consciousness of the dramatis personae.[12] Some of the examples in Jonah, discussed below, prove to be typical of the biblical pattern where an inside view is followed by a quick return to the outside world, as for example when the sailors "fear" and then "cry" to their gods (1:5) or when the Ninevites "believe" in God, then "call" for a fast (3:5). The investigation will show that the book of Jonah displays on a small scale a wide range of techniques that afford the reader temporary access to the inward experiences of characters. Thus, to say that the book of Jonah offers the reader inside views in a collection of books where inside views are frequently found says little.[13] The more difficult questions relate to degree (to what extent has a character's mind been revealed?), reliability (has the narrator's credibility been established?), and duration (to what extent has narrative time been prolonged due to the focus on the inner life?). Comparative statements in this survey will focus on the prophets, especially the Latter Prophets, since these books have not been discussed in this context.

Chapter 1

The opening chapter of Jonah provides eight inside views, four given by the omniscient narrator and four by the characters themselves. On all four occasions when the narrator provides inside views, they concern the sailors:

1. "And the sailors were afraid." (1:5a)
2. "And the men were afraid, greatly afraid." (1:10)
3. "And the men were afraid, greatly fearing the Lord." (1:16)
4. "For the men knew that he was fleeing from the presence of the Lord for he had told them." (1:10)

Coming from the omniscient and reliable narrator, these inside views require our absolute faith, but they have little bearing on plot development. Seen alongside a passage from the Former Prophets, these examples from Jonah might be described as surface or shallow inside views. For example, one finds prolonged views of Amnon in 2 Sam. 13:1–2 as well as of Jonadab (vs. 3) that have a much more significant bearing on plot:

> Some time passed. David's son Absalom had a beautiful sister whose name was Tamar; and David's son Amnon fell in love with her. Amnon was so tormented that he made himself ill

because of his sister Tamar, for she was a virgin and it seemed impossible to Amnon to do anything to her. But Amnon had a friend whose name was Jonadab . . . and Jonadab was a very crafty man.

"Fear" (ירא), one of the most familiar words the narrator uses to peer into the minds of the characters,[14] provides the reader in 1.–4. only with information she or he expects since all of the views are preceded by a description of the Lord's actions: "but the Lord hurled a great wind on the sea and there was a great storm on the sea so that the ship was about to break up" (vs. 4). While the penetration to their minds is not deep and certainly not surprising, the cumulative effect (they "were afraid" [vs. 5]; they "were afraid, greatly afraid" [vs. 10]; and then, they "were afraid, greatly fearing the Lord" [vs. 16])[15] highlights their surmounting anxiety as the storm builds ("the Lord hurled a great wind upon the sea" [vs. 4a]; then "the sea storms tempestuously" [vs. 11b], and then, "the sea storms tempestuously against them" [vs. 13b]). Here, these inside views provide no significant information that we would have assumed even if representation in this first example had been given entirely to the external world, but the cumulative effect draws us closer to the sailors.

The narrator also provides information about what the sailors know (4.) as compared to how they feel (1.–3.) in the opening scene. Since the reader already understands Jonah is fleeing from the presence of the Lord (vs. 3), the discrepancy in awareness at the expense of the characters calls attention to the different path characters and readers travel on the road from ignorance to enlightenment. Coming as indirect discourse—which in biblical narrative occurs much less frequently than direct discourse—and seen alongside 1.–3., inside view 4. suggests something that will become more obvious only in the chapters that follow: this artist's skill in achieving the ideological objective lies not in adherence to any one supreme manner of narration but rather in an ability to alter the strategy as he shows us his characters.

Inside views may be provided by the characters themselves, either through character-narrating statements ("So I [Jeremiah] went down to the potter's house, and . . . he reworked it into another vessel, as seemed good to him" [Jer. 18:3–4]) or, as is the case more frequently, through direct speech. These views are different from those that come from an all-knowing, trustworthy source because they come

from fallible observers who do not have free access to the internal
processes of others. In the book of Jeremiah this limited perspective
is highlighted by the narrator himself who explains why Jeremiah is
able to trick the officials who ask questions about the details of the
prophet's conversation with King Zedekiah. When asked about his
conversation, the prophet succeeds in keeping the content of his
advice to the king from the officials because, as the narrator relates,
"the conversation had not been overheard" (Jer. 38:27b).[16] Accord-
ingly, as shown below, the significance of the narrator's perspective
is matched only by God's. The remaining inside views in the first
chapter, two from the prophet and two from the sailors, are given
in direct speech:

5. "Perhaps the god(s) will give a thought to us so that we will
not perish." (1:6b)
6. "For you, Lord, as you have pleased you have done." (1:14b)
7. "I know that it is because of me that this great tempest is
upon you." (1:12b)
8. "the Lord, the God of the heavens, I fear, who made the sea
and dry land." (1:9)

Seen next to the narrator's statements (1.–4.), the sailors' pleas
(5.–6.) call attention to the way in which some information is beyond
human reach. Instead of entering God's mind, their words ("*perhaps
the god(s) will give a thought to us*" [vs. 6] and "*as you have pleased,
you have done*" [vs. 14]) reveal their anxiety and highlight for the
reader what their actions ("and they hurled the cargo which was on
the ship into the sea" [vs. 5]) had previously shown them to be:
innocent, desperate sailors seeking to save their lives.

Jonah's statements (7., 8.) are, technically speaking, inside views
since he reveals whom he "fears" (vs. 9) and what he "knows" (vs.
12). Statement 7. does not provide us with any new information,
and 8. serves to complicate judgment. If the prophet really fears the
Lord "who made the sea and the dry land" (vs. 9), then why does
he flee? Biblical narrative, notorious for its sparsity of detail, requires
considerable attention to be given to the nuances of the text, and
such complications in chapter 1 are mentioned here so that their
resolution and the emphasis on Jonah's inner life in the subsequent
chapters may be stressed.

Considered as a whole, these shallow inside views of the first
chapter, where characters' thoughts are mentioned and then passed

over, suggest that the author, like Homer, is more interested in
action in the external world ("Jonah rose to flee" [vs. 3]; "he went
down to Joppa" [vs. 3]; "the Lord hurled a wind" [vs. 4]; "they
hurled the cargo which was on the ship into the sea" [vs. 5]; "they
cast lots" [vs. 7]) than in dwelling on the thoughts of his characters.
Yet the quick shifts from the outer to the inner world allow for
reflection, foster realistic, dramatic tension, and reveal a strategy of
ambiguation and complication which is obvious even before chapter
1 ends. How does the author's strategy change by the time the
prophet completes his mission to the Ninevites and sits "east of the
city" (4:5) in the final chapter? The question will be answered in
due course, but first two general trends about Jonah's attitude at the
end of chapter 1 may be noted in an attempt to highlight the
ambiguation just before the prophet is hurled overboard.

Death Wish vs. Act of Compassion Hypotheses

Many commentators have attempted to explain Jonah's' attitude
when he asks the sailors to hurl him overboard in 1:12. The explanations tend to fall into one of two categories. On the one hand,
some suggest that Jonah's request to be hurled overboard reflects
his desire for death. Uriel Simon, commenting on 1:12, writes

כפי שבאונייה המסוערת העדיף הנביא להיות מוטל
הימה מלקרוא אל אלוהיו, כך לנוכח מחילת ה'
לנינוה הוא חזר וביכר למות מאשר להודות
בצדקת ה'...[17]

H.W. Wolff concludes his discussion of 1:12 in the following manner: "We hear only one thing: [Jonah] wants to die.... [He is]
seeking refuge from [the Lord] in death. Only the actual circumstances differ here from the circumstances in 4:3, 8; but we should
not assume that there is any essential difference between the plea
in 1:12 and the plea in 4:3, 8."[18]
In contrast to the many interpreters who view 1:12 as the prophet's
death wish,[19] another interpretation of vs. 12 may also be generally
described as the prophet's act of compassion on behalf of the innocent sailors. For example, André Feuillet concludes: "Jonas, qui
d'ailleurs n'a pas douté un seul instant de l'appel divin, ... sait par-
faitement que la tempête est due à sa résistance et demande lui-
même pour cette raison qu'on le jette dans la mer."[20] And James D.

Smart writes that "in order to save the lives of the heathen sailors and passengers on board the ship, Jonah commanded them to throw him overboard. This act was the natural consequence of all that Jonah has learned from the prophetic faith; both justice and mercy demanded of him this sacrifice of himself."[21]

Both interpretations share a distinct feature for in each instance a conclusion is drawn that *either* the prophet is seeking death *or* that he is acting out of compassion for the sailors. Variations on the "Death Wish" vs. "Act of Compassion" theses are likely to multiply as long as the continuum is ignored because as the discussion on inside views has already suggested, the narrator has strategically passed over explicit clues that would allow a satisfactory explanation for Jonah's thoughts at this point. Since mutually exclusive versions of reality are being projected at once through a single order of words, the frequent observation against the originality of the psalm in chapter 2 on grounds that it does not match the psychological portrayal of Jonah *at the end of chapter 1* must now be qualified on these grounds: the tendency toward ambiguous psychological portrayal reflected in the psalm is well in place *before* the prophet is thrown into the sea.

2:3–10 and 4:2–3: Jonah's Prayers

Jonah's prayers also provide the reader with a view of the prophet's mind at work on the world.

> 9. "I called from my distress;
>   Unto the Lord and he answered me.
> From the belly of Sheol I cried out;
>   You heard my voice.
> And you cast me to deep, into the heart of the seas,
>   And a river encircled me.
> All your breakers and your waves
>   Passed over me.
> And I said,
>   'I was cast away from your sight.
> Yet I will again look
>   Upon your holy temple.'
> Waters encompassed (my) neck;
>   (The) deep swirled around me.

> Reeds were wrapped around my head
>> To/At the roots of the mountains,
> I descended to the underworld;
>> Bars were upon me forever.
> Yet you brought my life up from the Pit,
>> O Lord, my God.
> My soul fainted within me;
>> I remembered the Lord.
> And my prayer came unto you,
>> Unto your holy temple.
> Those who regard vain idols,
>> Abandon their *ḥesed*.
> But I, in a voice of thanksgiving,
>> I will sacrifice to you.
> What I have vowed, I will pay.
>> Salvation is of the Lord!"
>
> (2:3–10)

Unlike the inside views in the opening chapter, these prayers are considerably longer and the penetration is also much deeper. The first prayers (9.) have received a considerable amount of attention,[22] and until recent years were viewed as a redactor's insertion which not only provided content to the prayer that Jonah supposedly prayed at 2:2 but also rectified what was perceived as a picture of the prophet's disobedient and arrogant attitude before the Lord in marked contrast to commendable actions displayed by the sailors and Ninevites in the first and third chapters respectively.

As suggested in the "Death Wish vs. Act of Compassion Hypotheses" above, one cannot discount the characterization of the prophet in chapter 2 with the opening chapter on grounds of irreconcilable incongruities or tensions because chapter 1 has revealed scant evidence of the prophet's mind at work. Throughout the first portion of the prayer, metaphors and language from the psalter continue to ambiguate rather than to elucidate, thus continuing the momentum of the opening scene.[23] A portion of the prayer contains what might be called narrative-type statements. Whether the prayer is viewed as allegorical,[24] satirical,[25] or as a psalm composed of an unusual mixture of thanksgiving and lament elements,[26] considerable agreement exists that would support the view that the psychological portrayal of the prophet in the closing words ("But I, in a voice of

thanksgiving, I will sacrifice to you; what I have vowed, I will pay"
[vs. 10]) suggests that Jonah has decided to obey the Lord's command, a promise that mirrors the sailors' previous actions (1:16).
Moreover, the prayer clearly indicates that the prophet is expressing
his praise in response to the divine act which led to his rescue.
Jonah's final words at the close of chapter 2 are striking in terms of
their relationship to the book's theme of salvation or deliverance.
In a statement of praise Jonah concludes, "Salvation is of the Lord!"
(vs. 10b). When he is delivered, both here and in 4:6, the prophet
offers thanks (2:10) and is happy (4:6). After the deliverance of the
Ninevites, which occurs between 2:10 and 4:6, the prophet's psychology is again foregrounded in the place of overt actions ("and it
displeased" him [4:1; see 14. below]), suggesting to the reader the
first incongruity between divine and human love. After being spewed
from the fish, Jonah does in fact arise and travel to Nineveh, according to the word of the Lord (3:3). After the dramatic events in
Nineveh, Jonah prays a second time.

> 10. "I pray, Lord, was this not my word when I was in my
> country? This is why I made haste to flee towards Tarshish,
> for I knew that you are a gracious God and compassionate, slow
> in coming to anger and great in *hesed* and repenting of evil.
> And now Lord, take, I pray, my life from me, for I prefer death
> to life." (4:2-3)

The prophet's prayer in chapter 4 provides a clearer picture of his
mind at work and shows him for what he really is, a prophet more
concerned with preserving his self-image than in accepting the
good news that the inhabitants of a large city have received God's
grace and been spared destruction. This prayer (10.) is the most
revealing and significant of inside views offered thus far. The four
shallow inside views which the narrator provided in the opening
scene (1.-4.) all related to the sailors. Jonah's prayers in chapter 2,
while containing more words and occupying a pivotal point in the
structure of the book, did not allow the reader to formulate a clear
picture of the prophet's true character. In fact, the reader may have
assumed (wrongly) that the prophet was then convinced that he
should "cry against" Nineveh in full accord with the Lord's command. And in chapter 3, the writer strategically allows the prophet
to fade into the background after proclaiming that the city would
be overthrown in forty days. Only retrospectively does the reader

begin to see that Jonah's prophetic prayer in 4:2 highlights what the narrator has *not* shared with us previously. Jonah's mind could have been opened through direct narrative statement, interior monologue, or by the prophet's own speech at any point along the text continuum. As the world of action is replaced by the world of thought and feeling, this momentary foregrounding of the character's psychology surprises us because it is of a character whose inner life has been shrouded in mystery until this point (4:2) of the text continuum.

Chapter 3

The discussion of the prayers together has taken us past chapter 3. The phrase וְנִינְוֵה הָיְתָה עִיר גְדוֹלָה לֵאלֹהִים (3:3) appears to indicate an inside view and is sometimes translated, "and Nineveh was a big city to God," that is, God considered the city to be big, significant, or important. Gabriël Cohn offers this type of translation ("und Ninive war eine grosse Stadt vor Gott") with some hesitation and points out that LXX does not retain the reference to God: "Dieser Zusatz bewirkt in der Regel eine Betonung der Bedeutung. . . . So übersetz G.[LXX] 'eine besonders grosse Stadt.' In unserer Übersetzung haben wir jedoch die Beziehung Gottes zur Stadt mitklingen lassen, ähnlich wie T[argum]."[27] The expression לֵאלֹהִים ("to God") in 3:3 is, however, probably best seen as one of several examples where the divine name is used as an epithet with an intensifying force. This point was made by the medieval commentators. Kimchi, commenting on the verse, pointed out that

כל דבר שרוצה להגדילו סומך אותו לאל דרך
הגדולה.[28]

If this translation is correct and לֵאלֹהִים is a means of expressing a superlative, then 3:3 should not be included as one of the inside views.

Various similarities exist between chapters 1 and 3. For example, both contain the divine commission, drastic actions from the foreigners as they attempt to escape God's wrath, and the prophet's conversation with foreigners. In the opening chapter, the narrator presents inside views of the sailors as a group ("the sailors were afraid" [vs. 5]) then of an individual leader within the group ("perhaps the god(s) will give a thought to us" [vs. 6]). This pattern (group→ leader) is repeated in chapter 3:

11. "And then the people of Nineveh believed in God." (3:5a)
12. "[And the king said,] 'Who knows? God may turn and be sorry, turn from the flaming of his anger so that we will not perish.'" (3:9)

The inside view of the king (12.) comes in the form of direct speech. Just as 5. and 6. demonstrated that characters do not have free access to the minds of others, his speech here ("*Who* knows, God *may* turn . . .") anticipates a double-sided truth that will become more obvious at 13. below: only the narrator assumes god-like comprehensiveness and delights in sharing his omniscience with us. Jack Sasson has observed that grammatical considerations suggest that this question in 3:9, which is introduced by מִי יוֹרֵעַ ("Who knows?"), is linked to the chief sailor's statement of 1:6. The Hebrew interrogative pronoun, "who," is in this instance followed by a participle. When this construction is placed at the beginning of a sentence (but not at the end) it introduces the same kind of wishful statement as those introduced with אוּלַי ("perhaps") as in 1:6.[29]

The people of Nineveh first "believe in God" (vs. 5) then "call a fast and dress themselves in sackcloth," but with respect to both thought and action certain events do not take place. Because of their absence, one may postulate that the book should not be viewed as a Jewish-Gentile tract with Jonah representing Israel. The universalist interpretation with its accompanying missionary implications suggests that the book of Jonah was written to correct the separatist tendency of the strict measures introduced by Ezra and Nehemiah.[30] Consider the radically different situation that ensues when Moses, the prophet par excellence, returns from the mountain at Sinai, calls the elders, and explains to them the words that the Lord has spoken. The people respond saying, "All that the Lord has spoken we will do" (Exod. 19:8). By contrast, the Ninevites' sudden turn in chapter 3 is much more open ended. There is no evidence that they embrace the Torah, acknowledge the Lord as the one true God, accept circumcision, or reject idolatry.[31] Instead, their actions mirror those of the sailors in the opening chapter whose desires to be rescued from drowning caused them to do whatever was necessary to avoid death.

Further consideration of the verb "believe" (אָמַן) and its object in this passage from Exodus also sheds light on Jonah 3:5. In Exod. 19:9, the Lord reassures Moses with these words: "Behold, I shall come to you in a thick cloud, in order that the people may hear

when I speak with you and may also believe in you" (וגם בך‎
יאמינו‎). Here, unlike the passage from Jonah, the prophet is the
object of the verb "to believe." With the spotlight away from Jonah
in 3:5–10, the reader presumes on the basis of much of the narration
through external and internal portrayal in the first three chapters,
that this is a story about the possible destruction or conversion of
the wicked Ninevites. At the end of chapter 3, one may actually
expect the story to end because the problem the Lord announced
at the beginning ("for their wickedness has come up before me"
[1:2]) has been resolved, and in the course of events the prophet's
disobedience has even had a good effect. The sailors not only addressed God by using his intimate name (vs. 14)[32] but also "slaughtered a slaughter-meal to the Lord and they vowed vows" (vs. 16).
Only in chapter 4 do we notice that the tale proves to be something
other than a story about the repentance of a foreign nation. As the
two principal characters are shown from within in the concluding
chapter, where the high frequency and depth of inside views is more
significant than what has come before, we discover that the author's
primary concern lies elsewhere.

This radical turn of events begins with an inside view of God, the
first supplied by the narrator:

> 13. "And God saw their deeds, how they turned from their evil
> ways, and God was sorry concerning the evil which he had said
> he would do to them and he did not do it." (3:10)

The word נחם‎, "be sorry," appears three times in this short section
(3:9, 3:10, and 4:2). Each time the reference is to God, but it comes
from three perspectives: from a Ninevite (3:9), from the narrator
(3:10), and from Jonah (4:2). From the narrator's perspective (13.),
God "sees" and is then "sorry" about the calamity that his prophet
had declared would come to the Ninevites. This dramatic event is
presented through God's eyes, and proves to be only the first in a
series of important developments which follow.[33]

Chapter 4

> 14. "And it displeased Jonah, a great evil, and he became hot
> with anger." (4:1)

The translation of this verse is difficult primarily because the subject of the initial verb, וירע ("displeased"), is elusive. An under-standing of the verb רע is important in considering this inside view. H. W. Wolff, in his *Studien zum Jonabuch*,[34] proposes a translation different than that in the LXX, Targum, Peshitta, and Vulgate by suggesting that Jonah is the subject of the verb. A different translation from the one Wolff has proposed may be made by eliminating a few options. Since Jonah is introduced into the sentence by way of a preposition, אל יונה "unto Jonah," he cannot be the subject of the sentence and since the feminine expression רעה גדולה "a great evil" would normally require a feminine verb (ותרע), one may sus-pect that the subject is understood as "it," i.e. God's actions described in 3:10. רע in the qal is frequently used with an implied subject.[35] Thus the use of the verb רע, whose force is strengthened by the accompanying cognate noun רעה,[36] is to be seen as a description of Jonah's attitude ("it displeased him") rather than the narrator's ex-plicit condemnation of Jonah ("he was bad/displeasing") as Wolff suggests. By hinting at the complexity of feeling and refraining from evaluation, the narrator complicates judgment as he reveals Jonah's attitude.

> 15. "And the Lord said, 'Is it right for you to become in-flamed?'" (4:4)
> 16. "And God said to Jonah, 'Is it right for you to become inflamed about the *kikayon*?'" (4:9a)
> 17. "And [Jonah] said, 'It is right for me to become inflamed, even to the point of death.'" (4:9b)

For the first time, the Lord provides an inside view of the prophet through direct speech. The narrator had already used חרה ("burn with anger") in 4:1 to describe Jonah's attitude, and in 4:4 the emphasis is made in the Lord's rhetorical question: "Is it right for you to become inflamed [חרה]?" From the reader's side, the nar-rator's portrayal is repeated in part through the Lord's authoritative words, and the emphasis on Jonah's inner life continues by means of key-word repetition a third time (i.e. 4:1→4:4→4:9a). When God's rhetorical question comes to Jonah a second time (16.), the first part of the question is repeated verbatim and then an additional word is added ("Is it right for you to become inflamed *about the kikayon* [על־הקיקיון]?") as if to emphasize the point to any reader who has missed it: the prophet's anger (i.e. "heat") has come about because of the shade that was lost over *his* head. Jonah insists in the strongest possible words that the *kikayon* is important to him. He loves it. He is "extremely happy" about it (יִשְׂמַח‎–4:6 . . . שָׂמְחָה   גְדוֹלָה), and when it withers, he is furious. The prophet is so mad that the thought of death seems better than the idea of living without the plant!

The third inside view in this series also contains the key word חרה. Now Jonah speaks, taking the Lord's words "Is it right for you to become inflamed?" to build even further on the original thought, "It is right for me to become inflamed, even to the point of death." In 15. Jonah was angry because Nineveh had *not been* destroyed. With 16. and 17. the prophet is so angry that he prefers death because the tree *has been* destroyed. The shift is vividly brought out as the narrator allows Jonah to reveal his feelings thus condemning himself with his own words.

18. "And Jonah was happy about the *kikayon*, extremely happy." (4:6b)

The verb "happy" (שׂמח) and its cognate forms appear in nine of the prophetic books within the collection of The Twelve, and its significance in the book of Jonah is best seen when comparisons are made. The word frequently refers or relates to groups of people living in a land ("Israel" [Hos. 9:1]; "Jerusalem" and "Zion" [Zeph. 3:16–17]) and is sometimes used in a collective/abstract sense ("sons of Zion" [Joel 2:23]; "children of Ephraim" [Zech. 10:7b]). Table 4 contains references to the word in all its forms in the other books of the Twelve and indicates that it never describes a prophet and only twice refers to an individual.[37]

Inside view 18. is significant, therefore, because it provides us with a rare glimpse into the mind of a prophet. When the Lord speaks to Hosea and commands him to take a wife of harlotry (Hos. 1:2), we may assume that the prophet felt something, but his thoughts are passed over as the action is described: "So he went and took Gomer, the daughter of Diblaim, and she conceived and bore him a son" (1:3). Scholes's and Kellogg's comments, if amended, would highlight an important feature of the prophetic literature where characterization is *sometimes* achieved through views from within.[38]

Jonah's happiness—emphasized in the Hebrew as extraordinary happiness—follows his expression of anger (4:2) and request for death (4:3) and highlights his self-centeredness. As mentioned in the "Death Wish vs. Act of Compassion Hypotheses," commentators are divided in their opinions about Jonah's request to be thrown overboard at the end of chapter 1, and both hypotheses are supported by the open-ended text there. In chapter 4 however, Jonah's request is unequivocally clear: this prophet desires to die *because* 120,000 people have been spared! Further, next to the pardon that God has extended to the wicked Ninevites, the gift of the *kikayon* to Jonah is certainly a small token. From the prophet's own person, his isolated concerns and pride, we begin to see how characterization through thought relates to rhetoric,[39] for at the end of the story, Jonah's feelings will be weighed against God's, and we will see, in Sheldon Blank's words, that "Jonah here is not the only one subject to disappointment and distress."[40]

19. "And the Lord said, 'You were concerned about the *kikayon* for which you did not labor nor cause to grow, which as a child of night came to be and as a child of night perished. And may I not be concerned about Nineveh, the great city, where there are more than 120,000 people who do not know their right hand from their left and many cattle?'" (4:10–11)

Table 4
The Word שמח ("Happy") among the Minor Prophets

Passage		Reference to
Hos.	7:3	king
	9:1	Israel
Joel	1:16	inhabitants of the land (1:2)
	2:21	land
	2:23	sons of Zion
Amos	6:13	those/the ones
Obad.	12	sons of Judah
Mic.	7:8	enemy
Hab.	1:15	he
Zeph.	3:14	daughter of Jerusalem
	3:17	Jerusalem and Zion
Zech.	2:14 (Ev 10)	daughter of Zion
	4:10	the seven
	8:19	house of Judah
	10:7 (2x)	Ephraim and children of Ephraim

This extraordinary view of the Lord represents only the second occasion since the very beginning of the story (1:2) where the Lord has revealed his thoughts. 4:10–11 is organized around another key word just as 15.–17. had been above. חום, "concern," "compassion," "pity," appears rarely in the Hebrew Bible as an expression of the Lord's feelings.[41] At the end of the book of Jonah, the Lord points out that Jonah has felt concern (חום) for the *kikayon*, and then in an attempt to bring Jonah's agreement at long last asks, "May I not be concerned about (חום) Nineveh?" Thus the book ends with a contrast between the Lord and Jonah, and the focus is on the great matter occupying the Lord. The prophet's emotions which had previously been emphasized starting with the first verse in chapter 4 (rage, disappointment, extraordinary happiness, frustration) are now summarily contrasted with the compassion the Lord feels for all of creation. In ideological terms, the silence at the end signals that the Lord is supremely authoritative.

Conclusion

A few general remarks will serve to integrate the discussion that has focused on the isolated verses. It may appear that some of the points have been overemphasized, and the high number of inside views considered by itself would certainly leave the wrong impression. For example, 1., 2., and 3. are similar and provide us only with information we would infer from the action. On the other hand, Jonah's direct speech at the beginning of chapter 4 (10.) is considerably more significant since it provides answers to questions the reader has posed from the start: What are Jonah's thoughts? Why is he not only reluctant but disobedient? By isolating these verses, one is able to see the significance of the fourth chapter where *only one* of the eleven verses consistently describes the events in the external world: "and God appointed a worm when the next dawn came up, and it struck the *kikayon* and it withered" (4:7). The observations about technique in chapter 4 confirm once again that this is a story about a prophet. The difference between shallow inside views with the sailors and Ninevites as compared to the more significant stress of the inner life with the Lord and Jonah suggests that the foreigners serve as a foil to the primary characters.[42]

The survey of passages has revealed that Scholes's and Kellogg's observations—such as "the inward life is assumed but not presented in primitive [i.e. Hebraic] narrative literature . . ." or "it may be that the technique of such presentation was simply not available to primitive narrators . . ." or "the character whose inward development is of crucial importance is primarily a Christian element . . ."—are flawed and much too general.[43] In fact, in Jonah and especially in the final chapter, the narrator frequently shows the characters in conflict by moving into and out of their minds. Seen next to examples from the modern period, we have pointed out that these isolated passages reveal that the author avoids prolonged or deep plunges into the minds of the characters, but sympathy or contempt may be heightened by the sharing of one character's thoughts and the withholding of other's ideas.

It has also been stressed that the sharing of an inside view puts the reader in an elevated or privileged position. The focus has been on only one of the various rhetorical resources at the command of the narrator. The rendering of the prophet Jonah and the Lord as characters in conflict proves to be one of the story's distinguishing marks and may even help explain its popularity.[44] We travel with Jonah. We fear and pity this prophet, as Aristotle might say, rather than detest and mock him since with the help of the narrator we see him in a view that in real life we never obtain of anyone but ourselves. Thus a number of difficulties arise when the book is interpreted as parody[45] or comedy.[46] As we experience Jonah's thoughts and feelings first hand, we discover that the story is too earnest for laughter. The analysis above allows us to affirm S. D. F. Goitein's observation of 1937: "Jonah is not painted with the brush of mockery or disdain, but drawn with the pencil of deep and sympathetic insight into human weakness."[47]

Chapter 8

The Ideological Plane:
Summary and Conclusion

It is not important what any of [the] characters are in this world;
[the author] is primarily interested in what the world is to the
characters.

—Boris Uspensky, quoting Mikhail Bakhtin

In the preceding chapters we have sought to reveal the author of
Jonah as an artist, one who manages the telling and in turn shapes
the audience's response. It should now be obvious that we do not
meet any character in the story directly. Rather, some of a character's
presence is mediated through his or her words and actions, the words
and actions of other characters, and the voice of the narrator. We
have in Jonah, a narrative that is conveyed by several voices, and
through the representation of events we gain a multifaceted perspective of the action. Content itself is a player in the ideological
game, and contrary to all that schools of theory preach, representation is not dissociated from evaluation. The ultimate goal of this
study is to move beyond matters of technique to the communication
of values and attitudes from text to reader through the medium of
a story about a prophet. Herein lies the real task of this narrative
poetics: to discover how individual words, phrases, and syntactic
arrangements function as means of evaluation. God, the people, even
the animals who inhabit this narrative world are all potential vehicles
of an evaluating or ideological point of view. To limit the analysis
to the narrow sphere of organization or expression is to overlook
the fact that ordering, point of view, causal chains, and the whole
lot reflect an ideology-bound model of reality. Such a full-working
poetics will illustrate that Jonah is an aesthetic as well as a social
text where content is produced within an ideological frame.

What are the ideological positions of the narrator and the characters? How are they expressed? Which, if any, of the characters
and events in the narrative world are evaluated or judged? And how
does a system of ideas shape the work? Even the norms that the
book embodies serve a unity that is realized in effects, rather than

144

in conceptual schemes. As characters perceive objects and events their views are often presented through their eyes and voices. At other times, the narrator, exercising privileges of omniscience and omnipotence, reports their conceptualizations. Sometimes a character's interest in an object or idea is invoked by a turn of events or by the actions of others. What we have in Jonah is a plurality of independent consciousnesses, each suggesting potentially valid perspectives where evaluation is carried out from several angles. Ideological material is sometimes external, that is, emerging from the narrated events themselves. At other times, it is internal, emerging from the conversation of characters or evaluation by the narrator. Stated succinctly, the unified position in this narrative world is that *God controls everything and is free to command not only the natural elements but the prophet as well, free to forecast impending doom, and free also to alter plans.* The profound rhetorical question at the end of the book leaves little doubt that this ideological unity is sought, but, like the prophet, we take many turns before it is delivered.

If the story of Jonah is filtered through various perspectives or points of view, we may understand the narrative events that stand in relation to each other as a matrix. Boris Uspensky, applying the theoretical insights of Mikhail Bakhtin, differentiates four levels of point of view: the phraseological level, the spatial and temporal level, the psychological level, and the ideological level.[1] Our main purpose in this chapter is to explore how the author, narrator, and characters view the world and how their viewpoints impact the ideological level. First, it may be worthwhile to supplement a few observations made previously in this study that correspond to Uspensky's scheme by considering the phraseological, the temporal and spatial, and the psychological levels before turning to the important, if difficult to recover, ideological level.

Language works at the phraseological level to indicate point of view. With each character or character group speaking the word רעה ("wickedness," "evil"), for example, the reader is given an opportunity to form impressions based on similar and contrasting views. The network of language in Jonah may also be observed as characters pray or cry out to God. For example, close examination at the phraseological level suggests that the author did not understand the design of extemporized prayer as uniquely Israelite; the arrangement of address, petition, and motivation testified to a universal capacity of prayer. A more focused look at the words of Jonah's prayers also signalled a change in point of view from chapter 2 to chapter 4. Initially, Jonah addresses the Lord and says,

> *you* heard my voice (vs. 3) . . . *you* cast me (vs. 4) . . . *your* breakers and *your* waves (vs. 4) . . . I was cast away from *your* sight yet I will again look upon *your* holy temple (vs. 5) . . . *you* brought my life up from the Pit, O Lord, my God (vs. 7) . . . I remembered *the Lord* (vs. 8) . . . my prayer came . . . unto *your* holy temple (vs. 8) . . . I will sacrifice to *you* . . . Salvation is of *the Lord!* (vs. 10)

After Nineveh, Jonah the introspect prays once again:

> *I* pray, Lord, was this not *my* word when *I* was in *my* country? This is why *I* made haste to flee towards Tarshish, for *I* knew that you are a gracious God, and compassionate, slow in coming to anger and great in *ḥesed* and repenting of evil. And now Lord, take, *I* pray, *my* life from *me*, for *I* prefer death to life. (4:2–3)

Jonah's words this time show us a different side of both the prophet and God than what we have seen thus far. At the beginning of the story, Jonah describes God to the sailors (and us) as the maker of the sea and dry land (1:9). He tells them (and reminds us) that God is at least partially responsible for their plight. After the events of the first three chapters, Jonah describes God once again, but this time as "gracious," "compassionate," "slow in coming to anger," "great in *ḥesed*," and "repenting of evil." These descriptions, part of Israel's common vocabulary (Num. 14:18; Pss. 86:15; 103:8; 145:8; Nah. 1:3; Neh. 9:17), have not merely been duplicated. Instead, Jonah's words give a new, qualifying picture of God.

Characterization of the Lord is accomplished by words such as "appoints," "speaks," "hurls," and a host of others. These words suggested a picture of God the creator, in complete control of plant, animal, and human life in this story. The wind, water, fish, Ninevites—virtually everything and everybody except Jonah—simply do what they are instructed to do. The Lord acts. Creation reacts. An examination at the phraseological level also revealed that the Lord's actions introduced by an infinitive verbal form succeed. However, activities performed by humans and introduced by an infinitive verbal form turn out to be unsuccessful.

דבר ("word") figures prominently at the phraseological level. It gains momentum as the tale unfolds. In the opening verse of the book, the narrator informs the reader that the Lord's "word" reaches Jonah. In parallel fashion, the narrator repeats the message in 3:1, this time giving greater emphasis to this "word" (3:2). In 3:3 Jonah arises and goes to Nineveh according to the Lord's "word." It is the "word" the prophet delivers that reaches the king in 3:6. Then in 3:10, God "sees their deeds" and "is sorry concerning the evil which he had said (דבר) he would do to them." With the fulfillment of God's "word" in chapter 3, the prophet is now able to express his thoughts in 4:2, which he does by saying, "was this not my word?" The contrast between divine and prophetic words is highlighted by Jonah's derogatory speech.

The narrator, free to tell us everything, often enlists his characters to participate in a play of perspectives. We have noted numerous instances where narration confirms dialogue and other occasions where dialogue confirms narration. One example of these partners-in-words was noted at the high point of the story:

> Narrator: "And he became inflamed." (4:1)
> Lord: "Is it right for you to become inflamed?" (4:4b)
> Lord: "Is it right for you to become inflamed about the *kikayon*?"
>   (4:9a)
> Jonah: "It is right for me to become inflamed." (4:9b)

Invoking three different voices, the writer throws the climax into bold relief. The acceleration eventually leads to the desired goal when Jonah gets his lesson about God's compassion. Many other examples could be cited, but these few make it clear that language signals point of view.

We had occasion to observe descriptions and events at the spatial and temporal level, and we have attempted to understand the author's use of time and space as purposeful. An interesting feature of dialogue in Jonah is the representation of setting by means of quoted speech that not only impacts characterization but also indicates space. Obviously, pictures or images of the setting are suggested by the narrator who tells us that Jonah went down to Joppa (1:3); that the men rowed hard to return the ship to land (1:13); that they picked Jonah up and threw him into the sea (1:15); that the people proclaimed a fast and put on sackcloth (3:5), and so forth. Many of the spatial coordinates are given in relationship to the prophet: Jonah ultimately finds sanctuary in the inner part of the ship (1:5), and then later in the body of the fish (2:1–2), before he is spewed up to the dry land (2:11), etc.

The four chapters themselves are marked by scenic boundaries. In chapter 1, Jonah is by (or at) the sea. In the next chapter, he is in the belly of the fish. In the third chapter, he is in Nineveh; and in (most of) the fourth, he is outside the city. Thus, the action in all four scenes is described in terms of the prophet's location.

The narrator also provides temporal coordinates: Jonah resides in the fish's belly for three days and three nights (2:1); Nineveh's size is measured in terms of the time it takes to walk through it (3:3); Jonah travels a one day's journey before proclaiming the message (3:4); and the proclamation itself is given in a time frame (3:4). By mentioning these extended periods of time, the author passes over much that transpires between the occasion of the Lord's commission in 1:2 and the final rhetorical question in 4:11. Temporal ordering figured prominently with respect to the reading process, and several deformations in chronological ordering suggested an artist at work. The true chronological order has been rearranged at a few points of the text continuum: the indirect speech reported at 1:10b does not follow a true chronological pattern; the narrator's description of the great fish that swallows Jonah in 2:1 may also be out of its true order (cf. the description of the sailors in 1:16 who remain on the ship after Jonah has been hurled into the sea); the reference to two prayers in chapter 2 suggests the author altered the true temporal sequence; and the prophet's railings against the Lord in 4:2 ("was this not my word?") is another example of the author's manipulation of temporal order to suit his purpose. Alterations like these suggest that the description of Jonah's exit from the city and glance back at Nineveh in 4:5 may not have been, as commentators have suggested, placed inadvertently.

The levels at which point of view is manifested often overlap. Take, for example, the two levels we have considered thus far, the phraseological and spatial levels. In the opening scene, Jonah's descent begins when he goes down to Joppa (1:3) and boards a ship, but it continues as he descends into the ship's recesses (1:5). Even the sailors' activity reinforces this movement. They cast lots that "fall" to Jonah (1:7), and then finally throw him overboard (1:15). This descent motif continues in the first half of the psalm, and is reversed beginning in 2:7b when Jonah recounts that the Lord brought him up from the Pit. The author also combines the phraseological and spatial levels by investing heavily in arising and sitting motions throughout the book. These descriptions begin in 1:2 where

Jonah is first commanded to "arise" and go to Nineveh, but "arises" in the next verse to flee towards Tarshish. In 1:6, the captain approaches the prophet and commands him "to arise" and to call upon his god(s). Eventually Jonah does "arise" and go to Nineveh (3:3), and in 3:6 the king, after learning of the proclamation, "arises" from his throne. Subsequently, Jonah "sits" under the booth in 4:5 as he anxiously awaits to see what will happen in the city. These space-words suggest a contrast between the king's standing and Jonah's sitting, and they underscore the inconsistency in attitude: the king is concerned that the Ninevites be spared at considerable discomfort to all including even the animals; Jonah, delighted to have the shade, hopes that the city will be destroyed. Descriptions of space allow the reader to contrast what one might expect to happen with what actually transpires. That is, these description also impact the ideological level.

With respect to Uspensky's third level of point of view, we have already seen that characterization by means of the inner life has implications at the psychological level. Biblical narrative, notorious for its sparsity of detail, requires that considerable attention be given to the nuances of characters' minds and mood. The works of Homer, Shakespeare, and Dickens suggest that at the level of plot, characters deprived of essential information ask questions and that the cumulative weight of their asking often affects psychological portrayal. The lack of subordinate clauses or recurrent character-statement qualifiers in the first chapter highlights the quick pace of the story while concurrently de-emphasizing the nuances of thought and feeling. Initially, the narrator focuses on the characters by describing what they do rather than on what they feel. While the glimpses of their minds at work on the world do not surprise us, the cumulative effect highlights their surmounting anxiety as the storm builds. Considered as a whole, shallow inside views of the first chapter, where characters' thoughts are mentioned and then passed over, suggest that the author is more interested in action in the external world than in dwelling on the thoughts of his characters. Yet these quick shifts from the outer to the inner world in Jonah 1 do allow for reflection and reveal a strategy of ambiguation and complication. The frequent observation against the originality of the psalm in chapter 2 on grounds that it does not match the psychological portrayal of Jonah *at the end of chapter 1* was qualified because the tendency toward ambiguous psychological portrayal reflected in the psalm is established in chapter 1. Jonah's mood in chapter 2 is suggested by a prayer that contains elements of both the "thanksgiving" and the "lament of the individual" psalm types. These types produce a prayer entirely consistent with the psychological portrayal of this prophet fleeing from the Lord, lamenting his situation as the reeds wrap around his head, and thankful for the deliverance from drowning that he had previously experienced. By focusing almost exclusively on the action of the Ninevites in chapter 3, the narrator continues to pass over Jonah's mind in misleading silence. The explicit references to Jonah's shifting attitude throughout chapter 4 contrast sharply with the descriptions at the psychological level in chapters 1–3, and even within the final chapter one notices much oscillation. Jonah reveals, and what a surprise it is to us, that he longs for death because of the very success of his mission. He desires to die *because* 120,000 are alive! He asks to die in 4:3, but then three verses later is "happy" (וישמח) about the *kikayon*, "extremely happy" (שמחה גדולה). He is angry (4:2), he wants to die (4:3), and he is extremely happy (4:6) within a short narrative space. Then, just after he experiences the cutting east wind and the heat of the sun on his head, he asks once again to die (4:8). Jonah's joy about the shade withers as quickly as the *kikayon* itself. He feels compassion, not for the *kikayon*, but for himself. The book ends with a contrast between the mind of the Lord and the mind of Jonah, and the focus is on a great matter occupying the Lord. All this attention at the psychological level has a profound impact, as will soon be suggested, at the ideological level.

In Jonah, these levels are integrally related. Indeed, they seldom work independently. They form a complex pattern of differences and identifications. At times two points of view concur only to be modified by a third. Sometimes two agree but diverge later in the story. From the temporal perspective, ideological expressions based on events from the past may come to have meaning for the present. The phraseological level affects the psychological; both in turn, are linked to images on the spatial and temporal level. Any, indeed all, of these perspectives, serve not only the immediate compositional goals of characterization or plot, but also function at the ideological level. Having concluded that each level struggles to assert itself by contact and conflict with the others, I now wish to suggest that the ideological plane is the most significant of the four and that the sometimes more easily retrieved phraseological, spatial and temporal, and psychological levels function largely as means for exposing the ideological.

When Uspensky discusses the ideological level, he writes, "We will look . . . at the most basic aspect of point of view, which may be manifested on the level which we may designate as ideological or evaluative . . . This level is least accessible to formalization, for its analysis relies, to a degree, on intuitive understanding."[2] As we consider the ideological point of view in Jonah, we may first of all ask who carries ideology in this story filtered through various perspectives. The author—by which we mean not the author's world view independent of the work, but the viewpoint that emerges from the organization of the book itself—the narrator, the characters, even the animals are all potential carriers of ideology. While the narrator and characters carry ideology, they do not all occupy the same position of authority. We have already observed that the foreigners appear on the literary stage just long enough to fulfill their role in the portrayal of the prophet and God. The Lord and Jonah are, on the other hand, multidimensional characters. With ideas distributed among the characters, one method of establishing unity is through hierarchal relationships. Textual voices may be plotted along a continuum from dominance to subordination with the author, narrator, Lord, and Jonah stationed at the authoritative end, and the sailors, Ninevites, animals, and plant at the other end. Members at the least authoritative end of the spectrum do not evaluate events as they happen, though they all function as a means for evaluation. Thus, every animate object is an *actual* carrier of the ideological point of view in Jonah.

Uspensky points out that the expression of point of view at the level of ideology is the least accessible of the four to formal study. But with the relationship of voices encoded in the text suggesting a hierarchy, this network provides specific means for discovering ideology. When all voices are observed on the same level of narration, the sorting of authority lines is complex, but in Jonah ideological transmission is recoverable because the voices are dominant or subordinate by virtue of their status and psychological positions.

The author—whose title is a constant reminder of the authority he or she can wield—works in alliance with the narrator. These partners are dominant carriers of ideology, and with respect to the ideological view, they do not disagree. In Sternberg's words, "The implied author and the narrator to whom he delegates the task of communication practically merge into each other . . . The biblical narrator is a plenipotentiary of the author, holding the same views, enjoying the same authority, addressing the same audience, pursuing the same strategy, self-effacement included. . . . No ironic distance separates these figures of maker and teller. They stand and fall together."[3] The narrator's high position is suggested in the opening words of the story. He tells us what happens, who speaks, whatever he chooses about these characters. As an omniscient, he can reveal anyone's mind, at any moment, and summarize blocks of time at will. Yet the narrator often shows remarkable restraint by allowing characters to speak for themselves. Even the self-imposed silence is another clue of the narrator's high degree of authority.

We noticed in chapter 3 of this study that the narrator assumes a prominent position in the first chapter of Jonah by addressing us in each of the verses except vs. 2. This role diminishes, and by chapter 4 we hear less from the narrator and considerably more from the Lord, another dominant carrier of ideology. The Lord emerges as a dominant carrier and as the supreme authority figure early in the narrative. The narrator establishes this position in the opening words of the narrative ("and the word of the Lord came") and then allows the Lord to reinforce it through speech ("'arise,' 'go'"). At times the Lord's authority is manifested only implicitly. In chapter 2, for example, when Jonah is in the belly of the fish, it is the prophet's words that remind us of the Lord's authority. Elsewhere, the words of other characters ("perhaps" "who knows?" and "for I knew that you are a gracious God") function in a similar fashion. Thus, even those at the lower end of the spectrum establish the Lord's position of authority. At other times, God's authority is explicitly revealed by the narrator. The Lord is the first and last character whose speech is quoted in the story, and in both instances, Nineveh is the focus. This organization appears to be part of a deliberate plan because, apart from the Lord's command of a dozen words in 1:2 (repeated with slight variation in chapter 3), the Lord has little to say in the opening chapters. The position of God's authority is maintained throughout. Whether launching a storm and then increasing it to the point where it virtually overwhelms the sailors, providing a fish and then commanding it to return Jonah to the dry land, sparing the Ninevites but *only* because of a change of mind, or appointing a bush, a worm, and an east wind in a short narrative space of three verses (4:6–8), the Lord establishes the rules in each chapter. Throughout, we see the Lord at the high end of the ideological spectrum in words and action on what Uspensky would call the phraseological, spatial and temporal, and psychological planes.

Of the human characters, Jonah is the most dominant carrier of ideology. His authority is suggested in several ways. First, only Jonah and God's presence is suggested in every one of the four chapters. Second, it is Jonah alone who hears from and who speaks to the Lord. The word comes to Jonah, but to no one else. Third, the author has Jonah keeping the message that he takes to Nineveh a secret from the audience. In addition, the prophet's complaint in 4:2 is surprising because his thoughts back in Israel were also withheld. Secrets like these establish Jonah's authority. Fourth, the prophet is the only character in the book who resists God's commands, even though he is aware of the perils involved (1:9). Initially, Jonah challenges God with actions, and by the end of the book, Jonah speaks as he sits in judgment of God. Jonah's position is also suggested by questions in the book. In separate scenes, three characters speak to or about God, and their words betray their perspectives: "Perhaps?" in 1:6; "Who knows?" in 3:9, and "Was this not my word?" in 4:2. These questions suggest radically different world views, and the audience has an advantage when it comes to evaluation because the characters are unaware of *every*one's speech. The sailors and Ninevites do not meet in the story, and we cannot be certain if Jonah hears either the sailors on board ship or the Ninevite king. None of the foreigners hear Jonah addressing God. Yet the audience is aware of all reported speech, and cumulatively, their words provide a means for evaluation.

Although the sailors and the Ninevites occupy a lower rung on the ideological ladder, they do have persuasive powers as agents of alignment. As ideological counterparts to Jonah, their quoted speech and the narrator's description of their actions demonstrate their important role: "'perhaps the god(s) will give a thought to us;'" "and the men rowed hard (trying) to return to the dry land;" "they slaughtered a slaughter-meal to the Lord and they vowed vows;"[4] "the people of Nineveh believed in God, and they called a fast and dressed themselves in sackcloth from the greatest to the least;" "and God saw their deeds, how they turned from their evil ways, and God was sorry concerning the evil;" etc. Even these characters do not merely "say something" without suggesting a worldview.

Animals and the natural order are not evaluators either, but they, too, are instruments of evaluation. They establish God's authority. Jonah informs the sailors on board ship that the Lord is the God of heaven, the maker of the sea and dry land. The actions of the story confirm Jonah's words because the sea creature, plant, insect, and hot winds obey God's words unhesitatingly. It will soon be suggested that chapter 4 is significant because it is the place of evaluation. We may anticipate this argument by noticing the important role that creation plays in the fourth chapter. Respect for animals seldom finds any expression in the Hebrew Bible (though see Deut. 22:6, 25:4, Prov. 12:10), but at the end of Jonah's tale, the Lord is motivated, at least in part, to have mercy on the city because of the animals. In chapter 3, the animals had figured almost comically ("they shall cover themselves with sackcloth, people and animals, and they shall call to God with might" [3:8]). The author makes a profound point about the animal kingdom by means of a reversal (from the comic to the tragic) while concurrently evaluating Jonah: both the cattle and the people who "do not know their right hand from their left" (4:11) evoke divine compassion; God's grace extends to nonhuman creatures as well. By drawing the cattle back into the picture, the Lord makes it clear that the decision to spare Nineveh is justified by the animals alone. They are worth more than the plant that Jonah has just recently grown to love. By asking to die just after the *kikayon* withers, Jonah implies that the plant had a right to stay alive. On what grounds could he overlook the many cattle that just happen to graze on Assyrian soil? The final words of the story concerning the animals might pass as an innocent coda, but the vocabulary of the king's edict in chapter 3 and God's final words at the end testify to their ideological weight. The author finally subordinates this whole mass of ideology to a single accent and unified point of view: God is free to command, to modify plans, and to have compassion on all of creation.

The Significance of Chapter 4

At several points of this study it has been suggested that the fourth chapter of Jonah is the high point of the story. It remains to be shown how the author uses art to enhance ideology at the book's terminus. Mikhail Bakhtin provides some insight: "Finally, the ideas of the author can be scattered sporadically throughout the whole work. They can appear in authorial speech as isolated sayings, as maxims, as whole arguments, or they can be placed in the mouth of one or another character—often in quite large and compact chunks."[5] One such ideological chunk exists in chapter 4 where *evaluation, in its most profound form, occurs* as Jonah emerges as a new center of interest. Toward the end we realize that the storyteller has misdirected us: judgment is not just for the Ninevites—and not even primarily for the Ninevites—whose wickedness had come up before the Lord (1:2), but for Jonah as well, a prophet of God who fulminates against an act of mercy.

The fourth chapter's ideological significance may be measured first of all in a series of reversals. These reversals—contrasting narrative situations, contrasting speech, sudden attention at one or more of the four levels of point of view, unexpected loss of life, etc.—are numerous. One such reversal was noted just above. The animals figured comically in chapter 3, but in chapter 4 the serious side of creation is emphasized. Other reversals in chapter 4 include the following: the sole presence of Jonah and the Lord; the narrator's diminished role; a new dialogue pattern; closures masquerading as resolution; a game; dramatic shifts in words and images; and Jonah's mood swings.

In the final chapter, and for the first and only time, two independent points of view are present—Jonah's on the one hand and the Lord and narrator's on the other. Their expressions at the psychological level have implications at the ideological plane. In chapter 4, both the prophet and the Lord reveal their feelings through speech, and as the world of action is replaced by the world of thought and feeling, this foregrounding is surprising since their inner lives had been shrouded in mystery throughout most of the story. This reversal in portrayal of the angry God who practically stops at nothing—a shipload of sailors were placed in danger because of the error of one—in pursuing his prophet, allows us to see clearly that the Lord is a God of compassion, endorsing that characterization to which Jonah objected in 4:2. At the very end, God reveals mercy which extends to the whole world of men, women, and animals.

Another reversal in chapter 4 is seen in the narrator's new, diminished role. We observed before that the narrator assumed a prominent role conveying information in most of the verses of the initial chapter. In fact, the narrator sets the stage at the beginning of each of the four chapters. With Jonah and the Lord conversing in chapter 4, the narrator's role soon becomes much less pronounced. Up until 4:1, the narrator had frequently described actions in the external world—a raging storm, cargo being hurled overboard, people dressing in sackcloth—and had on occasion revealed character's thoughts, though the revelation about what the sailors felt in chapter 1 was hardly surprising. But the opening in chapter 4 is alarming: the Lord's response to the Ninevites is what angers Jonah. The narrative voice, now more laconic at the beginning of this chapter, provides a surprising glimpse of the prophet. We may also notice that the narrator no longer mentions Nineveh by name in the final chapter.

A dialogue pattern has also been changed in the fourth chapter. In the first three chapters, Jonah's recorded direct speech to the Lord is found only at 2:3–10. The Lord addresses Jonah in direct speech twice in the first three chapters (1:2; 3:2). Consistently, in each of these initial chapters, when the Lord speaks to Jonah or when Jonah speaks to the Lord, the addressee does not offer a verbal response. It should now be apparent that such nonverbal replies are particularly important because Jonah and God are leading carriers of the ideological point of view. At the end, this trend is reversed. In 4:2–4, the Lord and prophet finally respond *verbally* to each other. The narrator then describes Jonah's actions just outside Nineveh (4:5–8a) before allowing God and Jonah to resume their dialogue in the closing verses (4:8b–11). In the final conversation between God and Jonah, the dialogue becomes packed with emotion and excitement as both characters continue to address each other: "And God said to Jonah, 'Is it right for you to become inflamed about the *kikayon?*' And [Jonah] said, 'It is right for me to become inflamed, even to the point of death'" (4:9). This quoted speech serves as a contrast to the silence, ambiguity, and indirection of the initial three chapters. Characterization had often been achieved by the narrator's direct statements. Now, characterization at the psychological level is achieved by important carriers of the ideological point of view, and anyone listening in can evaluate.

Another reversal centers on the question of who is on trial in this book? The Lord's command to the prophet to head to Nineveh because of "her wickedness" (1:2) propels our reading. The repetition at 3:2 redirects the prophet and reminds us that this story is about God's response to corrupt Nineveh. At the end of chapter 3, it appears that events crucial to the forecast have been resolved. After Jonah's short proclamation, "Yet in forty days and Nineveh will be overthrown," the people believe in God, begin fasting, and dress in sackcloth. After seeing their actions, God is "sorry concerning the evil which he had said he would do to them." The Ninevites are spared. The conflict is resolved. But we soon learn that this closure is only masquerading as resolution. At 4:6, the story can once again end on a happy note, at least from Jonah's perspective. Jonah has already expressed his anger, and the fate of the Ninevites is no longer of concern to him. Just after this second would-be resolution point, however, we discover that from God's standpoint, the prophet still needs a lesson on divine mercy. God uses the prophet's personal experiences and transposes the issues to a higher key. In the first three chapters, Nineveh is the object of God's wrath. In chapter 4, Jonah is. Nineveh is alluded to in chapter 4, but in both instances (4:5 and 4:11) it is Jonah who is portrayed or evaluated in relationship to Nineveh. Thus, both 3:10 and 4:6 masquerade as resolution, and just after them, the author sets a stage for evaluation.

After this second point of closure that masquerades as resolution, the Lord launches a game, thus allowing Jonah to dig his own grave verbally. The narrative becomes multidirectional once again as Jonah's feelings are weighed against God's. The opportunity for evaluation is now provided by this vast gulf that separates the two perspectives. The division is suggested by the pronouns of vss. 10–11, between אתה ("you," i.e. Jonah) and אני ("I," i.e. the Lord). The perspective of אתה is on the plant. The perspective of אני is on the creatures of Nineveh. Key words that had been used previously are drawn back into the picture. The emphasis on העיר הגדולה ("the great city") this time is not just on its immense size, but on its magnitude when compared to one single shade plant. It is during this game, this evaluation by means of a reversal, that these two perspectives bring us back to the very beginning of the story where Jonah chose to disobey the Lord. The word אבד ("perish") is also invoked once again (4:10). This catchword had been used before (in 1:6, 14; 3:9), and in each instance, the word was related to the foreigners' hope that they would not perish. In 4:10, the word is invoked for the first and only time to refer to an animate object that actually loses its life. In this case, the plant's dying provides Jonah an opportunity to rethink his position, and provides us an opportunity to evaluate him.

This perishing serves to demonstrate more than Jonah's trivial feelings. In the course of the game, Jonah answers with the same vocabulary as God:

LORD: ההיטב חרה לך "Is it right for you to become inflamed?" (4:9a)

JONAH: היטב חרה לי "It is right for me to become inflamed." (4:9b)

But at the conclusion, and in turning the tables once again, the Lord uses words we have not heard before:

אתה חסת על הקיקיון . . . ואני לא אחום על נינוה

"You were concerned about the *kikayon* . . . may I not be concerned about Nineveh?" (4:10–11)

Several things are at work here. The author's choice to have God avoid the theological vocabulary of the prophet opens a vast phraseological gulf that highlights the two different perspectives. God avoids the vocabulary crucial to chapter three [רעה ("evil"), נחם ("sorry"), שוב ("turn")], despite the fact that Jonah had previously used some of these words. The new and repeated word חום ("concerned") virtually replaces נחם ("sorry" of 3:10), a word that conveys a feeling associated with an act or plan that has taken place earlier. The Hebrew word חום, on the other hand, only concerns emotions of the present moment. The question never alludes to repentance, and certainly not to repentance as a precondition for God's change of mind. As Wolff has observed, "there is no recollection of the threat that has been withdrawn, or of the city's repentance, or even of the implicitly suggested fact that Nineveh is [the Lord's] creation. It is only what excites [the Lord's] compassion here and now that is mentioned."[6] What God does is to use new words at the very end to guide, to suggest, to invite Jonah to see the world in a new way, to see it as God sees it.

Another reversal that has implications at the ideological level concerns Jonah's mood swings. The fourth chapter's function at the ideological level can perhaps best be understood by reviewing and supplementing my argument that a central concern of chapter 4 is to focus on Jonah's mood. One interpretation—and there are certainly others—is that Jonah is preoccupied with himself. As Leslie Allen points out, "[Jonah's] attachment to [the plant] could not be very deep, for it was here one day and gone the next. [His] concern

was dictated by self-interest, not by a genuine love."[7] And Hans
Walter Wolff agrees when he writes that "the irony is unmistakable:
the change has nothing to do with Nineveh, and the problem of
God's word and God's justice. It is due solely to Jonah's own trivial
sense of well-being."[8] Jonah's mood in 4:8b is described *in terms of*
the now withered shade plant. His joy about the shade withers as
quickly as the *kikayon* itself. Of course, Jonah feels nothing *for* the
plant. Instead he misses its shade, just as earlier, he became angry
not because *Nineveh* suffered, but quite possibly because his repu-
tation as a prophet had been damaged. Jonah's actions and words
in chapter 4 reflect his reaction after proclaiming a message of doom
that is not realized. He is physically uncomfortable now just as he
was emotionally uncomfortable earlier. Shortly after the divine
change of heart, the prophet proceeds to let God know that he had
suspected this outcome from the very beginning. For this reason,
Jonah also reveals that he was not especially anxious to set out for
Nineveh in the first place. What he feels is obviously more important
to him than what God is able to do. His preoccupation with himself
cuts him off from God's change of heart. The Ninevites, fearing
death, had performed actions so that they might live. Jonah, after
learning that *they* had been spared, proceeds to twice ask that his
life be taken from him (4:3, 8). In this reversal, the reader discovers
that Jonah is the appalling one after all, the one more concerned
with himself than with the good news that God spared the Ninevites
after they turned from their evil ways. The Lord's concern for all
of creation overshadows Jonah's mood.

The technical choices of the storyteller in producing speech and
action like this in chapter 4 betray values and judgments. Cumulatively, these utterances produce an effect; the narrative combines
discourse from a number of subjects; and the network of voices
operating at different levels reveals distinct modes of consciousness.
Once again, attention at the psychological level has implications at
the ideological. At the very end, and after many turns, we are able
to perceive the merits of God's love and mercy as we see Jonah's
concern with himself contrasted with divine compassion. It is our
turning which now deserves attention.

Jonah as Nondidactic Literature

One point remains to be made. While Jonah's tale is highly
charged ideological literature, it does not belong to that extreme

variety of writing called didactic. The didactic genre not only advances the point of view in a militaristic fashion; it also subverts the whole order of the plot, the characters themselves, and the words they speak to the exigencies of doctrine.[9] With respect to compositional possibilities, the most easily recoverable ideological evaluation is carried out exclusively from such a single dominating point of view. This option, uninteresting at best, is not exercised in Jonah. Evaluation is carried out in a profound form in chapter 4, but we, like Jonah, take several wrong turns before we arrive. The variety of techniques observed throughout this study is matched by a blending of points of view, a play of perspectives.

The most fully reinforced nondidactic ideology is one that is, in Uspensky's words, polyphonic or "many voiced."[10] Polyphony refers to several independent and legitimate points of view that work and often struggle together to assert themselves. In place of one dominating, persistent voice, ideology in Jonah is realized by polyphonic means. The ultimate ideological goal is accomplished at the story's outcome, at the conclusion of the Lord's most prolonged speech, but it is also accomplished throughout and in more than one way. Jonah tells the sailors that he "fears" the Lord; the narrator points out that the sailors offer a sacrifice and make vows; we learn that the people of Nineveh believe in God, that they fast and dress in sackcloth, and that God has a change of heart; Jonah tells us that God is gracious, compassionate, and great in ḥesed. Ideology is handled implicitly by the ordering of values conferred by the plot sequence. The reader pieces it together from activity and speech. We constantly look to see if the characters or the narrator take similar or opposing stances to this prophet. Ultimately, we move from this polyphony, these worldviews, to a singular view of God. In chapter 4, the place of evaluation, the story ultimately proves to be about a prophet's apprehensions, fears, and struggles, and God's own hurt as well. In the end, God is both a commanding and a compassionate God, subject to distress and disappointment at the thought of losing 120,000 Ninevites and much cattle. The multidirectional moves of the author, the multivoiced views of the characters throughout the story, and our wrong turns highlight *how* the ideological point is made.

God does not condemn Jonah, but invites the prophet to condemn himself and admit that his anger has no merit. The Lord offers Jonah a practical lesson. Though the narrator reports on how Jonah feels after certain experiences, even a voice as strong as this one does not evaluate. Instead of appearing on stage to denounce (as any didactic would), the narrator allows us to watch as the Lord handles the prophet. The intentional silence at the end is an invitation for reflection: from the author's point of view, maybe Jonah is not the only one who needs to catch a glimpse of the world as God sees it.

A number of non-heavy-handed moves has been suggested throughout this study. Another strategy may be observed that illustrates that the book does not belong to the extreme class of didacticism. No one doubts that the many questions found in Jonah are distinct rhetorical devices.[11] It may, however, be less apparent that the author has other options because there are multiple ways of getting ideas across. Like the rude dinner guest who demands, "Give me the salt!" instead of asking for it; so too, our author can always phrase otherwise when it comes to speech, or pass over altogether. What *are* questions? And what are they doing in Jonah? Might they suggest that evaluation is accomplished through nondidactic means?

It is generally held that questions are openings that seek to be closed, and that they may be placed in either of two categories. One, the information-seeker, is the kind that people in the real world and characters in the narrative world ask routinely when deprived of information or when desiring new facts. The sailors ask Jonah where he is from, who his people are, etc. in 1:8 because they *need* to know. A rhetorical question, the second type and the only type found in chapter 4 of Jonah—yet another component in the reversal package—is any utterance that invokes the conditions of an interrogative but serves some further figurative purpose, either assertive or expressive. When the Lord says to Cain, "Where is your brother Abel?," Cain takes the Lord's rhetorical question to be of the information-seeking type and responds by saying, "I do not know; am I my brother's keeper?" (Gen. 4:9). Both Cain and the Lord have asked questions, but neither has asked for information. While the tradition of dividing questions into two categories is open to debate— in the largest sense, all questions are rhetorical because they assume a persuasive function in communication—the distinction is important to maintain so that the manner of evaluation in chapter 4 may be understood. The questions in Jonah are brief and pointed, and they operate at both the phraseological and ideological levels.[12]

The questions in chapter 1 serve to highlight the drama as the human characters attempt to get information from the prophet. First, the captain jabs Jonah with an accusing question, "How can you fall into a trance?!" in 1:6 just before the sailors bombard him with a series of their own in 1:8.[13] Then in vss. 10–11 they ask what he has done and what they should do with him. Each of the questions in the first chapter highlights the sailors' confused state of mind. The next question appears late in chapter 3 when the king of Nineveh concludes his proclamation with a wish. He says, "Who knows? God may turn" (vs. 9). Apart from the accusing question that the captain of the sailors addresses to Jonah in 1:6, the foreigners never evaluate the prophet. The author leaves that to the audience.

The two characters at the high end of the ideological spectrum, Jonah and the Lord, do not ask a single question in the first three chapters, but again, we notice a reversal in chapter 4 where both ask questions of the other. Now, the author exploits and seeks to change all in the speaker-addressee-audience triangle by invoking questions.

a. "Was this not my word when I was in my country?" (4:2)

Jonah asks the first question. The Lord will in turn ask three questions of Jonah. Much has already been said in this study about the important question Jonah asks in 4:2. Suffice it to say here that it shows the degree of the prophet's anger, and it sets a series of exchanges in motion. Jonah chooses to answer this question himself, and in so doing reveals he is angry because the Lord has proven to be just the sort of God the Hebrew Bible says the Lord is (Num. 14:18; Pss. 86:15; 103:8; 145:8; Nah. 1:3; Neh. 9:17).

The Lord, who had only issued commands to the prophet in the first and third chapters (three in 1:2, repeated in 3:2), and whose speech had not been recorded at all in chapter 2, is now only asking questions. The Lord begins the attempt to persuade the prophet by issuing commands, yet ends up trying to convince him (and us) by consistently asking short, compelling questions:

b. "Is it right for you to become inflamed?" (4:4)
c. "Is it right for you to become inflamed about the *kikayon*?" (4:9a)
d. "May I not be concerned about Nineveh . . . ?" (4:11)

Chapter 4 is loaded with a different kind of question, the so-called rhetorical type. Questions like these in Jonah 4 allow for a generalization: often the purpose of asking rhetorical questions is to cajole, convince, berate, affirm, denounce—in short, to change—the addressee. Their effectiveness depends not only on the words and their meaning but also on the way they are offered and received. As with any text, another component must be considered because dialogue is not only heard, but overheard. Our author has used a number of techniques to involve those who are listening in, and questions like these certainly draw the audience into the story in a significant way. Thus far, quite a few questions have not been answered. (We noticed earlier that Jonah does not respond to all of the questions the sailors asked in the first chapter.) But it does not concern the informed reader that many of the questions are left unanswered. We certainly know the answers to the sailors' inquiry. If the final chapter is the place of evaluation, and if all questions here are rhetorical, it will be worthwhile to see if (and how) answers are supplied.

The Lord responds to Jonah's death request with a question (b.) that highlights the unjustifiability of the prophet's anger. It is this question about Jonah's *right* to be angry that is now the focus. While Jonah's fleeing may have been understandable—Israelite prophets were notoriously reluctant, and the Ninevites were, from an Israelite perspective, notoriously wicked—the few words of the question define a new issue: on what grounds can Jonah's anger be justified? The Lord, exercising a divine prerogative, has altered the initial plan; the people of Nineveh are not overturned (נהפכת). Jonah no doubt understands that the Lord's words are a rhetorical question, and he is in no mood to answer with words.

The next question in this series (c.) also contains the key word חרה ("heat" or "anger"). When the Lord poses this rhetorical question, the first part of the interrogative is repeated verbatim from 4:4 and then a qualifying phrase is added ("Is it right for you to become inflamed *about the kikayon* [עַל־הקיקיון]?"). Once again the issue focuses on Jonah's *right* to become indignant, but this time it is prompted by Jonah's anger over the *kikayon*. The forecast of 1:2 and the action in Nineveh have now been reduced to the single issue of this shade plant. When the Lord asked the first question (b.), Jonah was angry because *Nineveh had not been destroyed*. Now, the prophet is so angry that he prefers death because the *tree has been destroyed*. Earlier, Jonah was indignant because the Lord was concerned about Nineveh. Now Jonah is angry because of the loss of shade over his head, and his anger is so real that the thought of death seems better than momentary discomfort. Question c. leaves the prophet little room to maneuver. He can't flee now. Jonah did not deign to answer question b., but now the additional words about the plant sting him into a reply. Like Cain, Jonah answers this question as though the Lord were asking for information and in so doing condemns himself with words: "It is right for me to be angry enough to die" (vs. 9b).

The final question (d.), like the previous one, also gains in momentum. To the very end, the question moves from the less important (Jonah's concern about the *kikayon*) to the more important (the Lord's attempt to educate the prophet), by means of a compelling question. It is organized around a key word, חום ("concern," "compassion," or "pity"), a word that rarely appears in the Hebrew Bible as an expression of the Lord's feelings. At the end of Jonah, the Lord points out that this prophet has felt חום for the *kikayon*, and then in an attempt to bring Jonah's agreement at long last, asks, "May I not feel חום for Nineveh?" The book ends with a contrast between the Lord and Jonah, and the object of their חום: a shrivelled plant and a city teeming with animals and people. The prophet's emotions, which had previously been emphasized starting with the first verse of the chapter (rage, disappointment, extraordinary happiness, frustration), are now summarily contrasted with the חום that the Lord has for all of creation. And it is done with a question.

As noted earlier, the preceding actions and God's rhetorical question to Jonah now point not so much to human (re)action as to God's sovereign freedom. God's change of mind abrogating the forecast of 3:4 does come *after* the Ninevites "turn from their evil ways" (3:10), but the decision to spare them rests ultimately with God. The human change of heart is a condition, but not the basis, for God's delivering compassion. In fact, even the king's question ("Who knows?") in 3:9 had acknowledged that repentance does not force God's hand.

It is the Lord who poses the important question (d.) to the prophet at the end, which, as a rhetorical question, invites a response from the audience. With a sense of disproportion accentuated, the audience gains a perspective on the folly of human anger when compared with divine sorrow. The reader may expect some reaction to the final question, because earlier the reaction of the people after the Lord's actions had been reported (cf. 1:5, 10, 16; 3:5; 4:1, 6). And indeed, Jonah had just answered the previous rhetorical question. But here, at the very end, the reader is left without any reply to the book's central question. The author does *not* bring the plot to a neat end. There is an *attempt* to align Jonah's perspective with the Lord's, but is Jonah convinced? Is he angrier? Even the silence is an ideological tool. In retrospect, we see that the narrator is more of a reporter (Jonah became angry; he was happy; he was extremely happy) than an evaluator. At the story's outcome, the final question has not only expressive implications, but, from the reader's side, persuasive force as well. By responding to Jonah with a question, the Lord stresses the supremacy of compassion and upsets the possibility of looking for a rational coherence of God's ways with the world. The author leaves no unambiguous dogma or decree. Just the mystery of divine compassion. God's final question to Jonah is, at the phraseological level, the longest in the book, and, at the ideological, the most significant.

Conclusion

Jonah's tale is implicated in ideology from the very beginning. What we are allowed to see with the mind's eye motivates and shapes the representation. The characters and events that constitute this narrative world are presented according to different worldviews, and the main human character, Jonah, is revealed to us not only in terms of the evaluative system of the author, but also from the point of view of other characters' actions and words. Multiple ideological viewpoints suggest a fairly complex network of relationships. The technical choices that the author makes throughout betray values and judgments of which some may be unaware, but which are available to anyone who reads or hears the story. The psychological and ideological relationships among narrator, characters, narrative events, author, and audience give rise to an ideological system. More than a pure contemplation of pattern, this is a book where art serves ideology.

Notes

Preface

1. Cf. the translations, for example, in A. T. Murray, trans., *Iliad*, vol. 2, Loeb Classical Library (Cambridge: Harvard University Press, 1939), 167, and William Benjamin Smith and Walter Miller, trans., *The Iliad of Homer* (New York: Macmillan, 1944), 334. I wish to thank Katerina Katsarka Whitley for helping me with the Greek.

Introduction

1. Robert Alter, *The Art of Biblical Narrative* (New York: Basic Books, 1981), 189.
2. Paul D. Duke alludes to such criticism in *Irony in the Fourth Gospel* (Atlanta: John Knox Press, 1985), 2.

Chapter 1: What Is Poetics?

1. See, for example: Peter Edward Fink, S.J., "A Poetics of Christian Sacraments: A Dialogue with Paul Ricoeur" (Ph.D. dissertation, Emory University, 1976); James Allen Rimbach, "Animal Imagery in the Old Testament: Some Aspects of Hebrew Poetics" (Ph.D. dissertation, Johns Hopkins University, 1972); Meir Sternberg, *The Poetics of Biblical Narrative: Ideological Literature and the Drama of Reading* (Bloomington: Indiana University Press, 1985); Adele Berlin, *Poetics and Interpretation of Biblical Narrative* (Sheffield: Almond Press, 1983); Robert Funk, *The Poetics of Biblical Narrative* (Sonoma, California: Polebridge Press, 1988); Erhard Güttemanns, "What is 'Generative Poetics'?: Theses and Reflections concerning a New Exegetical Method," *Semeia* 6 (1976): 1–21; Jonathan Culler, *Structuralist Poetics* (Ithaca: Cornell University Press, 1975); Shlomith Rimmon-Kenan, *Narrative Fiction: Contemporary Poetics* (London and New York: Methuen, 1983); Boris Uspensky, *A Poetics of Composition*, translated by Valentina Zavarin and Susan Wittig (Berkeley: University of California, 1973); *Poetics: International Review for the Theory of Literature; Poetics Journal; Poetics Today; PTL: A Journal for Descriptive Poetics and Theory of Literature.*
2. Benjamin Hrushovski, "On the Boundaries of the Study of Literature" [Hebrew], *Hasifrut* 1 (1968): 1–10.
3. Alan Mintz, "On the Tel Aviv School of Poetics," *Prooftexts* 4 (1984): 218.

4. Benjamin Hrushovski, "Poetics, Criticism, Science: Remarks on the Fields and Responsibilities of the Study of Literature," *PTL* 1 (1976): v.
5. Hrushovski, "Boundaries," 1.
6. Hrushovski, "Poetics," vi.
7. As George M. Landes's article ("Linguistic Criteria and the Date of the Book of Jonah," *Eretz-Israel* 16 [1982]: 147–70) on the so-called Aramaisms in Jonah suggests. He concludes, "The complete lack of Persian or Greek loan words, together with the paucity of characteristics distinctive of L[ate] B[iblical] H[ebrew], including Aramaisms, suggests not only that the traditional dating of Jonah in the time of Ezra and Nehamiah (sic.) or later is in error, but also that it is quite unlikely that our author, while writing in this period, was deliberately archaizing the language of his story to bring it into conformity with its obvious preexilic setting" (p. 163). Jack Sasson's caveat (cited in Landes, "Linguistic," 170, n. 153) is also relevant: "Thus, it is our opinion that, despite an enormous literature on the subject, dating a Hebrew text on literary and linguistic bases will continue to be a most unreliable approach as long as our extra-biblical corpus of Hebrew vocabulary remains as sparse as it is presently" (Jack M. Sasson, *Ruth: A New Translation with a Philological Commentary and a Formalist-Folklorist Interpretation* [Baltimore and London: Johns Hopkins University Press, 1979]), 244. Cf. also Jack Sasson's remarks on this subject in *Jonah: A New Translation with Introduction, Commentary, and Interpretation*, AB, vol. 24b (New York: Doubleday, 1990), 204–5.
8. The work of George M. Landes ("The Kerygma of the Book of Jonah: The Contextual Interpretation of the Jonah Psalm," *Int* 21 [1967]: 3–31), Jack Sasson (*Jonah*), Gabriël H. Cohn (*Das Buch Jona* [Assen: Van Gorcum, 1969]), Ludwig Schmidt ("*De Deo:*" *Studien zur Literarkritik und Theologie des Buches Jona, des Gesprächs zwischen Abraham und Jahwe in Gen 18:22ff. und von Hi 1* [Berlin: Walter de Gruyter, 1976]), and Alan Jon Hauser ("Jonah: In Pursuit of the Dove," *JBL* 104 [1985]: 21–37) has done much to repair such scholarly omissions. On the other hand, Jonathan Magonet's book (*Form and Meaning: Studies in Literary Techniques in the Book of Jonah* [Bern/Frankfurt: Herbert Lang/Peter Lang, 1976]) is helpful, but the numerous charts, tables, and elaborate computations often distract from the biblical book's narrative art.
9. For one such view, see O. B. Hardison, Jr.'s comments in Aristotle, *Poetics*, translated by Leon Golden and commentary by O. B. Hardison, Jr. (Englewood Cliffs, N.J.: Prentice-Hall, 1968), 55. For a brief discussion on Aristotelian influence during and after the Renaissance, see Robert S. Crane, *The Language of Criticism and the Structure of Poetry* (Toronto: University of Toronto Press, 1953), 80–83 and 94–95.
10. Crane, *Language*, 3, 43, and 65.
11. Cf. the comments and accompanying observation at n. 25 below.

12. One of his earliest articles was written with Menakhem Perry ("The King through Ironic Eyes: The Narrator's Devices in the Biblical Story of David and Bathsheba and Two Excursuses on the Theory of the Narrative Text" [Hebrew], *Hasifrut* 1 [1968]: 263–92), which later appeared in a revised form in Sternberg's book (*Poetics*, chap. 6) and then in *Poetics Today* 7 (1986): 275–322. In addition to his two books (*Poetics* and *Expositional Modes and Temporal Ordering in Fiction* [Baltimore and London: Johns Hopkins University Press, 1978]), some of his articles (excluding those incorporated in *Poetics*) show how his thoughts have developed on the topic since 1968: "Temporal Ordering, Modes of Expositional Distribution, and Three Models of Rhetorical Control in the Narrative Text," *PTL: A Journal for Descriptive Poetics and Theory of Literature* 1 (1976): 295–316; "Between the Truth and the Whole Truth in Biblical Narrative: The Rendering of the Inner Life by Telescoped Inside View and Interior Monologue" (Hebrew), *Hasifrut* 29 (1979): 110–46; "Ordering the Unordered: Time, Space, and Descriptive Coherence," *Yale French Studies* 61 (1981): 60–88; "Point of View and the Indirections of Direct Speech," *Language and Style* 15 (1982): 67–117; "Proteus in Quotation-Land: Mimesis and the Forms of Reported Discourse," *Poetics Today* 3 (1982): 107–56; "Deictic Sequence: World, Language and Convention," in *Essays on Deixis*, edited by Gisa Ruah (Tübingen: Gunter Narr Verlag, 1983); "Language, World and Perspective in Biblical Narrative Art: Free Indirect Discourse and Modes of Covert Penetration" (Hebrew), *Hasifrut* 32 (1983): 88–131; "Mimesis and Motivation: The Two Faces of Fictional Coherence," in *Literary Criticism and Philosophy*, edited by Joseph P. Strelka (University Park and London: Pennsylvania State University Press, 1983); "The World from the Addressee's Viewpoint: Reception as Representation, Dialogue as Monologue," *Style* 20 (1986): 295–318.

A group of approximately twenty New Testament scholars discussed his book on the poetics of Hebrew biblical narrative at a round table during the 1988 annual SBL meeting in Chicago.

13. Sternberg, *Poetics*, 44.

14. The *anti*-didactic tendency of biblical narrative is discussed in Sternberg, *Poetics*, 37–39, 156–57, 177–78, 340–41, 483, 493–95.

15. Sternberg, *Poetics*, 98.

16. Boris Uspensky, *A Poetics of Composition*, translated by Valentina Zavarin and Susan Wittig (Berkeley: University of California, 1973); Mikhail Bakhtin, *Problems of Dostoevsky's Poetics* (Minneapolis: University of Minnesota Press, 1984); Michael Holquist, ed., *The Dialogic Imagination: Four Essays by M. M. Bakhtin* (Austin and London: University of Texas Press, 1981); Robert Polzin, *Moses and the Deuteronomist: A Literary Study of the Deuteronomic History (Part 1)* (New York: Seabury Press, 1980) and

Samuel and the Deuteronomist: A Literary Study of the Deuteronomic History (*Part Two*) (San Francisco: Harper & Row, 1989). For a bibliography on critical books and articles devoted to applying the theory of Bakhtin and his associates see Polzin, *Samuel*, 230, n. 3.

17. Homer, *The Odyssey*, translated by E. V. Rieu (Baltimore: Penguin Books, 1959), 118.

18. Ibid., 164.

19. Ibid., 220.

20. Ibid., 290.

21. William Shakespeare, *Julius Caesar*, III, iii, lines 5–8.

22. Charles Dickens, *Oliver Twist* (New York: Washington Square Press, 1970), 108.

23. Though for one attempt, cf. William Whallon's article and statement: "On the basis of style, the Hebraic mind or world view cannot be distinguished from the intelligence behind the *Odyssey* or *Iliad*." ("Old Testament Poetry and Homeric Epic," *CompLit* 18 [1966]: 113).

24. Douglas Stuart, *Hosea-Jonah*, Word Biblical Commentary, vol. 31 (Waco: Word Books, 1987), 443.

25. Phyllis Lou Trible, "Studies in the Book of *Jonah*" (Ph.D. dissertation, Columbia University, 1963), 59.

26. Trible, "Studies," 63; cf. also her comments about how the remaining versions also reflect MT "for the most part."

27. Cf. Meir Sternberg's remarks on the corrupt nature of 1 Sam. 13:1 in *Poetics*, 14.

28. Robert Polzin, *Samuel and the Deuteronomist: A Literary Study of the Deuteronomic History* (San Francisco: Harper & Row, 1989), 110. An earlier remark is also apropos: "The text offers two alternatives: the intricacy happened 'by chance' or 'it is [the author's] hand that strikes us.' . . . Is the narrative hand 'crude'—what critics usually mean when they write *redactional*—or 'careful'—what I mean when I write *authorial*" (56–57). Cf. also Jack Sasson's comments concerning modifications to the received Hebrew text (*Jonah*, 210).

29. Jack Sasson's philological commentary, *Jonah*, is foremost in this respect. The work of Phyllis Trible ("Studies," 1–65) and George M. Landes ("Linguistic," 147–70) is also outstanding. Cf. also Leslie C. Allen, *The Books of Joel, Obadiah, Jonah and Micah*, NICOT, vol. 5 (Grand Rapids: Eerdmans, 1975), 202–35; Julius A. Bewer, *The Book of the Twelve Prophets*, ICC (Edinburgh: T. & T. Clark, 1961), 28–65; Cohn, *Buch*, 12–19; Norman H. Snaith, *Notes on the Hebrew Text of Jonah* (London: Epworth, 1945); Meinrad Stenzel, "Altlateinische Canticatexte im Dodekapropheton," *ZNW* 46 (1955): 31–60 (esp. 54–60); Stuart, *Hosea*, 444, 454–55, 468–69, 481, 484, 499; Hans Walter Wolff, *Obadiah and Jonah*, translated by Margaret Kohl (Minneapolis: Augsburg, 1986), 106–08,

126–27, 144–45, 160–61; W. Wright, *The Book of Jonah in Four Semitic Versions: Chaldee, Syriac, Aethiopic, and Arabic with Corresponding Glossaries* (London: Williams and Norgate, 1857).

Chapter 2: The RSV, NRSV, and Jonah

1. Expansions, which included Apocryphal and Deutero-Canonical books, were made in 1957 and 1977.
2. I am indebted to Bruce Metzger, Robert Dentan, and Walter Harrelson (*The Making of the New Revised Standard Version of the Bible* [Grand Rapids: Eerdmans, 1991]) for some of my general observations in this introductory section.
3. Work on the RSV was carried out in stages: the Hebrew Bible was added to the New Testament and the Apocrypha and Deutero-Canonical works were added subsequently.
4. Metzger, *The Making*, 13.
5. The dates in this summary are based on the publication of both Jewish and Christian Scriptures.
6. Metzger, *The Making*, 7.
7. A list of recent studies on the feminine God would not be practical since virtually every academic press is now turning out books on the subject. A few recent titles include Alice Bach, ed., *The Pleasure of Her Text: Feminist Readings of Biblical and Historical Texts* (Philadelphia: Trinity Press International, 1990); Elisabeth Schüssler Fiorenza, *In Memory of Her: A Feminist Theological Reconstruction of Christian Origins* (New York: Crossroad, 1983); Marija Gimbutas, *The Language of the Goddess* (San Francisco: HarperCollins, 1989); Susanne Heine, *Matriarchs, Goddesses, and Images of God: A Critique of a Feminist Theology* (Minneapolis: Augsburg, 1989); Ann Loades, ed., *Feminist Theology* (Louisville: Westminster/ John Knox Press, 1990); Phyllis Trible, *God and the Rhetoric of Sexuality* (Philadelphia: Fortress Press, 1978).
8. *The New Oxford Annotated Bible with the Apocrypha* (RSV), edited by Herbert G. May and Bruce M. Metzger (New York: Oxford University Press, 1977) and *The New Oxford Annotated Bible with the Apocryphal/ Deuterocanonical Books* (NRSV), edited by Bruce M. Metzger and Roland E. Murphy (New York: Oxford University Press, 1991).
9. So Jack M. Sasson, *Jonah: A New Translation with Introduction, Commentary, and Interpretation*, AB (New York: Doubleday, 1990), 83 citing W. Rudolph, "Joel-Amos-Obadja-Jona," in *Kommentar zum alten Testament* 13.2 (Gütersloh: Gerd Mohn, 1971): 334.
10. Including Sasson, *Jonah*, 83–84.
11. BDB, 277, hi. 3.
12. See footnote at translation in chapter 1.
13. See, for example, Sasson's discussion, *Jonah*, 278.

14. Sasson, *Jonah*, 286–87.
15. Leslie C. Allen, *The Books of Joel, Obadiah, Jonah, and Micah*, NICOT, vol. 5 (Grand Rapids: Eerdmans, 1975), 230.
16. Metzger, *The Making*, 73.
17. Cf. Robert Dentan's discussion on this issue and his observation that changes like this one were not made "just for the sake of being modern" (*The Making*, 20).
18. 1:3, 4, 13 (twice); 2:1, 7, 10; 4:1, 7, 9. In addition, the *vav* is translated as "meanwhile" in 1:5.
19. 1:3, 4, 5, 13 (twice); 2:7, 10; 3:8; 4:1, 7, 9.
20. Sasson, *Jonah*, 246–47.
21. The *locus classicus* of nation's turning from their evil ways and God changing God's mind about forecasted disaster is Jer. 18:8.
22. This observation is made by Sasson, *Jonah*, 266, who refers to F. I. Andersen and D. N. Freedman's work, *Amos. A New Translation, with Introduction and Commentary*, AB, vol. 24a (Garden City, NY: Doubleday & Company, 1989), 639–79.
23. According to Sasson (*Jonah*, 271) the oldest Massoretic division of Jonah, which may even antedate Qumran, suggests the following separation: a) 1:1–2:10; b) 2:11–4:3; c) 4:4–11.
24. Sasson, *Jonah*, 270.
25. Ibid., 113.
26. Hans Walter Wolff, *Obadiah and Jonah*, trans. Margaret Kohl (Minneapolis: Augsburg, 1986), 107.
27. Allen, *Joel*; Douglas Stuart, *Hosea-Jonah*, WBC, vol. 31 (Waco: Word Books, 1987); Wolff, *Obadiah* (English translation by Margaret Kohl).
28. Sasson, *Jonah*, 260; Stuart, *Hosea*, 494; and Wolff, *Obadiah*, 145, n. 9a.
29. The NRSV's occasional omission of original words without any notes to clue the reader is, in my view, a weakness. For an omission in the New Testament, cf. Mark 1:21 where "immediately" (εὐθὺς), a key Markan word, has been dropped.
30. Though the insight is at least as old as Gesenius (§120g). Cf. also H. M. Orlinsky, ed., *Notes on the New Translation of the Torah* (Philadelphia: Jewish Publication Society, 1969), 34–35 cited by Sasson, *Jonah*, 69. Sasson, commenting on the two verbal forms, concludes, "In turn, the verb that is affected by the auxiliary . . . no longer maintains its primal meaning, but is attenuated to convey volition rather than direction" (p. 70).
31. Sasson, *Jonah*, 149.
32. Allen, *Joel*, 213, 230; André Lacocque and Pierre-Emmanuel Lacocque, *The Jonah Complex* (Atlanta: John Knox Press, 1981), xviii–xxi; Sasson, *Jonah*, 144, 270, 300; Stuart, *Hosea-Jonah*, 467, 498; and Wolff, *Obadiah*, 125, 159–60.
33. In addition to the four examples listed, the paratactic style is not main-

tained in the NRSV at 1:3, 5, 6, 7, 9, 12, 14; 2:2, 3; 3:1, 4, 5, 6, 7, 8, 9, 10; 4:2, 5, 6, 8, 9. (I consider such words as "so," "but," "meanwhile," "then," and "yet" as preserving the Hebrew conjunction.) Paratactic style in the NRSV is maintained at 4:4, 9, 11. Inconsistency within a single verse (1:8) is observed in the NRSV which translates the conjunction from MT on one occasion ("And of what people are you?") and omits it on another ("Where do you come from?").

34. Though it does not always. Cf. 1:3.

Chapter 3: The Narrator and Characters

1. Wayne Booth, *The Rhetoric of Fiction* (Chicago: University of Chicago Press, 1983 edition), 153.
2. With respect to the narrator and with much reservation, the third person, masculine, singular pronoun is used throughout.
3. With these three isolated examples, grief or disappointment is conveyed by the image of the heart (לב) or eyes (עין).
4. Meir Sternberg, *The Poetics of Biblical Narrative: Ideological Literature and the Drama of Reading* (Bloomington: Indiana University Press, 1985), 183.
5. Sasson, *Jonah*, 85.
6. For a discussion on the importance of naming, see the first section entitled, "Jonah and the Lord," below.
7. For an illuminating discussion of the expositional material at the beginning of the book of Job, see Meir Sternberg, *Expositional Modes* (Baltimore: Johns Hopkins University Press, 1978), 23–26.
8. *Jonah*, 97.
9. Commentators sometimes wrestle with the question about where the sailors found animals to sacrifice while on board the ship. Jack Sasson (*Jonah*, 139–40) records some imaginative answers proposed through the ages and then quotes from Jean Rougé's *Ships and Fleets of the Ancient Mediterranean* (Middleton, Conn: Wesleyan University Press, 1981), 199–200. Rougé observes that ancient seafarers offered sacrifices while on board ship whenever faced with life-threatening dangers, a phenomenon that is attested by figurative representations of ships which have an altar at the stern. Sasson also refers to tales that suggest animals were taken on board for this purpose (see, for example, Raphael Patai, "Jewish Seafaring in Ancient Times," JQR 32 [1941]: 24).
10. Vss. 1, 3, 4, 5, 6, 7, 8, 9, 10, 11, 12, 13, 14, 15, and 16 all begin with a conjunction.
11. See especially, Uriel Simon, "The Book of Jonah: Structure and Meaning" (Hebrew), in *Isaac Leo Seeligmann Volume: Essays on the Bible and the Ancient World*, vol. 2, edited by Alexander Rofé and Yair Zakovitch (Jerusalem: E. Rubinstein Publishing House, 1983), 298–317. The fol-

lowing sources are also helpful: Baruch Halpern and Richard Elliott Friedman, "Composition and Paronomasia in the Book of Jonah," *HAR* 4 (1980): 87–89; Terence E. Fretheim, *The Message of Jonah: A Theological Commentary* (Minneapolis: Augsburg Press, 1977), 55–56; Douglas Stuart, *Hosea-Jonah*, Word Biblical Commentary, vol. 31 (Waco: Word Books, 1987), 481; Phyllis Lou Trible, "Studies in the Book of *Jonah*" (Ph.D. dissertation, Columbia University, 1963), 186–90; Hans Walter Wolff, *Obadiah and Jonah*, translated by Margaret Kohl (Minneapolis: Augsburg, 1986), 145; James S. Ackerman, "Jonah," in *The Literary Guide to the Bible*, edited by Robert Alter and Frank Kermode (Cambridge: Harvard University Press, 1987), 238.

12. The issue of portrayal from within is discussed in chapter 7, "Representation of the Inner Life: A Case for Inside Views."

13. According to Leslie Allen, *The Books of Joel, Obadiah, Jonah, and Micah*, NICOT (Grand Rapids: Eerdmans, 1976), 231, n. 16. For an extended discussion on the various proposals, see Trible, "Studies," 92–102.

14. Such as Kimchi, Ibn Ezra, and some early Christian exegetes. Norbert Lohfink ("Jona ging zur Stadt hinaus [Jon 4,5]," *BZ* 5 (1961): 191, n. 29) points out that vs. 5 is part of a pattern of chronological deformation used to highlight religious reactions; cited in Allen, *Books*, 231, n. 16.

15. I agree with George Landes who has also argued as I do in this context. Cf. George M. Landes, "The Kerygma of the Book of Jonah: The Contextual Interpretation of the Jonah Psalm," *Int* 21 (1967): 27, n. 65.

16. Robert Alter, *The Art of Biblical Narrative* (New York: Basic Books, 1981), 65 and Robert Polzin, *Samuel and the Deuteronomist: A Literary Study of the Deuteronomic History* (San Francisco: Harper & Row, 1989), 156. Polzin also points out that Bakhtin discusses this phenomenon "at length and brilliantly . . . throughout his writings" (*Samuel*, 42). While working independently, Jack Sasson and I reached similar conclusions concerning the relationship between narration and dialogue. For example, when commenting on 3:10 (cf. my third chapter below) he writes, "The verse replays previous vocabulary and constructions in order to reinforce the connection between cause (the Ninevites' plan of actions) and effect (God's change of mind)" (*Jonah*, 263).

17. *Jonah*, 123.

18. For different perspectives on this issue, cf. the comments at n. 33 of chapter 7 and the discussion there. The important function of chapter 4 at the ideological plane is discussed in the final chapter.

19. A similar phenomenon is observed at 4:11 when the Lord addresses Jonah, and asks, "And may *I* not pity Nineveh" (pronominal subject, negative particle, verb, object). Jack Sasson discusses these rhetorical principles in *Jonah*, 93, 118, and 119.

20. *Jonah*, 119. Sasson also points out that such departures from the usual word order are more common in poetry and legalistic writing. Such

exists in Jonah at chapter 2 and at the royal proclamations at 3:4 and 3:7.

21. The same phenomenon, with a different idiom, is evident in Gen. 18:12. "So Sarah laughed to herself (lit. "in her midst"), saying, 'After I have grown old, and my husband is old, shall I have pleasure?'" Finally, Gen. 18:17–21 may also be considered an example of interior monologue or possibly soliloquy. Here the narrator gives us no clue with the reporting verb that the Lord speaks "in his heart / midst," but the context clearly suggests that God is alone when "speaking."

22. Jack Sasson's discussion is the best I am aware of on this topic. I draw from his commentary (*Jonah*, 232–33) in the discussion above.

23. Jonathan Magonet, *Form and Meaning: Studies in Literary Techniques in the Book of Jonah* (Bern/Frankfurt: Herbert Lang/Peter Lang, 1976), 19–22.

24. Magonet, *Form*, 21.

25. The Ninevites and sailors are considered a single-collective character in this discussion.

26. Scholars have pointed out the importance of paronomasia and play on words in Jonah before, though infrequently calling attention to its impact on characterization. In addition to the standard commentaries, see, for example, Halpern and Friedman, "Composition," 79–92. Other words are emphasized in Jonah. For example, notice the contrast focused around the word "hurl" (טול; Hi., הטיל) in 1:4, 12, 15.

27. Sternberg, *Poetics*, 331. It is surprising that Jack Sasson observes that Jonah is the only character who receives a name in the book (*Jonah*, 86, 249), especially when his comments about the characters using the special name for the Lord (i.e. the tetragrammaton) are so convincing (pp. 98, 103, 118–19, 131–32, 257, 261–63).

28. Jack Sasson cites Job 1:19 and indicates that the רוח גדולה ("great wind") typically comes from God (*Jonah*, 94).

29. Wolff, *Obadiah*, 102.

30. Sasson, *Jonah*, 83.

31. See the discussion and examples listed in Magonet, *Form*, 31.

32. Trible, "Studies," 225.

33. Alter, *The Art*, 70.

34. Cf. the comments in "Omniscient vs. Limited Perspectives" above.

35. Sternberg, *Poetics*, 37. Cf. also his statements on 38, 156–57, 340–41, and 494–95.

36. Cf. n. 18 above.

37. My thoughts are derived in large part from Sheldon Blank's excellent article, "'Doest Thou Well to Be Angry?'—A Study in Self-Pity," *HUCA* 26 (1955): 29–41. Using the rhetorical question at the end of Jonah as a starting point, Blank demonstrates that the "admittedly somewhat uncommon theme" of human self-pity and divine suffering is conveyed in a few passages from the Hebrew Bible such as Jer. 45 and Hos. 11:8.

38. Sternberg, *Poetics*, 99.

39. Ibid., 318–20.

40. Hans Walter Wolff, *Studien zum Jonabuch* (Nuekirchen-Vluyn: Neukirchener, 1965), 118. Translation: the first person expression appears five times in v. 2 alone ("this is indeed what *I* thought when *I* was still in *my* own country; therefore *I* likewise wanted to make haste to flee because *I* knew . . .") and four times in the short v. 3 ("Take, Lord, *my* spirit from *me*, for *my* dying is better than *my* living").

41. Sasson, *Jonah*, 226; cf. also 72–75, 87, 227.

42. Terence E. Fretheim, "Jonah and Theodicy," *ZAW* 90 (1978): 230–33. I wish to express my gratitude to George M. Landes for calling this point to my attention.

43. George M. Landes has suggested that Jonah's words, "the Lord, the God of heaven, I fear" (vs. 9), may be intended as a response to the sailors' initial question, "On whose account has this evil happened to us?" (personal correspondence). Perhaps, but I don't see a causal connection between Jonah's statement and their first question. Jack Sasson concludes that Jonah answers only the last question (*Jonah*, 115 and 126).

44. I am indebted to George M. Landes for this insight. Carl A. Keller overlooks this ironic contrast between Jeremiah and Jonah as he attempts unsuccessfully to suggest parallels between the two prophets. He writes, "La demande de mourir (. . . Jér. 20. 14–18; . . . Jon. 4. 3, 8, 9) exprime 'la lassitude et le dégoût devant un mystère dont ces hommes étaient les confidents sans pouvoir le comprendre.' . . . Voilà des appréciations plus justes de la personnalité de Jonas et de sa destinée! Nous sommes loin des épithètes injurieuses citées au début de ce travail. Le drame de Jonas est interprété en fonction de la 'servitude' du prophète" (Carl A. Keller, "Jonas. Le portrait d'un prophète," *TZ* 21 [1965]: 338–39). Translation: The request to die (. . . Jer. 20:14–18; . . . Jon. 4:3, 8, 9) expresses "the weariness and distaste in front of a mystery of which these men were the confidants without power to understand it" . . . Here are some fairer appreciations of the personality of Jonah and of his destiny! We are far from the insulting epithets cited at the beginning of this work. The drama of Jonah is interpreted as a function of the "servitude" of the prophet.

45. Polzin, *Samuel*, 149.

Chapter 4: Jonah and the Reading Process

1. George Landes, "The Kerygma of the Book of Jonah: The Contextual Interpretation of the Jonah Psalm," *Int* 21 (1967): 3–31.

2. Ibid., 31.

3. Meir Sternberg, *The Poetics of Biblical Narrative: Ideological Literature and the Drama of Reading* (Bloomington: Indiana University, 1985), 186.

4. Indeterminacy is a large issue in philosophy and literary theory. See, for example, Charles Altieri, "The Hermeneutics of Literary Indeterminacy: A Dissent from the New Orthodoxy," *NLH* 10 (1978): 71–99; John Fizer, "Indeterminacies as Structural Components in Semiotically Meaningful Wholes, " *PTL* 4 (1979): 119–31; Lawrence W. Hyman, "Indeterminacy in Literary Criticism," *Soundings* 59 (1976): 345–56; Michael Riffaterre, "Interpretation and Undecidability," *NLH* 12 (1981): 227–42. For a discussion related to biblical studies, see Peter D. Miscall, *1 Samuel: A Literary Reading* (Bloomington: Indiana University, 1986), xvi, 34–35, 60–65, 113–114, 120–25, 181, 184–85.

5. Meir Sternberg, *Expositional Modes and Temporal Ordering in Fiction* (Baltimore and London: Johns Hopkins University, 1978), 52.

6. Martin Price, "The Irrelevant Detail and the Emergence of Form," in *Aspects of Narrative*, edited by J. Hillis Miller (New York: Columbia University, 1971), 86.

7. Sternberg, *Poetics*, 235.

8. Sternberg, *Expositional*, 50–51.

9. The "ideal reader," an important though elusive subject, relates indirectly to this discussion. Especially helpful is Robert DeMaria, Jr.'s "The Ideal Reader: A Critical Fiction," *PMLA* 93 (1978): 463–74. For different perspectives, cf. Robert Rogers, "Amazing Reader in the Labyrinth of Literature," *Poetics Today* 3:2 (1982): 31–46; James R. Kincaid, "Coherent Readers, Incoherent Texts," *CI* 3 (1977): 781–802; Tamar Yacobi, "Reader and Norms in Fictional Communication" (Hebrew), *Hasifrut* 34 (1985): 5–34. A collection of essays that contains a significant introduction may be found in Susan R. Suleiman and Ingre Crosman, *The Reader in the Text: Essays on Audience and Interpretation* (Princeton: Princeton University, 1980).

10. Cf. Meir Sternberg's discussion in "What is Exposition? An Essay in Temporal Delimitation," in *The Theory of the Novel: New Essays*, edited by John Halperin (New York: Oxford University Press, 1974), 25–70.

11. For a discussion on temporal ordering, see Sternberg, *Expositional Modes.*

12. Julius A. Bewer, *The Book of the Twelve Prophets*, ICC (Edinburgh: T. & T. Clark, repr. 1961), 21.

13. W. Neil "Jonah, the book of," in *IDB*, vol. 2, edited by G. A. Buttrick (Nashville: Abingdon, 1962), 967.

14. Samuel Sandmel, *The Hebrew Scriptures* (New York: Alfred A. Knopf, 1963), 495.

15. While the point is made by Jack Sasson (*Jonah*, 194), his position on the psalm's role is unlike that of Bewer, Neil, and Sandmel quoted just above. In fact, Sasson later points out that the kind of disparities between the poetry and prose sections which have frequently been noted are, in fact, "organic to the distinctive dictions" of the two media (p. 202).

16. See for example, Peter Weimar, "Jonapsalm und Jonaerzahlung," *BZ*

28 (1984): 438. He suggests through his structural and literary analysis that the prose narrative once existed without the poetic prayer. Uriel Simon has written an extensive and enlightening article on the structure of the book ("The Book of Jonah: Structure and Meaning" [Hebrew], in *Isaac Leo Seeligmann Volume: Essays on the Bible and the Ancient World,* vol. II, edited by Alexander Rofé and Yair Zakovitch [Jerusalem: E. Rubinstein, 1983], 291–317) but does not mention why the psalm is not considered in his discussion. For other perspectives that are related to this general trend, see Otto Eissfeldt, *The Old Testament: An Introduction,* translated by Peter R. Ackroyd (New York: Harper & Row, 1965), 406; A. R. Johnson, "Jonah 2:3–10: A Study in Cultic Fantasy," in *Studies in Old Testament Prophecy,* edited by H. H. Rowley (Edinburgh: T. & T. Clark, 1950), 82–83; Carl A. Keller, "Jonas. Le portrait d'un propète," *TZ* 21 (1965): 329–49; Phyllis Trible, "Studies in the Book of Jonah," Ph.D. Dissertation, Columbia University (1963), 31–40, 75–81, 89.

17. George Landes's article contributed to a shift in understanding with respect to the poetic prayer. S. D. F. Goitein anticipated some of the more recent arguments when he stated that "Jonah's attitude to his mission [throughout chapter 2] was deliberately left obscure." Goitein did not explore the ambiguity because, in his words, "I do not like to dwell on the prayer" ("Some Observations on Jonah," *JPOS* 17 [1937]: 69). Other scholars who have argued for the literary unity of the prayer and the prose framework, though for completely different reasons than I am proposing here, include: A. Jepsen, "Anmerkungen zum Buche Jona," *Wort-Gebot-Glaube: Walter Eichrodt zum 80. Geburtstag* (ATANT 59; Zürich: Zwingli, 1970): 297–305; Duane L. Christensen, "The Song of Jonah: A Metrical Analysis," *JBL* 104 (1985): 217–31; John C. Holbert, "Deliverance Belongs to Yahweh!: Satire in the Book of Jonah," *JSOT* 21 (1981): 59–81; James S. Ackerman, "Satire and Symbolism in the Song of Jonah," in *Traditions in Transformation: Turning Points in Biblical Faith,* edited by Baruch Halpern and Jon D. Levenson (Winona Lake, Ind.: Eisenbrauns, 1981), 213–46.

18. A catalogue of all who have discussed Jonah 2:3–10 exclusively in terms of the book's terminus would serve little purpose since it would include the vast majority of commentators, both ancient and modern.

19. Meir Sternberg discusses the "hindsight fallacy" and "hindsight misreading" in *Expositional Modes,* 70–71, 73, 85, 321, and my thoughts stem from his discussion. His more recent book on biblical narrative (see n. 3 above) offers many significant observations which result when reading is understood as a process.

20. See the extended foreign nation oracles in e.g. Ezek. 27–32; Isa. 13, 15–19; Jer. 46–51; Amos 1–2:3; Obadiah; Nah. 1–3. Elisha, the only other prophet commissioned to travel to a foreign land, speaks to Hazael on three occasions in the short passage of 2 Kgs. 8:7–15: "Elisha said

to him, 'Go, say to him, "You shall certainly recover;" but the Lord has shown me that he shall certainly die'" (v. 10); "Elisha answered, 'The Lord has shown me that you are to be king over Aram'" (v. 13b).

21. *The Books of Joel, Obadiah, Jonah, and Micah* (NICOT; Grand Rapids: Eerdmans, 1976) 199, n. 108, and cf. his comment on pp. 198–99.

Chapter 5: The Multiple Reports of Prayer in Jonah

1. The discussion about Jonah 2, when considered in its entirety, has certainly gravitated towards source at the expense of discourse analysis. Apparently, C. G. Hensler (in *Animadversiones in quaedam duodecim prophetarum minorum loca*, according to Peter Friedrichsen, *Kritische Uebersicht der verschiedenen Ansichten von dem Buch Jonas* [Leipzig: Friedr. Christ. Wilh. Vogel, 1841], 52, n. 1 cited by George Landes, "The Kerygma of the Book of Jonah: The Contextual Interpretation of the Jonah Psalm," *Int* 21 [1967]: 3, n.2) was the first to call attention to what were perceived as incongruities between the psalm which comprises most of chapter 2 and the prose narrative. Practically all subsequent research on Jonah 2:3–10 has attempted to "prove" or "disprove" Hensler's thesis. See footnotes 16 and 17 in chapter 4 for a short bibliography on this issue.

2. Jonah 2:3 and 2:6–8 refer to a distinct prayer, one which Jonah voiced before he was swallowed by the fish. See, "The Prayers of Chapter 2" below.

3. Throughout this discussion, reference is made to a single author of the Jonah story. The present state of research suggests that no definitive answer to the authorship question will be found. If consensus is reached and if two or more authors are responsible for the canonical text, a substitution of "final" author or "editor" is all that is required for the "author" above.

4. Elias Bickerman, *Four Strange Books of the Bible: Jonah, Daniel, Koheleth, Esther* (New York: Schocken, 1967), 12.

5. John Calvin, *Commentaries on the Twelve Minor Prophets*, vol. 3, translated by John Owen (Grand Rapids: Eerdmans, 1950), 75, n.1.

6. Leslie C. Allen (*The Books of Joel, Obadiah, Jonah, and Micah* [NICOT Grand Rapids: Eerdmans, 1976], 182) includes Jacques Ellul (*The Judgment of Jonah*, translated by G. W. Bromiley [Grand Rapids: Eerdmans, 1971]) and Gabriël H. Cohn (*Das Buch Jona im Lichte der biblischen Erzählkunst* [Assen: Van Gorcum, 1969]) in this category with Ibn Ezra.

7. Jerome T. Walsh, "Jonah 2, 3–10: A Rhetorical Critical Study," *Bib* 63 (1982): 225. It is worthwhile to notice that some commentators do not address the issue of single or multiple prayers in chapter 2. See, for

example, John C. Holbert, "'Deliverance Belongs to Yahweh!': Satire in the Book of Jonah," *JSOT* 21 (1981): 71. Scholars who have perceived the two prayers in chapter 2 include Terence E. Fretheim, *The Message of Jonah: A Theological Commentary* (Minneapolis: Augsburg Press, 1977), 101, and esp. George Landes, who concludes, "the tense meaning of the verb forms, not only in [2:3] but also where the psalm describes the previous experience of the poet [2:6–8], is consistently preterite, and no linguistic machinations can legitimately turn them into presents. . . . Jonah recalls an already experienced affliction" (Landes, "The Kerygma," 15).

8. Pss. 142:2 (אזעק; impf.) and 102:2 (שמעה; impv.), for example.
9. George M. Landes, "The Jonah Psalm (Jon. 2:3–10) Revisited," in a paper delivered at the annual SBL meeting in Dallas, Texas, December, 1983.
10. Cf. Leslie McFall's statistics in appendix 1 of *The Enigma of the Hebrew Verbal System* (Sheffield: Almond Press, 1982), 187. Jack Sasson translates the entire psalm with present tense verbs (cf. *Jonah*, 160, 163–64). I disagree with this choice of verbs based on the issues already mentioned.
11. According to Jack Sasson, this image is unique to Jonah and suggests "despair of the darkest hue" (*Jonah*, 172).
12. James S. Ackerman, "Satire and Symbolism in the Song of Jonah," in *Traditions in Transformation in Biblical Faith*, ed. Baruch Halpern and Jon D. Levenson (Winona Lake, Ind.: Eisenbrauns, 1981), 220.
13. "Le sens du livre de Jonas," *RB* 54 (1947): 344. Translation: Jonah's fish is, like the crows of Elijah or the she-ass of Balaam, part of the animal world placed by God for the service of the prophetic cause. . . . the fish is not presented as a punishment. Feuillet makes a similar point in an earlier article, "Les sources du livre de Jonas," *RB* 54 (1947): 182: "le poisson garde le prophète sain et sauf et le ramène au rivage" (the fish keeps the prophet safe and sound and takes him to the seashore).
14. See Landes, "The Kerygma," 13, n. 42, and the evidence that was assembled by Hans Schmidt, *Jona. Eine Untersuchung zur vergleichenden Religionsgeschichte* (Göttingen: Vandenhoeck & Ruprecht, 1907), 96–155. For the salutary character of the dolphin and its Mediterranean provenance, see N. Glueck, *Deities and Dolphins* (New York: Farrar, Straus and Giroux, 1965), 316, 353, and 356.
15. Bickerman, *Four*, 12.
16. Cf. the footnotes at the translation in chapter 1.
17. For an extended treatment on this subject, see Jack White Corvin, "A Stylistic and Functional Study of the Prose Prayers in the Historical Narratives of the Old Testament," (Ph.D. dissertation, Emory University, 1972) and A. Wendel, *Das freie Laiengebet im vorexilischen Israel* (Leipzig: Ex Oriente Lux., 1932). Moshe Greenberg discusses the prayer pattern (address, petition, motivation) in *Biblical Prose Prayer as a Window*

to the Popular Religion of Ancient Israel (Berkeley and Los Angeles: University of California Press, 1983).

18. See also, Gen. 32:10–13 (Evv 9–12). The isolated examples that follow are intended to be suggestive rather than exhaustive and to highlight the fact that the sailors' prayer follows the pattern of Israelite prayer.

19. In Leviticus, the Lord addresses Moses frequently and Aaron occasionally, but there are no reports of prayer.

20. A high frequency of prayers with these elements are found in Jeremiah. See, for example, Jer. 14:7–9; 15:15–18; 17:14–18; 18:19–23.

21. Neh. 3:36–37 (Evv 4:4–5).

22. Greenberg, *Prose Prayer*, 61, n. 7.

23. James B. Pritchard, ed., *Ancient Near Eastern Texts Relating to the Old Testament* (Princeton: Princeton University Press, 1950), 80, lines 37–40.

24. Pritchard, *Ancient*, 24.

25. As explained above, the reader learns only subsequently that Jonah prays twice after being hurled overboard, once before and once after being swallowed by the fish.

26. Cf. esp. "Analogy along Generic Lines: Prose and Poetry in Jonah" below.

27. In the following list, the = sign represents a verbatim correspondence between some of the words in the verses. Jonah 2:3a = Pss. 18:7, 30:3; 118:5; 120:1; Jonah 2:3b = Ps. 130:2; Jonah 2:4b = Ps. 42:8b; Jonah 2:5a = Ps. 31:23a; Jonah 2:6a = Pss. 18:5; 69:2; Jonah 2:8a = Pss. 142:4; 143:4; Jonah 2:8b = Pss. 5:8b; 18:7; Jonah 2:9a = Ps. 31:7a; Jonah 2:10a = Pss. 42:5b; 50:14; 66:13; Jonah 2:10b = Ps. 3:9. This type of information is readily available, though with considerable inconsistency, in the standard commentaries.

28. Sasson, *Jonah*, 80.

29. This pattern of address, motivation, petition occurs less frequently than address, petition, motivation in the Hebrew Bible. The implications are discussed under "Analogy along Generic Lines" below.

30. Cf. the footnotes at the translation in chapter 1.

31. Apparently, Allen (*The Books*, 198–99) is the only commentator who has noticed the close relationship between these two parts of the prayers.

32. Feuillet, "Les sources," 161–86, esp. 167–83.

33. See n. 27 above and the remarks in the "Imagery" section at the end of the next chapter.

34. See, H. A. Brongers, "Bemerkungen zum gebrauch des adverbiaken Weʿattah im Alten Testament," *VT* 15 (1965): 296–99.

35. For another example, notice the way the prophet expands Elisha's injunction to say, "Thus says the Lord: I anoint you king over Israel," to "Thus says the Lord the God of Israel: I anoint you king over the people of the Lord, over Israel. You shall strike down the house of your master

Ahab, so that I may avenge on Jezebel the blood of my servants the prophets, and the blood of all the servants of the Lord. For the whole house of Ahab shall perish; I will cut off from Ahab every male, bond or free, in Israel. I will make the house of Ahab like the house of Jeroboam son of Nebat, and like the house of Baasha son of Ahijah. The dogs shall eat Jezebel in the territory of Jezreel, and no one shall bury her" (2 Kings 9:3 and 9:6–10).

36. For a discussion on the Bible's variations in repetition, see, Meir Sternberg, "The Structure of Repetition: Strategies of Informational Redundancy" in his book, *The Poetics of Biblical Narrative* (Bloomington: Indiana University Press, 1985), 365–440.

37. For a discussion on the words, see Baruch Halpern and Rich Elliott Friedman, "Composition and Paronomasia in the Book of Jonah," *HAR* 4 (1980): 79–82; Joel Rosenberg, "Jonah and the Prophetic Vocation," *Response* 22 (1974): 23–26; Cohn, *Buch*, 62–77, and Phyllis Trible, "Studies in the Book of *Jonah*" (Ph.D. dissertation, Columbia University, 1963), 239–41.

38. Cf. the discussion in Chapter 7. The parallel structures in these chapters is outside our present concern and has been treated on many occasions. See esp., Jonathan Magonet, *Form and Meaning: Studies in Literary Techniques in the Book of Jonah*, Beitrage zur biblischen Exegese und Theologie 2 (Bern/Frankfurt: Herbert Lang/Peter Lang, 1976), 55–63; Uriel Simon "The Book of Jonah" [Hebrew], in *Isaac Leo Seeligmann Volume: Essays on the Bible and the Ancient World*, vol. 2, edited by Alexander Rofé and Yair Zakovitch (Jerusalem: E. Rubinstein Publishing House, 1983), 291–317, and Cohn, *Buch*, 48–51.

39. Meir Sternberg has provided an extensive treatment on the subject of analogy with special reference to it impact on delineation of character, and the definition above is from his book, *Poetics*, 365. The entry "analogy" in the index (542–43) provides the page numbers to the extended discussion. Cf. also his work on this topic in "Patterns of Similarity: Part and Whole in Biblical Composition: A Literary Text! Problems in the Poetics and Interpretation of Biblical Narrative" [Hebrew and with Manakhem Perry], *Hasifrut* 2 (1970): esp. 633–37; "Delicate Balance in the Story of the Rape of Dinah: Biblical Narrative and the Rhetoric of the Narrative Text," *Hasifrut* 4 (1973): esp. 228–30. For other views, see, Wallace Stevens, "Effects of Analogy," *YR* 75 (1986): 255–70, and L. Alonso-Schökel, "Erzählkunst im Buche der Richter," *Bib* 42 (1961): 143–72.

40. Earlier, the younger brother had said to the wife, "You are like a mother to me, and your husband is like a father to me" ("The Story of the Two Brothers," in Pritchard, *Ancient*, 24).

41. Pritchard, *Ancient*, 76, 77, 82, 83, 87, 88 and 95.

42. Cf. Leslie Allen's observation above in n. 21 of chapter 4.

Chapter 6: Jonah and Poetry

1. *Njal's Saga*, trans. Magnus Magnusson and Hermann Palsson (Harmondsworth: Penguin Books, 1987), 171, 173, and 193.

2. James Kugel, *The Idea of Biblical Poetry: Parallelism and Its History* (New Haven and London: Yale University Press, 1981), 61, 63, 69, 85, and 94.

3. For mixed reviews, see, Baruch Halpern, *JR* 65 (1985): 118–20; Daniel Grossberg, *BTB* 12 (1982): 95–96; Patrick Miller, *Theology Today* 39 (1982): 331–34; Stephen A. Geller, *JBL* 102 (1983): 625–26. On the favorable side, see Calvin S. Brown *CompLit* 34 (1982): 361, and, for the most critical of all, James Barr, *TLS* (December 25, 1981): 1506.

4. Kugel, *Idea*, 88.

5. Jerome T. Walsh, "Jonah 2, 3–10: A Rhetorical Critical Study," *Bib* 63 (1982): 219–29; Duane L. Christensen, "The Song of Jonah: A Metrical Analysis," *JBL* 104 (1985): 217–31; Frank M. Cross, "Studies in the Structure of Hebrew Verse: The Prosody of the Psalm of Jonah," in *The Quest for the Kingdom of God: Studies in Honor of George E. Mendenhall*, edited by H. B. Huffmon, F. A. Spina, A. R. W. Green (Winona Lake, Indiana: Eisenbrauns, 1983), 159–67. I have intentionally looked outside the commentaries for what appears to be more focused discussions. Additionally, I have sought to focus on articles from a restricted period of time to avoid "stacking the deck" with representative examples from earlier centuries to the modern era. (See for example, E. Sievers, *Metrische Studien* [Leipzig: Teubner, 1901], 482–85 who included the initial two chapters of Jonah in his metrical analysis of the book and Wilhelm Erbt, *Elia, Elisa, Jona. Ein Beitrag zur Geschichte des IX. und VIII. Jahrhunderts* [Leipzig: Eduard Pfeiffer, 1907], 48–49 who divided the book into two separate literary sources different from the distinction today.) In addition to the research on this topic in the commentaries, mention should also be made of Landes's comments (George M. Landes, "The Kerygma of the Book of Jonah: The Contextual Interpretation of the Jonah Psalm," *Int* 21 [1967]: 3–31, esp. 6, 15–21) which relate primarily to structure and parallelism, and Peter Weimar, "Jonapsalm und Jonaerzählung," *BZ* 28 (1984): esp. 52–63.

6. These selected quotes are from Walsh, "Jonah 2," 219, 220, n. 2, and p. 221, n. 4.

7. Walsh, "Jonah 2," 221.

8. See, Masako K. Hiraga, "Eternal Stillness: A Linguistic Journey to Basho's Haiku about the Cicada," *Poetics Today* 8 (1987): 5–18.

9. Cross's justification for deletions such as the conjunction on נהר ("river") in vs. 4 is a serious mistake which reveals his tendency to arrange the text in such a way so that the pattern fits the argument. Cross writes, "the conjunction beginning colon 6 [vs. 4] is to be suppressed in view

of its rarity elsewhere in the poem in this position, and the notorious tendency for its introduction in the course of textual transmission" (p. 162; the exact form of וּנָהָר ["and a river"] occurs also in Gen. 2:10; Isa. 19:5; and Job 14:11), and elsewhere, "one suspects that the original reading of the . . ." (p. 161).

10. Cross, "Studies," 166.

11. Benjamin Hrushovski, "Prosody, Hebrew," *EJ*, vol. 13, edited by Cecil Roth (Jerusalem: Keter Publishing House, 1971), 1195–1203. Perhaps some significance is to be attached to the fact that this nonbiblical scholar, who is a leading authority in the area of comparative literature, has been able to articulate the major principles of biblical verse in such a clear and concise fashion. In what follows, I also draw insight from Adele Berlin's book, *The Dynamics of Biblical Parallelism* (Bloomington: Indiana University Press, 1985).

It is discouraging to find Robert Lowth quoted and credited with promoting the study of parallelism to a place of prominence in biblical studies *and* to have Hrushovski's insight completely ignored in almost all of the recent discussions in major books on biblical poetry, as for example, Kugel, *Idea*; M. O'Connor, *Hebrew Verse Structure* (Winona Lake, Indiana: Eisenbrauns, 1980); W. G. E. Watson, *Classical Hebrew Poetry: A Guide to its Techniques*, *JSOT* Supplement Series 26 (Sheffield: JSOT, 1983). I agree with Robert Alter's two observations about Hrushovski's article: "extraordinary compact paragraphs on biblical versification . . . [offering] an account of the system that seems to me thoroughly convincing because of its elegant simplicity and its lack of strain" (*The Art of Biblical Poetry* [New York: Basic Books, 1985], 8) and "in a few packed paragraphs, Hrushovski manages to cut through generations of confusion and to offer a general account of biblical prosody at once plausible and elegantly simple, avoiding the far fetched structures and the strained terminology of his predecessors" (*The Art of Biblical Narrative* [New York: Basic Books, 1981], 14–15). Further support for Hrushovski's views, which, along with Adele Berlin's book (*Dynamics*), serve as a base in the discussion below, may also be found indirectly in David Noel Freedman's admirably candid admission about his experience as a scholar specializing in the study of biblical poetry: "I have tried more complex methods of counting, distinguishing between long and short vowels, and even adding in consonants in order to secure an exact calculation of the time-span of a poetic unit. For the most part, I think it has been wasted effort . . ." (David Noel Freedman, "Pottery, Poetry, and Prophecy: An Essay on Biblical Poetry," *JBL* 96 [1977]: 12).

12. "Versets" is Hrushovski's term, which Robert Alter adopts for the basic syntactical unit commonly designated as hemistich or colon. I have retained "versets" as the designation in the disussion on Jonah 2:3–10 below, though I had not made the connection of cola and colon to

intestinal organs and soft drinks before Robert Alter pointed it out (Alter, *Poetry*, 9).

13. The 3 plus 2 stress pattern is frequently noted, as for example in the standard commentaries and Walsh, "Jonah, 2," 220.

14. Alter, *Poetry*, 9.

15. George Buchanan Gray, *The Forms of Hebrew Poetry* (London: Hodder & Stoughton, 1915), 49–52.

16. Robert Alter uses most of these symbols in *Poetry*, e.g., p. 29. I have altered them slightly for the discussion of Jonah 2:3–10. George M. Landes has called my attention to problems associated with a few of these designations. Because of the rich imagery, it is difficult (not to mention distracting) to assign such symbols to individual lines. Other observations than those presented above (such as the secondary quality of complementariness in lines 6 and 11) might also be made, but in the interest of clarity they have been omitted here.

17. In vs. 3 of chapter 1, for example, Jonah "arises," "flees," "goes down," "finds a ship," and "goes down in it."

18. Ps. 103:10 contains a negative particle-prepositional phrase-verb-preposition sequence which is matched exactly in the corresponding verset.

19. Landes, "The Kerygma," 8, n. 22.

20. Jack Sasson's comments on Jonah 2 became available after I had written these statements regarding a shift in person. I agree with his point that "this shift in voice is part of the poet's arsenal" (*Jonah: A New Translation with Introduction, Commentary, and Interpretation*, AB [New York: Doubleday, 1990], 173).

21. The literary examples are from R. R. K. Hartman and F. C. Stork, *Dictionary of Language and Linguistics* (London: Applied Science Publishers, 1972), 9, 22, 49.

22. Roman Jakobson, "Closing Statement: Linguistics and Poetics," in *Style in Language*, edited by Thomas A. Sebeok (Cambridge: MIT Press, 1960), 371. See also, Benjamin Hrushovski's discussions in "The Meaning of Sound Patterns in Poetry: An Interaction Theory," *Poetics Today* 2 (1980): 39–56, and "Do Sounds Have Meaning? The Problem of Expressiveness of Sound Patterns in Poetry" [Hebrew], *Hasifrut* 1 (1968): 410–20.

23. James Muilenburg, "Poetry," *EJ*, vol. 13, edited by Cecil Roth (Jerusalem: Keter Publishing House, 1971), 680.

24. Cf. n. 16 in Chapter 4, "Jonah and the Reading Process."

25. See, P. Kyle McCarter's illuminating discussion of the imagery in Jonah 2 along with Pss. 18 (2 Sam. 22), 66, and 69 under the rubric of "river ordeal" in "The River Ordeal in Israelite Literature," *HTR* 66 (1973): 403–12.

26. Jack Sasson, relying on figures supplied by David Noel Freedman, writes, "In the case that immediately interests us, Jonah's psalm, there are 3

such particles in a poem of 81 words (3.7 percent), while there are 93 such particles in the 608 words of narrative (15.3 percent). These percentages compare favorably with what obtains in other segments of Scripture" (*Jonah*, 162). Cf. also F. Anderson and A. Forbes, "Prose Particle' Count in the Hebrew Bible," in *The Word of the Lord Shall Go Forth: Essays in Honor of David Noel Freedman in Celebration of His Sixtieth Birthday*, edited by Carol Meyers and M. O'Connor (Winona Lake, Indiana: Eisenbrauns, 1983), 165–83 and David Noel Freedman, "Prose Particles in the Poetry of the Primary History," in *Biblical and Related Studies Presented to Samuel Iwry*, edited by Ann Kort and Scott Morschauser (Winona Lake, Indiana: Eisenbrauns, 1985), 49–61.

27. According to Moshe Greenberg, praying and prayers are mentioned "about 140 times" outside of the Psalter and more than half of these lack the verbal formulations (*Biblical Prose Prayer as a Window to the Popular Religion of Ancient Israel* [Berkeley and Los Angeles: University of California Press, 1983], 7 and 59, n. 3).

28. The quotation is taken from Robert Polzin (*Moses and the Deuteronomist: A Literary Study of Deuteronomic History* [New York: Seabury, 1980], 20) who cites Mikhail Bakhtin's *Problems of Dostoevsky's Poetics* (Ann Arbor, Ardis Pubs., 1973).

Chapter 7: Representation of the Inner Life: A Case for Inside Views

1. Elias Bickerman, "Les deux erreurs du prophète Jonas," *RHPR* 45 (1965): 232.

2. "There was a commentator who said the number of books and commentaries that have been written about this small book, the book of Jonah, exceeds the number of verses within the book itself" (Zalman Shazar, "The Book of Jonah" [Hebrew], *BMik* 47 (1971): 432).

3. The following observations about the consensus must be made with some qualification. Benoit Trépanier concludes that "we are in the presence of a historical narrative" ("The Story of Jonas," *CBQ* 13 [1951]: 15). Cf. also John C. Holbert's n. 1 in "'Deliverance Belongs to Yahweh!': Satire in the Book of Jonah," *JSOT* 21 (1981): 75: "Let the reader not think, however, that the historical question is not still asked. G. C. Aalders in *The Problem of the Book of Jonah* (London) in 1948 was still seeking to defend the history of nearly all particulars. Elias Bickerman in his stimulating analysis of Jonah in *Four Strange Books of the Bible* (New York: 1967) notes (p. 4) that in 1956 one Catholic encyclopedia had accepted this view and in 1962 a Protestant biblical dictionary had also. See even more recently the comments of J. H. Stek in 'The Meaning of the Book of Jonah,' *CTJ* 4 (1969): 23–50."

4. James Ackerman, "Jonah" in *The Literary Guide to the Bible*, edited by Robert Alter and Frank Kermode (Cambridge: Harvard University Press, 1987), 234.

5. Adele Berlin, "A Rejoinder to John A. Miles, Jr., with Some Observations on the Nature of Prophecy," *JQR* 66 (1975): 230. Chaim Lewis notes that "we cannot but wonder why the book of Jonah lodges among the minor prophets" in "Jonah—A Parable for Our Time," *Judaism* 21 (1972): 160, and James D. Smart's conclusion is similar to many offered in the standard commentaries: "the book of Jonah stands fifth among the books of the twelve minor prophets, but it is quickly apparent to the reader that it is of a nature very different from the others" (James D. Smart, "The Book of Jonah," *IB*, vol. 6 [Nashville: Abingdon, 1956], 871).

6. Carl A. Keller, "Jonas. Le portrait d'un prophète," *TZ* 21 (1965): 329–40.

7. André Feuillet, "Les sources du livre de Jonas," *RB* 54 (1947): 161–86.

8. Keller, "Jonas," 337. Translation: There, he [Jonah] enjoys a privileged status. The sailors pray fervently and they offer sacrifices—but God rests mute. The inhabitants of Nineveh "believe" and they give way to all manifestations of anguish, of submission, of a restrained hope—God sees them, but he does not reveal himself. Jonah prays—and God answers him. Jonah desires to die—God makes a plant grow that consoles him. Jonah is exasperated by the disappearance of the plant—God speaks to him, at length, with an untiring solicitude. Jonah alone can hear God, Jonah alone is initiated in the mysteries of divine love: Jonah is the unique intermediary between God and men. Jonah alone "knows" God because it is to him alone that God makes himself known.

9. Cf. Robert Alter's comment about the narrator, "At times he may choose to make us wonder but he never misleads us" in *The Art of Biblical Narrative* (New York: Basic Books, 1981), 184 and also Meir Sternberg's treatment in *The Poetics of Biblical Narrative: Ideological Literature and the Drama of Reading* (Bloomington: Indiana University Press, 1985), 33, 51, 59–85, 90, 116–18, 126, 130–31, 178–79, 181–85, 234–35, 245–46, 321, 327, 345–46, 379–82, 386, 389, 395–401, 410–15, 430, 453–55, 475–77, 502, 504. For a different perspective and critical assessment of Sternberg's reading, see Danna Nolan Fewell and David M. Gunn, "Tipping the Balance: Sternberg's Reader and the Rape of Dinah," *JBL* 110 (1991): 193–211. For observations about the narrator's reliability in the New Testament, see R. Alan Culpepper, *Anatomy of the Fourth Gospel* (Philadelphia: Fortress Press, 1984), 19.

10. Robert Scholes and Robert Kellogg, *The Nature of Narrative* (Oxford, London, New York: Oxford University Press, 1966), 166. Cf. also Wayne Booth's observation of this development among New Testament writers:

"For us it may seem strange that the writers of the Gospels would claim so much knowledge of what Christ is feeling and thinking. 'Moved with pity, he stretched out his hand and touched him' (Mark 1:41)" in *The Rhetoric of Fiction* (Chicago and London: University of Chicago Press, 1983), 18, n. 10.

11. Scholes and Kellogg, *Nature*, 164, 165, 166, and 175. Meir Sternberg also points to weaknesses in this view in "Between the Truth and the Whole Truth in Biblical Narrative: The Rendering of the Inner Life by Telescoped Inside View and Interior Monologue" (Hebrew), *Hasifrut* 29 (1979): 110, 119, 120, 135, and 141 as well as in *Poetics*, 247 and 477.

12. See for example, Erich Auerbach's discussion of Virginia Woolf's *To the Lighthouse*, Marcel Proust's *A la recherche du temps perdu*, and James Joyce's, *Ulysses* in chapter 20, "The Brown Stocking," of *Mimesis: The Representation of Reality in Western Literature*, translated by Willard R. Trask (Princeton: Princeton University Press, 1974), 525–53.

13. In Genesis, for example, a preliminary list of inside views would include the following: 2:25; 3:1; 3:5; 3:6; 3:7; 4:4–5; 6:2; 6:5; 6:6; 6:8; 6:11; 6:12; 7:1; 7:11; 8:20; 13:10; 16:4; 18:12; 18:17–20; 19:14; 19:33; 19:35; 20:11; 21:9; 21:16; 24:67; 25:28; 26:7 (2x); 27:23; 27:41 (2x); 28:8 29:18; 29:20; 29:30; 31:2; 31:32; 32:8; 32:20; 34:3; 34:7; 34:13; 34:18; 34:19; 37:3; 37:4; 37:5; 37:8; 37:11; 37:33; 38:11; 38:14; 38:15; 39:19; 40:23; 42:4; 42:7; 42:23; 42:35; 43:18; 43:30; 45:1 and 48:10.

  Meir Sternberg's article ("Between the Truth") contains numerous examples of "telescoped inside views" and interior monologue including: Gen. 17:17; 19:33; 19:35; 25:28; 25:34; 34:7; 34:18; 39:7; Exod. 2:12; 4:14; 11:8; Num. 12:3; Judg. 8:20; 15:2; 1 Sam. 18:8, 9, 12; 20:30; 20:34; 25:3; 25:36; 26:12; 2 Sam. 3:11, 4:1, 12:19; 13:1–3; 13:15; 24:1; 1 Kings 20:43; 2 Kings 6:11; 10:4; 25:26; Esther 1:12; 2:15; 2:17; 7:6; 7:7; Neh. 4:1. For other discussions see also Meir Sternberg, "Language, World and Perspective in Biblical Narrative Art: Free Indirect Discourse and Modes of Covert Penetration" (Hebrew), *Hasifrut* 32 (1983): 88–131, esp. 102–106 and 109–14; Meir Sternberg, "The World from the Addressee's Viewpoint: Reception as Representation, Dialogue as Monologue," *Style* 20 (1986): 295–318; Adele Berlin, *Poetics and Interpretation of Biblical Narrative* (Sheffield: Almond Press, 1983), 37–38, 61–62; Shimon Bar Efrat, *The Art of the Biblical Story* (Hebrew) (Tel Aviv: Sifriat Hapoalim, 1979), 83–88.

14. The word also appears three or more times in the individual books of Joel, Zephaniah, Haggai, Zechariah, and Malachi and frequently in short, isolated passages in Isaiah and Jeremiah. See for example Isa. 8:12 (twice) and 8:13; Isa. 41:5, 10, 13, 14; Jer. 32:21, 39, 40 and Jer. 42:11 (twice) and 42:16.

15. The editors of BHK and BHS suggest that "unto the Lord" is an

"addition," one of their frequent observations which is made without support from any text tradition. Why would an editor or scribe be *more* likely to add this than the author?

16. The literal translation is "for the conversation was not heard." When rendered in the active voice, the subject is implied as translated above.

17. "Just as on the tempestuous ship the prophet preferred to be thrown overboard into the sea rather than to call upon his God, thus in the presence of the Lord's pardon in Nineveh he once again preferred to die rather than to admit to the righteousness of the Lord . . ." (Uriel Simon, "The Book of Jonah," in *Isaac Leo Seeligmann Volume: Essays on the Bible and the Ancient World*, vol. 2, edited by Alexander Rofé and Yair Zakovitch [Jerusalem: E. Rubinstein Publishing House, 1983], 301).

18. H. W. Wolff, *Obadiah and Jonah*, translated by Margaret Kohl (Minneapolis: Augsburg, 1986), 118.

19. S. D. F. Goitein, "Some Observations on Jonah," *JPOS* 17 (1937): 68; Leslie C. Allen, *The Books of Joel, Obadiah, Jonah and Micah*, NICOT (Grand Rapids: Eerdmans, 1976), 211; André and Pierre-Emmanuel Lacocque, *The Jonah Complex* (Atlanta: John Knox Press, 1981), 47.

20. André Feuillet, "Le sens du livre de Jonas," *RB* 54 (1947): 344. Translation: Jonah, who moreover did not doubt the divine call for a single instant, . . . knows perfectly well the storm is due to his resistance and for this reason he himself asks that they throw him into the sea. Jack Sasson's position is similar. He offers insight into the word נשׂא ("lift up," vs. 12) which appears at first glance to be "hardly necessary;" after all, the sailors to not need instructions about how to get Jonah into the sea. Sasson discusses this word and Jonah's instructions to the sailors at the narrative, psychological, and semantic levels (pp. 124–25).

21. Smart, "The Book," 883–84. Other examples of this general view may be found in George M. Landes, "The Kerygma of the Book of Jonah," *Int* 21 (1967): 22–23; L. H. Brockington, "Jonah," in *Peake's Commentary on the Bible*, ed. Matthew Black and H. H. Rowley (London: Thomas Nelson, 1962), 628; J. Ellul, *The Judgment of Jonah*, translated by G. W. Bromiley (Grand Rapids: Eerdmans, 1971), 36; Grace I. Emmerson, "Another Look at the Book of Jonah," *ExpT* 88 (1976–1977): 86–87.

22. For bibliographies on the discussion of the prayers in chapter 2, see esp. James Ackerman, "Satire and Symbolism in the Song of Jonah," in *Traditions in Transformation: Turning Points in Biblical Faith*, edited by Baruch Halpern and Jon D. Levenson (Winona Lake, Ind.: Eisenbrauns, 1981), 214, n. 1 and Jerome T. Walsh, "Jonah 2, 3–10: A Rhetorical Critical Study," *Bib* 63 (1982): 219, n. 1.

23. Cf. n. 27 in chapter 5, "The Multiple Reports of Prayer in Jonah."

24. James D. Smart suggests that Jonah represents Israel and that the great fish symbolizes the exile ("The Book," 874). Another allegorical interpretation may be found in P. R. Ackroyd, *Exile and Restoration: A Study*

of Hebrew Thought of the Sixth Century B.C. (London: SCM, 1968), 244. Terence E. Fretheim reaches a similar conclusion, though with some reservation, in *The Message of Jonah: A Theological Commentary* (Minneapolis: Augsburg, 1977), 22, 30–31.

25. as James Ackerman does. While some may argue that the psalm does not necessarily move the entire work "in the direction of satire and compel an ironic reading throughout" (Ackerman, "Satire," 216), Ackerman certainly succeeds in showing that "the song of Jonah merits our special attention, because it is unusual in its rhetorical flourishes, depicting a part of the prophet's state of mind that is not elsewhere so extensively expressed" (p. 244).

26. as George M. Landes has suggested, "The Jonah Psalm (Jon. 2:3–10) Revisited" in a paper delivered at the annual SBL meeting in Dallas, Texas, December, 1983.

27. Gabriël H. Cohn, *Das Buch Jona im Lichte der biblischen Erzählkunst* (Assen: Van Gorcum, 1969), 17. Translation: In principle, this addition causes an emphasis on the expression. . . . Thus the G. [LXX] translates, "an especially large city." In our translation we have, however, allowed the relationship of God to the city to resonate, as in the T[argum].

28. "Any word desiring intensification may be joined to אֵל as a means of intensification." This reference to Kimchi is made by D. Winton Thomas, "A Consideration of Some Unusual Ways of Expressing the Superlative in Hebrew," *VT* 3 (1953): 211. Thomas includes Jonah 3:3 along with Gen. 23:6, 30:8; Ex. 9:28; 1 Sam. 14:15; Pss. 36:7; 80:11, and Job 1:16 to illustrate how divine names are used to express the superlative. For an earlier, opposing view, see F. Prat, "Le nom divin est-il intensif en hébreu?" *RB* 10 (1901): 497–511.

29. Sasson, *Jonah*, 260.

30. The history of this interpretation has been well summarized by Uriel Simon, "The Book," 291–98.

31. This view has been expressed and discussed at length both by Ronald E. Clements ("The Purpose of the Book of Jonah," VTSup 28 [1974]: 16–28) and Uriel Simon: "In [the Ninevite] reaction upon this there is no hint of collective-international treatment, as there is no hint of individual or collective hatred. . . . And also Jonah, from his side, is far from being a hater of foreigners" (Uriel Simon, "The Book," 293). See also, Cohn, *Das Buch*, 99, n. 4.

32. Notice their confession earlier in the chapter: "they cried out each to his god(s)" [vs. 5], and the chief sailor commands Jonah, "Call upon your god(s)." He hopes that "the god(s)" will not destroy them [vs. 6].

33. In the discussion that follows, I attempt to explain why I agree with the claim that chapter 4 is the climax to this story. See for example, Simon, "The Book of Jonah" (Hebrew), esp. 298, who reaches a similar conclusion, though by a completely different route, as he examines the

structure of the book in order to emphasize the way in which *ḥesed* is established as the central theme. The importance of Jonah 4 at the ideological level is discussed in chapter 9. For a different perspective, see Feuillet, "Le sens," 342: "C'est à la prédication de Jonas dans Ninive que l'auteur veut en venir, et le chapitre III est donc le centre de l'ouvrage." Translation: It is the preaching of Jonah in Nineveh that the author seeks to highlight, and chapter 3 is therefore the center of the work.

34. Biblische Studien 47 (Neukirchen: Neukirchener, 1965), 38–40. Cf. also G. I. Davies, "The Uses of R'' Qal and the Meaning of Jonah IV 1," *VT* 27 (1977): 105.

35. Gen. 21:12; 2 Sam. 11:25; 1 Chr. 21:7; Neh. 2:10; 13:8; and with some qualification also in Gen. 48:17.

36. For examples and a discussion of the strengthening of a verbal idea with a cognate substantive see GKC, §117, p–q.

37. The "king" in Hos. 7:3 and "he" in Hab. 1:15.

38. See their quotation and the comments at n. 11 above.

39. Of course, the word "rhetoric" may carry a negative connotation in American English. I am using the word here in the positive sense to refer to the persuasive aspect of communication.

40. Sheldon Blank, "'Doest Thou Well to be Angry?' A Study in Self-Pity," *HUCA* 26 (1955): 30.

41. Ezek. 20:17; Hans Walter Wolff indicates that only on this one occasion does the Bible reveal that the Lord has had "compassion" with the word חום (*Obadiah*, 174).

42. An example of a similar strategy may also be found in the contrasting representation among characters in *Emma* where Jane Austen refrains from offering extended inside views of Jane Fairfax thus allowing sympathy to build for Emma. Cf. Wayne C. Booth's discussion in *Rhetoric*, 248–49.

43. Cf. n. 11 above.

44. This observation is made with reference to the Book of the Twelve. Jonah is frequently compared to Elijah (esp. 1 Kings 17–19) and Jeremiah (esp. Jer. 18 and Jer. 36). See for e.g. Trépanier, "The Story," 9, 10, and 14; Lacocque, *Complex*, 5, 6, 10, and 11; Cohn, *Das Buch*, 81; Cohn, "Jonah, the Book of," in *EJ*, vol. 10, edited by Cecil Roth (Jerusalem: Keter Publishing House, 1971), 173; André Feuillet, "Les sources," 168–69 and 171–76; Ackerman, "Satire," 223, n. 18; Ackerman, "Jonah," 239; Hans Walter Wolff, *Obadja und Jona* BKAT 14/3 (Neukirchen: Neukirchener, 1977), 60, 66, 75, 78, 80, 120, 126, 127, 129, 130, 131, 141, and 143; Wolff, *Studien*, 5 and 6; and Keller, "Jonas," 331, 336, 338, and 339. None of these sources offers a discussion of the inside views found, for example, in 1 Kings 17:17; 17:22; 18:3; 18:7; 19:3; 19:4; 19:13; 19:21; Jer. 18:4; 19:5–10; 19:12; or 19:23. A subsequent investi-

gation which is beyond the scope of this study might explore the relationship of Jonah to Jeremiah and Elijah in this context.

45. John A. Miles, "Laughing at the Bible: Jonah as Parody," *JQR* 65 (1975): 168–81.

46. Judson Mather ("The Comic Art of the Book of Jonah," *Soundings* 65 [1982]: 280–91) interprets the book as "a rich comic invention" consisting of "the devices of burlesque and parody" (p. 280).

47. Goitein, "Some Observations," 74.

Chapter 8: The Ideological Plane: Summary and Conclusion

1. Boris Uspensky, *A Poetics of Composition: The Structure of the Artistic Text and Typology of a Compositional Form*, trans. Valentina Zavarin and Susan Wittig (Berkeley: University of California Press, 1973).

2. Uspensky, *A Poetics*, 8.

3. Meir Sternberg, *The Poetics of Biblical Narrative: Ideological Literature and the Drama of Reading* (Bloomington: Indiana University Press), 75.

4. By including God's intimate name in 1:16, the author grants the sailors their own recognition of God's character.

5. Mikhail Bakhtin, *Problems of Dostoevsky's Poetics*, translated by Caryl Emerson (Minneapolis: University of Minnesota Press, 1984), 84.

6. Hans Walter Wolff, *Obadiah and Jonah*, translated by Margaret Kohl (Minneapolis: Augsburg, 1986), 175. Cf. also the comments of Jack M. Sasson, *Jonah: A New Translation with Introduction, Commentary, and Interpretation*, AB (New York: Doubleday, 1990), 318.

7. Leslie C. Allen, *The Books of Joel, Obadiah, Jonah, and Micah*, NICOT, vol. 5 (Grand Rapids: Eerdmans, 1975), 234.

8. Wolff, *Obadiah*, 171.

9. Sternberg, *Poetics*, 37.

10. Uspensky, *A Poetics*, 10.

11. Twelve questions (1:6; 1:8 (4x); 1:10, 1:11; 3:9; 4:4; 4:2; 4:9; 4:11) and possibly thirteen (1:8a) or fourteen (2:5b) are invoked in Jonah. See the discussion on the status of 1:8a and 2:5b in Sasson, *Jonah*, 112–15 and 179–82.

12. Every character who addresses Jonah asks him at least one question—the captain of the sailors in 1:6; the sailors in 1:8,10,11; and the Lord in 4:4,9,11. In addition, the king asks a question in 3:9 and Jonah asks the Lord a question in 4:2.

13. The captain's speech and the speech of the sailors in 1:10 are both introduced with מַה. מַה is usually translated as an interrogative pronoun (what?), but may also be understood as an expression of surprise (cf. the comments of Wolff, *Obadiah*, 116).

Bibliography

Books and Dissertations

Ackroyd, Peter R. *Exile and Restoration: A Study of Hebrew Thought of the Sixth Century B.C.* London: SCM Press, 1968.

Allen, Leslie C. *The Books of Joel, Obadiah, Jonah, and Micah.* New International Commentary on the Old Testament, vol. 5, Grand Rapids: Eerdmans, 1975.

Alter, Robert. *The Art of Biblical Narrative.* New York: Basic Books, 1981.

———. *The Art of Biblical Poetry.* New York: Basic Books, 1985.

Aristotle. *Poetics.* Translated by Leon Golden and commentary by O. B. Hardison, Jr. Englewood Cliffs, N.J.: Prentice-Hall, 1968.

Auerbach, Erich. *Mimesis: The Representation of Reality in Western Literature.* Translated by Willard R. Trask. Princeton: Princeton University Press, 1974.

Bach, Alice, ed. *The Pleasure of Her Text: Feminist Readings of Biblical and Historical Texts.* Philadelphia: Trinity Press International, 1990.

Bakhtin, Mikhail. *Problems of Dostoevsky's Poetics.* Translated by Caryl Emerson. Minneapolis: University of Minnesota Press, 1984.

Bar Efrat, Simon. *The Art of the Biblical Story* (Hebrew). Tel Aviv: Sifriat Hapoalim, 1979.

Barton, John. *Reading the Old Testament: Method in Biblical Study.* Philadelphia: Westminster Press, 1984.

Baudissin, Wolf Wilhelm Grafen. *Einleitung in die Bücher des Alten Testamentes.* Leipzig: S. Hirzel, 1901.

Bentzen, Aage. *Introduction to the Old Testament,* vol. 2. Copenhagen: G. E. C. Gads, 1949.

Berlin, Adele. *The Dynamics of Biblical Parallelism.* Bloomington: Indiana University Press, 1985.

———. *Poetics and Interpretation of Biblical Narrative.* Sheffield, England: Almond Press, 1983.

Bewer, Julius A. *The Book of the Twelve Prophets.* The International Critical Commentary. Edinburgh: T. & T. Clark, 1961.

Bickerman, Elias. *Four Strange Books of the Bible: Jonah, Daniel, Koheleth, Esther.* New York: Schocken, 1967.

Blake, William, and John Donne. *The Complete Poetry and Selected Prose of John Donne and the Complete Poetry of William Blake.* New York: The Modern Library, 1941.

Booth, Wayne. *The Rhetoric of Fiction.* Chicago and London: University of Chicago Press, 1983.

Brown, Francis, S. R. Driver, and Charles A. Briggs, eds. *A Hebrew and English Lexicon of the Old Testament.* Oxford: Clarendon Press, 1953.

Calvin, John. *Commentaries on the Twelve Minor Prophets,* vol. 3. Translated by John Owen. Grand Rapids: Eerdmans, 1950.

Childs, Brevard. *Introduction to the Old Testament as Scripture.* Philadelphia: Fortress Press, 1979.

Cohn, Gabriël H. *Das Buch Jona im Lichte der biblischen Erzählkunst,* Assen: Van Gorcum, 1969.

Corvin, Jack White. "A Stylistic and Functional Study of the Prose Prayers in the Historical Narratives of the Old Testament." Ph.D. dissertation, Emory University, 1972.

Crane, Robert S. *The Language of Criticism and the Structure of Poetry.* Toronto: University of Toronto Press, 1953.

Croce, Benedetto. *Aesthetic.* Translated by Douglas Ainslie. London: Macmillan and Co., 1922.

Culler, Jonathan. *The Pursuit of Signs: Semiotics, Literature, Deconstruction.* Ithaca: Cornell University Press, 1981.

———. *Structuralist Poetics: Structuralism, Linguistics, and the Study of Literature.* Ithaca: Cornell University Press, 1975.

Culpepper, R. Alan. *Anatomy of the Fourth Gospel.* Philadelphia: Fortress Press, 1984.

Dahood, Mitchell. *Psalms I:1–50.* Anchor Bible, vol. 16. Garden City: Doubleday, 1966.

De Wette, Wilhelm Martin Leberecht. *A Critical and Historical Introduction to the Canonical Scriptures of the Old Testament.* Translated by Theodore Parker. Boston: Charles C. Little and James Brown, 1843.

Dickens, Charles. *Oliver Twist.* New York: Washington Square Press, 1970.

Driver, Samuel R. *A Treatise on the Use of the Tenses in Hebrew.* Oxford: The Clarendon Press, 1892.

Duke, Paul. *Irony in the Fourth Gospel.* Atlanta: John Knox Press, 1985.

Eissfeldt, Otto. *The Old Testament: An Introduction.* Translated by Peter R. Ackroyd. New York: Harper & Row, 1965.

Ellul, Jacques. *The Judgment of Jonah.* Translated by G. W. Bromiley. Grand Rapids: Eerdmans, 1971.

Erbt, Wilhelm. *Elia, Elisa, Jona. Ein Beitrag zur Geschichte des IX. und VIII. Jahrhunderts.* Leipzig: Eduard Pfeiffer, 1907.

Fink, S. J., and Peter Edward. "A Poetics of Christian Sacraments: A Dialogue with Paul Ricoeur." Ph.D. dissertation, Emory University, 1976.

Fiorenza, Elisabeth Schüssler. *In Memory of Her: A Feminist Theological Reconstruction of Christian Origins.* New York: Crossroad, 1983.

Fish, Stanley. *Is There a Text in This Class? The Authority of Interpretive Communities.* Cambridge: Harvard University Press, 1980.

Frei, Hans. *The Eclipse of Biblical Narrative: A Study in Eighteenth and*

Nineteenth Century Hermeneutics. New Haven and London: Yale University Press, 1974.

Fretheim, Terence E. *The Message of Jonah: A Theological Commentary.* Minneapolis: Augsburg Press, 1977.

Friedrichsen, P. *Kritische Uebersicht der verschiedenen Ansichten von dem Buch Jonas.* Leipzig: Friedr. Christ. Wilh. Vogel, 1841.

Funk, Robert. *The Poetics of Biblical Narrative.* Sonoma, California: Polebridge Press, 1988.

Gadamar, Hans-Georg. *Truth and Method.* New York: Crossroad, 1985.

Gimbutas, Marija. *The Language of the Goddess.* San Francisco: HarperCollins, 1989.

Glueck, N. *Deities and Dolphins.* New York: Farrar, Straus and Giroux, 1965.

Gordon, Alex R. *The Prophets of the Old Testament.* London: Hodder & Stoughton, 1916.

Gray, George Buchanan. *The Forms of Hebrew Poetry.* London: Hodder & Stoughton, 1915.

Greenberg, Moshe. *Biblical Prose Prayer as a Window to the Popular Religion of Ancient Israel.* Berkeley and Los Angeles: University of California Press, 1983.

Hartman, R. R. K., and F. C. Stork. *Dictionary of Language and Linguistics.* London: Applied Science Publishers, 1972.

Heine, Susanne. *Matriarchs, Goddesses, and Images of God: A Critique of a Feminist Theology.* Minneapolis: Augsburg, 1989.

Henshaw, Thomas. *The Latter Prophets.* London: George Allen & Unwin, 1958.

Holquist, Michael, ed., *The Dialogic Imagination: Four Essays by M. M. Bakhtin.* Austin and London: University of Texas Press, 1981.

Homer. *Iliad,* vol. 2 (Loeb Classical Library). Translated by A. T. Murray. Cambridge: Harvard University Press, 1939.

———. *The Iliad of Homer.* Translated by William Benjamin Smith and Walter Miller. New York: Macmillan, 1944.

———. *The Odyssey.* Translated by E. V. Rieu. Baltimore: Penguin Books, 1959.

Iser, Wolfgang. *The Implied Reader: Patterns of Communication in Prose Fiction from Bunyan to Beckett.* Baltimore: Johns Hopkins University Press, 1974.

Kautzsch, E., and A. E. Cowley, eds. *Gesenius' Hebrew Grammar.* 2d English ed. Oxford: Clarendon Press, 1910.

Koehler, Ludwig and Walter Baumgartner. *Lexicon in Veteris Testamenti Libros.* Leiden: E. J. Brill, 1958.

Kugel, James. *The Idea of Biblical Poetry: Parallelism and Its History.* New Haven and London: Yale University Press, 1981.

Lacocque, André, and Pierre-Emmanuel Lacocque. *The Jonah Complex.* Atlanta: John Knox Press, 1981.

Loades, Ann, ed. *Feminist Theology*. Louisville: Westminster/John Knox Press, 1990.

Lotman, Jurij. *The Structure of the Artistic Text*. Translated by Ronald Vroon. Ann Arbor: Michigan Slavic Contributions, 1977.

McFall, Leslie. *The Enigma of the Hebrew Verbal System*. Sheffield, England: Almond Press, 1982.

Magonet, Jonathan. *Form and Meaning: Studies in Literary Techniques in the Book of Jonah*, Beitrage zur biblischen Exegese und Theologie 2. Bern and Frankfurt: H. and P. Lang, 1976.

Mailloux, Steven. *Interpretive Conventions: The Reader in the Study of American Fiction*. Ithaca and London: Cornell University Press, 1982.

Metzger, Bruce M., Robert C. Dentan and Walter Harrelson. *The Making of the New Revised Standard Version of the Bible*. Grand Rapids: Eerdmans, 1991.

Miscall, Peter D. *1 Samuel: A Literary Reading*. Bloomington: Indiana University Press, 1986.

Njal's Saga. Translated by Magnus Magnusson and Hermann Palsson. Harmondsworth: Penguin Books, 1987.

O'Connor, M. *Hebrew Verse Structure*. Winona Lake, Indiana: Eisenbrauns, 1980.

Polzin, Robert. *Moses and the Deuteronomist: A Literary Study of the Deuteronomic History (Part One)*. New York: Seabury, 1980.

———. *Samuel and the Deuteronomist: A Literary Study of the Deuteronomic History (Part Two)*. San Francisco: Harper & Row, 1989.

Pritchard, James B., ed. *Ancient Near Eastern Texts Relating to the Old Testament*. Princeton: Princeton University Press, 1950.

von Rad, Gerhard. *Old Testament Theology*, vol. 2. Translated by D. M. G. Stalker. New York: Harper & Row, 1965.

Rimbach, James Allen. "Animal Imagery in the Old Testament: Some Aspects of Hebrew Poetics." Ph.D. dissertation, John Hopkins University, 1972.

Rimmon-Kenan, Shlomith. *Narrative Fiction: Contemporary Poetics*. London and New York: Methuen, 1983.

Rougé, Jean. *Ships and Fleets of the Ancient Mediterranean*. Translated by Susan Frazer. Middleton, Conn.: Wesleyan University Press, 1981.

Sandmel, Samuel. *The Hebrew Scriptures*. New York: Alfred A. Knopf, 1963.

Sasson, Jack M. *Jonah: A New Translation with Introduction, Commentary, and Interpretation*. The Anchor Bible. New York: Doubleday, 1990.

———. *Ruth: A New Translation with a Philological Commentary and a Formalist-Folklorist Interpretation*. Baltimore: Johns Hopkins University Press, 1979.

Schmidt, Hans. *Jona. Eine Untersuchung zur vergleichenden Religionsgeschichte*. Gottingen: Vandenhoeck & Ruprecht, 1907.

Schmidt, Ludwig. *"De Deo:" Studien zur Literarkritik und Theologie des Buches Jona, des Gesprächs zwischen Abraham und Jahwe in Gen 18:22f. und von Hi 1.* Berlin: Walter de Gruyter, 1976.

Scholes, Robert, and Robert Kellogg. *The Nature of Narrative.* Oxford, London, New York: Oxford University Press, 1966.

Sellin, E. *Introduction to the Old Testament.* New York: George H. Doran, 1923.

Shakespeare, William. "Julius Caesar." In *William Shakespeare: The Complete Works.* Edited by Alfred Harbage. New York: Viking Press, 1977.

Sievers, Eduard. *Metrische Studien.* Leipzig: Teubner, 1901.

Snaith, Norman H. *Notes on the Hebrew Text of the Book of Jonah.* London: Epworth, 1945.

Steinmann, Jean. *Le Livre de la Consolation d'Israël et les Prophètes du Retour de l'Exil.* Paris: Les Éditions du Cerf, 1960.

Sternberg, Meir. *Expositional Modes and Temporal Ordering in Fiction.* Baltimore and London: Johns Hopkins University Press, 1978.

———. *The Poetics of Biblical Narrative: Ideological Literature and the Drama of Reading.* Bloomington: Indiana University Press, 1985.

Steuernagel, D. Carl. *Lehrbuch der Einleitung in das Alte Testament.* Tübingen: J. C. B. Mohr, 1912.

Stuart, Douglas. *Hosea-Jonah.* Word Biblical Commentary, vol. 31. Waco: Word Books, 1987.

Suleiman, Susan R., and Ingre Crosman. *The Reader in the Text: Essays on Audience and Interpretation.* Princeton: Princeton University Press, 1980.

Trible, Phyllis. *God and the Rhetoric of Sexuality.* Philadelphia: Fortress Press, 1978.

———. "Studies in the Book of *Jonah*." Ph.D. dissertation, Columbia University, 1963.

Tromp, Nicholas J. *Primitive Conceptions of Death and the Nether World in the Old Testament.* Rome: Pontifical Biblical Institute, 1969.

Uspensky, Boris. *A Poetics of Composition: The Structure of the Artistic Text and Typology of a Composition.* Translated by Valentina Zavarin and Susan Wittig. Berkeley and Los Angeles: University of California, 1973.

Vanoni, Gottfried. *Das Buch Jona: Literar-und formkritische Untersuchung* (Arbeiten zu Text und Sprache im Alten Testament, 7) St. Ottilien: Eos Verlag, 1978.

Watson, Wilfred G. E. *Classical Hebrew Poetry: A Guide to its Techniques,* Journal for the Study of the Old Testament Supplement Series 26. Sheffield, England: Journal for the Study of the Old Testament, 1983.

Watts, John D. W. *The Books of Joel, Obadiah, Jonah, Nehemiah, Habakkuk, and Zephaniah.* The Cambridge Bible Commentary. Cambridge: Cambridge University Press, 1975.

Wendel, Adolf. *Das freie Laiengebet im vorexilischen Israel.* Leipzig: Ex Oriente Lux, 1932.

Witzenrath, Hagia. *Das Buch Jona: Eine Literatur-Wissenschaftliche Untersu-chung* (Arbeiten zu Text und Sprache im Alten Testament, 6) St. Ottilien: Eos Verlag, 1978.

Wolff, Hans Walter. *Obadiah and Jonah.* Translated by Margaret Kohl. Minneapolis: Augsburg, 1986.

———. *Obadja und Jona,* Biblischer Kommentar Altes Testament 14/3. Neukirchen-Vluyn: Neukirchener, 1977.

———. *Studien zum Jonabuch,* Biblische Studien 47. Nuekirchen-Vluyn: Neukirchener, 1965.

Wright, W. *The Book of Jonah in Four Semitic Versions: Chaldee, Syriac, Aethiopic, and Arabic with Corresponding Glossaries.* London: Williams and Norgate, 1857.

Articles and Parts of Books

Abramson, Glenda. "The Book of Jonah as a Literary and Dramatic Work." *Semitics* 5 (1977): 36–47.

Ackerman, James S. "Jonah." In *The Literary Guide to the Bible.* Edited by Robert Alter and Frank Kermode. Cambridge. Harvard University, 1987.

———. "Satire and Symbolism in the Song of Jonah." In *Traditions in Transformation: Turning Points in Biblical Faith.* Edited by Baruch Halpern and Jon D. Levenson. Winona Lake, Ind.: Eisenbrauns, 1981.

Albright, W. F. "Are the Ephod and the Teraphim Mentioned in Ugaritic Literature?" *Bulletin of the American Schools of Oriental Research* 83 (1941): 39–42.

Alonso-Schökel, L. "Erzählkunst im Buche der Richter." *Biblica* 42 (1961): 143–72.

Altieri, Charles. "The Hermeneutics of Literary Indeterminacy: A Dissent from the New Orthodoxy." *New Literary History* 10 (1978): 71–99.

Anderson, F. and A. Forbes. "Prose Particle' Count in the Hebrew Bible." In *The Word of the Lord Shall Go Forth: Essays in Honor of David Noel Freedman in Celebration of His Sixtieth Birthday.* Ed. Carol Meyers and M. O'Connor. Winona Lake, Indiana: Eisenbrauns, 1983.

Band, Arnold J. "Swallowing Jonah: The Eclipse of Parody." *Prooftexts* 10 (1990): 177–95.

Barr, James. Review of *The Idea of Biblical Poetry: Parallelism and Its History,* by James Kugel. *Times Literary Supplement* (December 25, 1981): 1506.

Berlin, Adele. "A Rejoinder to John A. Miles, Jr., with Some Observations on the Nature of Prophecy." *Jewish Quarterly Review* 66 (1975): 227–35.

Bickerman, Elias. "Les deux erreurs du prophète Jonas." *Revue d'histoire et de philosophie religieuses* 45 (1965): 232–64.

Blank, Sheldon. "'Doest Thou Well to be Angry?' A Study in Self-Pity." *Hebrew Union College Annual* 26 (1955): 29–41.

Brockington, L. H. "Jonah." In *Peake's Commentary on the Bible*. Edited by Matthew Black and H. H. Rowley. London: Thomas Nelson, 1962.

Brongers, H. A. "Bemerkungen zum gebrauch des adverbiaken Weattah im Alten Testament." *Vetus Testamentum* 15 (1965): 289–99.

Brown, Calvin S. Review of *The Idea of Biblical Poetry: Parallelism and Its History*, by James Kugel. *Comparative Literature* 34 (1982): 361–63.

Budde, Karl. "Vermutungen zum 'Midrash des Buches der Könige.'" *Zeitschrift für die alttestamentlich Wissenschaft* 12 (1892): 37–51.

Burrows, Miller. "The Literary Category of the book of Jonah." In *Translation and Understanding the Old Testament: Essays in Honor of H. G. May*. Edited by Harry Thomas Frank and William L. Reed. Nashville: Abingdon Press, 1970.

Carson, D. A. "Understanding Misunderstanding in the Fourth Gospel." *Tyndale Bulletin* 33 (1982): 59–91.

Cheyne, T. K. "Jonah." In *Encyclopaedia Biblica*, vol. 2. Edited by T. K. Cheyne and J. Sutherland Black. New York: Macmillan, 1901.

Christensen, Duane L. "The Song of Jonah: A Metrical Analysis." *Journal of Biblical Literature* 104 (1985): 217–31.

Clements, Ronald E. "The Purpose of the Book of Jonah." *Vetus Testamentum Supplements* 28 (1975): 16–28.

Cohn, Gabriël H. "Jonah, the Book of." *Encyclopedia Judaica*, vol. 10. Edited by Cecil Roth. Jerusalem: Keter Publishing House, 1971.

Cross, Frank M. "Studies in the Structure of Hebrew Verse: The Prosody of the Psalm of Jonah." In *The Quest for the Kingdom of God: Studies in Honor of George E. Mendenhall*. Edited by H. B. Huffmon, F. A. Spina, A. R. W. Green. Winona Lake, Indiana: Eisenbrauns, 1983.

Cross, Frank M., and David Noel Freedman. "The Song of Miriam." *Journal of Near Eastern Studies* 14 (1955): 237–50.

Davies, G. I. "The Uses of R'' Qal and the Meaning of Jonah IV 1." *Vetus Testamentum* 27 (1977): 105–11.

DeMaria, Robert, Jr. "The Ideal Reader: A Critical Fiction." *Publications of the Modern Language Association* 93 (1978): 463–74.

Díaz, S.J., José Alonso. "Paralelos entre la narración del libro de Jonás y la parábola del hijo pródigo." *Biblica* 40 (1959): 632–40.

Dozeman, Thomas B. "Inner-Biblical Interpretation of Yahweh's Gracious and Compassionate Character." *Journal of Biblical Literature* 108 (1989): 207–23.

Dürr, Lor. "Hebr. ‏נפשׁ‎ = akk. napištu = Gurgel, Kehle.." *Zeitschrift für die alttestamentlich Wissenschaft* 43 (1925): 262–69.

Dyck, Elmer. "Jonah among the Prophets: A Study in Canonical Context." *Journal of the Evangelical Theological Society* 33 (1990): 63–73.

Emmerson, Grace I. "Another Look at the Book of Jonah." *Expository Times*, 88 (1976–1977): 86–88.

Feuillet, Andre. "Le sens du livre de Jonas." *Revue biblique* 54 (1947): 340–61.

———. "Les sources du livre de Jonas." *Revue biblique* 54 (1947): 161–86.

Fewell, Danna Nolan and David M. Gunn. "Tipping the Balance: Sternberg's Reader and the Rape of Dinah." *Journal of Biblical Literature* 110 (1991): 193–211.

Fizer, John. "Indeterminacies as Structural Components in Semiotically Meaningful Wholes." *PTL: A Journal of Descriptive Poetics and Theory of Literature* 4 (1979): 119–32.

Freedman, David Noel. "Did God Play a Dirty Trick on Jonah at the End?" *Bible Review* 6 (1990): 26–31.

———. "Pottery, Poetry, and Prophecy: An Essay on Biblical Poetry." *Journal of Biblical Literature* 96 (1977): 5-26.

Freedman, David Noel. "Prose Particles in the Poetry of the Primary History." In *Biblical and Related Studies Presented to Samuel Iwry*. Edited by Ann Kort and Scott Morschauser. Winona Lake, Indiana: Eisenbrauns, 1985.

Fretheim, Terence E. "Jonah and Theodicy." *Zeitschrift für die alttestamentlich Wissenschaft* 90 (1978): 227–37.

Geller, Stephen A. Review of *The Idea of Biblical Poetry: Parallelism and Its History*, by James Kugel. *Journal of Biblical Literature* 102 (1983): 625–26.

Goitein, S. D. F. "Some Observations on Jonah." *Journal of the Palestine Oriental Society* 17 (1937): 63–77.

Grossberg, Daniel. Review of *The Idea of Biblical Poetry: Parallelism and Its History*, by James Kugel. *Biblical Theology Bulletin* 12 (1982): 95–96.

Güttemanns, Erhard. "What is 'Generative Poetics'?: Theses and Reflections concerning a New Exegetical Method." *Semeia* 6 (1976): 1–21.

Halpern, Baruch. Review of *The Idea of Biblical Poetry: Parallelism and Its History*, by James Kugel. *Journal of Religion* 65 (1985): 118–20.

——— and Richard Elliott Friedman. "Composition and Paronomasia in the Book of Jonah." *Hebrew Annual Review* 4 (1980): 79–92.

Hauser, Alan Jon. "Jonah: In Pursuit of the Dove." *Journal of Biblical Literature* 104 (1985): 21–37.

Hiraga, Masako, K. "Eternal Stillness: A Linguistic Journey to Basho's Haiku about the Cicada." *Poetics Today* 8 (1987): 5–18.

Holbert, John C. "'Deliverance Belongs to Yahweh!': Satire in the Book of Jonah." *Journal for the Study of the Old Testament* 21 (1981): 59–81.

Hrushovski, Benjamin. "Do Sounds Have Meaning? The Problem of Expressiveness of Sound Patterns in Poetry" (Hebrew). *Hasifrut* 1 (1968): 410–20.

———. "The Meaning of Sound Patterns in Poetry: An Interaction Theory." *Poetics Today* 2 (1980): 39–56.

———. "On the Boundaries of the Study of Literature" (Hebrew). *Hasifrut* 1 (1968): 1–10.

———. "Poetics, Criticism, Science: Remarks on the Fields and Responsibilities of the Study of Literature." *PTL: Journal for Descriptive Poetics and Theory of Literature* 1 (1976): iii–xxxv.

Hrushovski, Benjamin. "Prosody, Hebrew." *Encyclopedia Judaica*, vol. 13. Edited by Cecil Roth. Jerusalem: Keter Publishing House, 1971.

Hyman, Lawrence, W. "Indeterminacy in Literary Criticism." *Soundings* 59 (1976): 345–56.

Jakobson, Roman. "Closing Statement: Linguistics and Poetics." In *Style in Language*. Edited by Thomas A. Sebeok. Cambridge: MIT Press, 1960.

Jepsen, Alfred. "Anmerkungen zum Buche Jona." In *Wort-Gebot-Glaube: Walter Eichrodt zum 80. Geburtstag*, Abhandlungen zur Theologie des Alten un Neuen Testaments, 59. Edited by Hans Joachim Stoebe, Johann Jakob Stamm, and Ernst Jenni. Zurich: Zwingli Verlag, 1970.

Johnson, A. R. "Jonah 2:3–10: A Study in Cultic Fantasy." In *Studies in Old Testament Prophecy*. Edited by H. H. Rowley. Edinburgh: T. & T. Clark, 1950.

Keller, Carl A. "Jonas. Le portrait d'un prophète." *Theologische Zeitschrift* 21 (1965): 329–40.

Kincaid, James R. "Coherent Readers, Incoherent Texts." *Critical Inquiry* 3 (1977): 781–802.

Landes, George M. "Jonah: A Mashal?" In *Israelite Wisdom: Theological and Literary Essays in Honor of Samuel Terrien*. Edited by J. G. Gammie, et al. Missoula, Montana: Scholars Press, 1978.

———. "The Jonah Psalm (Jon. 2:3–10) Revisited." Paper delivered at the annual Society of Biblical Literature meeting in Dallas, Texas, December, 1983.

———. "The Kerygma of the Book of Jonah: The Contextual Interpretation of the Jonah Psalm." *Interpretation* 21 (1967): 3–31.

———. "Linguistic Criteria and the Date of the Book of Jonah." *Eretz-Israel* 16 (1982): 147–70.

Lewis, Chaim. "Jonah—A Parable for Our Time." *Judaism*, 21 (1972): 159–63.

Lohfink, S.J., Norbert. "Jona ging zur Stadt hinaus (Jon 4,5)." *Biblische Zeitschrift* 5 (1961): 185–203.

McCarter, P. Kyle. "The River Ordeal in Israelite Literature." *Harvard Theological Review* 66 (1973): 403–12.

Magonet, Jonathan. "Jonah, Book of." In *The Anchor Bible Dictionary*, vol. 3. Edited by David Noel Freedman. New York: Doubleday Press, 1992.

Mather, Judson. "The Comic Art of the Book of Jonah." *Soundings* 65 (1982): 280–91.

Miles, John A. "Laughing at the Bible: Jonah as Parody." *Jewish Quarterly Review* 65 (1975): 168–81.

Miller, Patrick. Review of *The Idea of Biblical Poetry: Parallelism and Its History*, by James Kugel. *Theology Today* 39 (1982): 331–34.

Mintz, Alan. "On the Tel Aviv School of Poetics." *Prooftexts* 4 (1984): 215–35.

Muilenburg, James. "Poetry." *Encyclopedia Judaica*, vol. 13. Edited by Cecil Roth. Jerusalem: Keter Publishing House, 1971.

Neil, William. "Jonah, the book of." In *Interpreter's Dictionary of the Bible*, vol. 2. Edited by George A. Buttrick. Nashville: Abingdon Press, 1962.

Nielsen, Eduard. "Le message primitif du livre de Jonas." *Revue d'histoire et de philosophie religieuses* 59 (1979): 499–507.

Patai, Raphael. "Jewish Seafaring in Ancient Times." *Jewish Quarterly Review* 32 (1941): 1–26.

Pelli, Moshe. "The Literary Art of Jonah." *Hebrew Studies* 20–21 (1979–1980): 18–28.

Prat, F. "Le nom divin est-il intensif en hébreu?" *Revue biblique* 10 (1901): 497–511.

Price, Martin. "The Irrelevant Detail and the Emergence of Form." In *Aspects of Narrative*. Edited by J. Hillis Miller. New York: Columbia University Press, 1971.

Riffaterre, Michael. "Interpretation and Undecidability." *New Literary History* 12 (1981): 227–42.

Rofé, Alexander. "Classes in the Prophetical Stories: Didactic Legenda and Parable." VTSup 26 (1974): 143–64.

Rogers, Robert. "Amazing Reader in the Labyrinth of Literature." *Poetics Today* 3 (1982): 31–46.

Rosenberg, Joel. "Jonah and the Prophetic Vocation." *Response* 22 (1974): 23–26.

Ryan, Marie-Laurie. "Toward a Competence Theory of Genre." *Poetics* 8 (1979): 307–37.

Shazar, Zalman. "The Book of Jonah" (Hebrew). *Bet Mikra* 47 (1971): 432–437.

Simon, Uriel. "The Book of Jonah: Structure and Meaning" (Hebrew). In *Isaac Leo Seeligmann Volume: Essays on the Bible and the Ancient World*, vol. 2. Edited by Alexander Rofé and Yair Zakovitch. Jerusalem: E. Rubinstein Publishing House, 1983.

Smart, James D. "The Book of Jonah." *The Interpreter's Bible*, vol. 6. Nashville: Abingdon, 1956.

Stenzel, Meinrad. "Altlateinische Canticatexte im Dodekapropheton." *Zeitschrift für die neutestamentliche Wissenschaft* 46 (1955): 31–60.

Sternberg, Meir. "Between the Truth and the Whole Truth in Biblical Narrative: The Rendering of the Inner Life by Telescoped Inside View and Interior Monologue" (Hebrew). *Hasifrut* 29 (1979): 110–46.

———. "Deictic Sequence: World, Language and Convention." In *Essays on Deixis*. Edited by Gisa Ruah. Tübingen: Gunter Narr Verlag, 1983.

———. "Language, World and Perspective in Biblical Narrative Art: Free Indirect Discourse and Modes of Covert Penetration" (Hebrew). *Hasifrut* 32 (1983): 88–131.

————. "Mimesis and Motivation: The Two Faces of Fictional Coherence." In *Literary Criticism and Philosophy*. Edited by Joseph P. Strelka. University Park and London: Pennsylvania State University Press, 1983.

————. "Ordering the Unordered: Time, Space, and Descriptive Coherence." *Yale French Studies* 61 (1981): 60–88.

————. "Point of View and the Indirections of Direct Speech." *Language and Style* 15 (1982): 67–117.

————. "Proteus in Quotation-Land: Mimesis and the Forms of Reported Discourse." *Poetics Today* 3 (1982): 107–56.

————. "Temporal Ordering, Modes of Expositional Distribution, and Three Models of Rhetorical Control in the Narrative Text." *PTL: A Journal for Descriptive Poetics and Theory of Literature* 1 (1976): 295–316.

————. "The World from the Addressee's Viewpoint: Reception as Representation, Dialogue as Monologue." *Style* 20 (1986): 295–318.

———— and Menakhem Perry. "Caution: A Literary Text! Problems in the Poetics and Interpretation of Biblical Narrative" (Hebrew). *Hasifrut* 2 (1970): 608–63.

Stevens, Wallace. "Effects of Analogy." *Yale Review* 75 (1986): 255–70.

Thomas, D. Winton, "A Consideration of Some Unusual Ways of Expressing the Superlative in Hebrew." *Vetus Testamentum* 3 (1953): 209–224.

Trépanier, Benoit. "The Story of Jonas." *Catholic Biblical Quarterly* 13 (1951): 8–16.

Walsh, Jerome T. "Jonah 2,3–10: A Rhetorical Critical Study." *Biblica* 63 (1982): 219–29.

Weimar, Peter, "Jon 2,1–11: Jonapsalm und Jonaerzählung." *Biblische Zeitschrift* 28 (1984): 43–68.

Whallon, William. "Old Testament Poetry and Homeric Epic." *Comparative Literature* 18 (1966): 113–31.

Yacobi, Tamar. "Reader and Norms in Fictional Communication" (Hebrew). *Hasifrut* 34 (1985): 5–34.

Index

1. Topics

aesthetics, 7–8
ambiguation, 8, 13, 46, 68, 87, 94, 132–34, 149, 156
analogy, 96, 97–101, 181 n. 39; defined, 99
archaeology, 24
art/artist, 1, 6, 7, 9, 12, 31, 53, 69, 70, 96, 111, 123, 127, 130, 144, 148, 154, 165, 167 n. 8, 169 n. 28
artistic and ideological principles, 2, 8–9, 61, 67, 72, 122, 123, 130, 154–55, 165

Bible, 1–2; aetiological tales in, 7; as non-didactic literature, 7–8, 67, 159–65; dates in, 7; genealogies in, 7; law passages in, 7
breve, 105

call narratives, 80; Jonah's response to, 78–81
causality, 57, 115, 144
characterization, 6, 8, 26, 27–28, 44, 45–72, 81, 89–90, 94, 99, 100, 123, 124–43, 144, 147, 149, 156; by ambiguation, 134; by contrast, 60–61; by key words, 61–62, 95, 125, 157; by meager means, 101; collective, 59, 60; impact of translation on, 44; of Jonah, 39–40, 46, 52, 55–58, 61, 67, 68–69, 81, 84–88, 93–96, 98, 101, 114–15, 131–36, 139–40, 146, 148–50, 152–53, 155, 157, 159; of Jonah and foreigners, 27–28, 31, 47–50,

61–63, 88, 100, 142; of Jonah and the Lord, 27–28, 36, 52–54, 56–58, 60, 63–64, 67–70, 72, 73–82, 101, 109–18, 138–42, 146, 147, 150, 151, 156–59, 161–65; of the Lord, 34–35, 40–42, 46, 50–53, 98, 123, 136, 138–42, 146, 152, 155, 160, 162; of the sailors and Ninevites, 9, 11, 26–27, 28–29, 32–33, 37–38, 42–44, 51–52, 55–56, 59–60, 64, 66, 70–71, 84–85, 89, 129–32, 137–38, 151, 153; outside book of Jonah, 58–59, 60, 70–71, 90–93, 96, 97–98, 123, 125–26, 129–31, 137, 141, 161; through dialogue, 58, 66–71, 84, 111
characters, biblical, 7–8, 46–47, 58–64, 117, 130–31, 137; naming of, 63
chiasms, 104–106
closure, 59–60, 79, 155; at 3:10, 59–60, 138, 157; at 4:6, 157
cola, 105
contrasts: in conjugation, 115; in grammatical person, 114–15; in sound, 117–18; in tense, 115
couplets, 105

Dead Sea Scrolls. *See* Qumran
dialogue, 64–66, 69, 125–26, 147, 155, 156, 163; absence of, 67; and narration, 2, 54–58, 64–65, 173 n. 16; as narrative event, 65; and representation of scenery, 65–66; and reversals in portrayal, 68; between Jonah and the Lord, 36, 60
didactic writing, 7, 160–61

203

3. Authors and Scholars, Ancient and Modern

Weiser, A., 15, 53
Wellhausen, J., 13, 15, 16
Wendel, A., 179 n. 17
Whallon, W., 169 n. 23
Whitley, K., 166 n. 1
Wolff, H. W., ix, 13, 15, 16, 38,
Wolff, *continued*
    41, 43, 63, 68, 132, 139, 158,
    159, 169 n. 29, 171 nn. 26, 27,
    28, 32, 173 n. 11, 174 n. 29,
    175 n. 40, 188 n. 18, 190 nn.
    41, 44, 191 nn. 6, 8, 13
Woolf, V., 2, 187 n. 12
Wood, K., x

Yacobi, T., 176 n. 9

4. Characters (biblical)

N.B. Characters from the story of
Jonah are discussed *passim*
throughout the book.

Aaron, 8, 180 n. 19
Ahab, 181 n. 35
Abel, 161
Abigail, 19, 48
Abraham, 58, 90
Absalom, 129
Adam, 19
Ahab, 95
Ahijah, 181 n. 35
Amnon, 129, 130
Amon, 54
Amos, 60

Bathsheba, 81, 97
Baasha, 54, 181 n. 35
Bezalel, 98
Bildad, 109

Cain, 160
Christ, 20

David, 8, 45, 49, 81, 94, 97, 125,
    126, 129

Diblaim, 140
Dinah, 123, 181 n. 39

Elijah, 47, 93, 95, 96, 190–91
    n. 44
Elisha, 177 n. 20, 180 n. 35
Eliphaz, 109
Esau, 58
Esther, 126
Eve, 19
Ezekiel, 58, 59, 128
Ezra, 137

Gideon, 8
Gilead, 48
Goliath, 49
Gomer, 140

Haman, 75
Hamor, 123
Hazael, 177 n. 20
Hosea, 128, 140

Isaac, 90
Isaiah, 60, 79

Jacob, 8, 58, 70, 71, 123
Jael, 24
Jehoash, 54
Jephthah, 48
Jeremiah, 47, 60, 71, 79, 93, 125,
    130, 131, 175 n. 44, 191 n. 44
Jeroboam, 54
Jesse, 125
Jesus, 19
Jezebel, 95, 181 n. 35
Job, 48, 49, 125
Jonadab, 129, 130
Joseph, 75, 126

Laban, 70, 71
Levi, 123

Moses, 3, 60, 78, 79, 90, 91, 93,
    95, 97–98, 137, 180 n. 19